D1579317

MILTON'S PARADISE LOST

BOOKS I AND II

JOHN MILTON

PARADISE LOST

BOOKS I AND II

EDITED BY
A. W. VERITY

CAMBRIDGE
AT THE UNIVERSITY PRESS
1952

CAMBRIDGE UNIVERSITY PRESS
Cambridge, New York, Melbourne, Madrid, Cape Town,
Singapore, São Paulo, Delhi, Mexico City

Cambridge University Press
The Edinburgh Building, Cambridge CB2 8RU, UK

Published in the United States of America by Cambridge University Press, New York

www.cambridge.org
Information on this title: www.cambridge.org/9781107641570

First published 1952
First edition 1893
Second edition 1894
Reprinted 1897, 1899, 1900, 1902, 1905, 1907, 1910, 1913, 1915,
1917, 1919, 1924, 1928, 1931, 1934, 1941, 1945, 1947, 1950
Third edition, Revised and Re-set 1952
First paperback edition 2013

A catalogue record for this publication is available from the British Library

ISBN 978-1-107-64157-0 Paperback

CONTENTS

NOTE TO FIRST EDITION

THE text of the books of *Paradise Lost* in this volume is that of the first edition, with the slight corrections of the second. In Book I. 703 and Book II. 282 I hold, as do most editors, that the readings of the second edition are not corrections but mere *errata*.

In referring to Milton's prose-works I have used the edition published in "Bohn's Standard Library".

Most of the Biblical, and many of the classical, allusions mentioned in the *Notes* have been pointed out by previous editors.

The brief additions to the first section of the *Appendix* are taken from Mr James' Lecture on the recently issued *Revelation of Peter*. I hope that the three new sections throw some fresh light on points of interest. In two of them I have to acknowledge the very kind assistance of Mr R. D. Hicks, of Trinity College. In the last I have tried to trace at greater detail than is attempted in any edition known to me the literary and historical allusions that centre round the famous catalogue of names in Book I. 582–7.

The sub-librarian of Trinity College, Mr W. White, helped me to detect some of the misreadings in Marvell's "Commendatory Verses" as commonly printed. And a friend compiled the *Index* of words.

A. W. V.

Bournemouth
30 *January* 1893

NOTE TO SECOND EDITION

THE chief change in this edition is that the *Glossary* has been recast and for the most part rewritten, the words being increased in number but treated more simply. A fresh section, "F", has been added to the *Appendix*.

A. W. V.

16 *August* 1894

NOTE TO THIRD EDITION

MR VERITY'S edition of *Paradise Lost* for which the demand, after so many years, is unabated, has now been re-set in a more modern typographical style. The opportunity has been taken of making a few slight alterations in the *format* of the book.

Cambridge
1952

INTRODUCTION

LIFE OF MILTON

MILTON's life falls into three clearly defined divisions. The first period ends with the poet's return from Italy in 1639; the second at the Restoration in 1660, when release from the fetters of politics enabled him to remind the world that he was a great poet; the third is brought to a close with his death in 1674. *Paradise Lost* belongs to the last of these periods; but we propose to summarise the main events of all three.

John Milton was born on December 9, 1608, in London. He came, in his own words, *ex genere honesto*. A family of Miltons had been settled in Oxfordshire since the reign of Elizabeth. The poet's father had been educated at an Oxford school, possibly as a chorister in one of the College choir-schools, and imbibing Anglican sympathies had conformed to the Established Church. For this he was disinherited by his Roman Catholic father. He settled in London, following the profession of scrivener. A scrivener combined the occupations of lawyer and law-stationer. It appears to have been a lucrative calling; certainly John Milton (the poet was named after the father) attained to easy circumstances. He married about 1600, and had six children, of whom several died young. The third child was the poet.

The elder Milton was evidently a man of considerable culture, in particular an accomplished musician, and a composer whose madrigals were deemed worthy of being printed side by side with those of Byrd, Orlando Gibbons and other leading musicians of the time. To him, no doubt, the poet owed the love of music of which we see frequent indications in the poems.[1] Realising, too, that in his son

[1] Milton was very fond of the organ; see *Il Penseroso*, 161, note. During his residence at Horton Milton made occasional

lay the promise and possibility of future greatness, John
Milton took the utmost pains to have the boy adequately
educated; and the lines *Ad Patrem* show that the ties of
affection between father and child were of more than
ordinary closeness.

Milton was sent to St Paul's School about the year 1620.
Here two influences, apart from those of ordinary school-
life, may have affected him particularly. The headmaster
was a good English scholar; he published a grammar containing many extracts from English poets, notably Spenser;
it is reasonable to assume that he had not a little to do with
the encouragement and guidance of Milton's early taste for
English poetry.[1] Also, the founder of St Paul's School,
Colet, had prescribed as part of the school-course the study
of certain early Christian writers, whose influence is said to
be directly traceable in Milton's poems and may in some
cases have suggested his choice of sacred themes.[1] While
at St Paul's, Milton also had a tutor at home, Thomas
Young, a Scotchman, afterwards an eminent Puritan
divine—the inspirer, doubtless, of much of his pupil's
Puritan sympathies. And Milton enjoyed the signal
advantage of growing up in the stimulating atmosphere of
cultured home-life. Most men do not realise that the word
'culture' signifies anything very definite or desirable before
they pass to the University; for Milton, however, home-
life meant, from the first, not only broad interests and
refinement, but active encouragement towards literature
and study. In 1625 he left St Paul's. Of his extant English
poems[2] only one, *On the Death of a Fair Infant*, dates from

journeys to London to hear, and obtain instruction (probably
from Henry Lawes) in, music. It was an age of great musical
development. See "Milton's Knowledge of Music" by Mr
W. H. Hadow, in *Milton Memorial Lectures* (1908).

[1] See the paper "Milton as Schoolboy and Schoolmaster" by
Mr A. F. Leach, read before the British Academy, Dec. 10, 1908.

[2] His paraphrases of *Psalms* cxiv, cxxxvi scarcely come under
this heading. Aubrey says in his quaint *Life* of Milton: "Anno
Domini 1619 he was ten yeares old, as by his picture [the
portrait by Cornelius Jansen]: and was then a poet."

his school-days; but we are told that he had written much
verse, English and Latin. And his early training had done
that which was all-important: it had laid the foundation of
the far-ranging knowledge which makes *Paradise Lost*
unique for diversity of suggestion and interest.

Milton went to Christ's College, Cambridge, in the
Easter term of 1625, took his B.A. degree in 1629, proceeded M.A. in 1632, and in the latter year left Cambridge.
The popular view of Milton's connection with the University will be coloured for all time by Johnson's unfortunate
story that for some unknown offence he "suffered the
public indignity of corporal correction". For various
reasons this story is now discredited by the best judges. It
is certain, however, that early in 1626 Milton did have some
serious difficulty with his tutor, which led to his removal
from Cambridge for a few weeks and his transference to
another tutor on his return later in the term. He spoke of
the incident bitterly at the time in one of his Latin poems,
and he spoke of Cambridge bitterly in after years. On the
other hand he voluntarily passed seven years at the University, and resented strongly the imputations brought against
him in the " Smectymnuus " controversy that he had been
in ill-favour with the authorities of his college. Writing in
1642, he takes the opportunity "to acknowledge publicly
with all grateful mind, that more than ordinary favour and
respect, which I found above any of my equals at the hands
of those courteous and learned men, the fellows of that
college wherein I spent some years: who at my parting,
after I had taken two degrees, as the manner is, signified
many ways how much better it would content them that
I would stay; as by many letters full of kindness and loving
respect, both before that time, and long after, I was
assured of their singular good affection towards me".[1]

[1] *An Apology for Smectymnuus, P. W.* III. 111. Perhaps Cambridge would have been more congenial to Milton had he been
sent to Emmanuel College, long a centre of Puritanism. Dr John
Preston, then Master of the college, was a noted leader of the
Puritan party.

And if we look into those uncomplimentary allusions to Cambridge which date from the controversial period of his life we see that the feeling they represent is hardly more than a phase of his theological bias. He detested ecclesiasticism, and for him the two Universities (there is a fine impartiality in his diatribes) are the strongholds of what he detested: "nurseries of superstition"—"not yet well recovered from the scholastic grossness of barbarous ages"—given up to "monkish and miserable sophistry", and unprogressive in their educational methods. But it may fairly be assumed that Milton the scholar and poet, who chose to spend seven years at Cambridge, owed to her more than Milton the fierce controversialist admitted or knew. A poet he had proved himself before leaving the University in 1632. The short but exquisite ode *At a Solemn Music* and the *Nativity Hymn* (1629) were already written.

Milton's father had settled at Horton in Buckinghamshire. Thither the son retired in July, 1632. He had gone to Cambridge with the intention of qualifying for some profession, perhaps the Church.[1] This purpose was soon given up, and when Milton returned to his father's house he seems to have made up his mind that there was no profession which he cared to enter. He would choose the better part of studying and preparing himself, by rigorous self-discipline and application, for the far-off divine event to which his whole life moved.

It was Milton's constant resolve to achieve something that should vindicate the ways of God to men, something great that should justify his own possession of unique powers—powers of which, with no trace of egotism, he proclaims himself proudly conscious. The feeling finds

---

[1] Cf. Milton's own words: "the church, to whose service, by the intentions of my parents and friends, I was destined of a child, and in my own resolutions" (*The Reason of Church Government*, *P.W.* II. 482). What kept him from taking orders was primarily his objection to Church discipline and government: he spoke of himself as "Church-outed by the prelates".

repeated expression in his prose; it is the guiding-star that shines clear and steadfast even through the mists of politics. He has a mission to fulfil, a purpose to accomplish, no less than the most fanatic of religious enthusiasts; and the means whereby this end is to be attained are devotion to religion, devotion to learning, and ascetic purity of life.

This period of self-centred isolation lasted from 1632 to 1638. Gibbon tells us among the many wise things contained in that most wise book the *Autobiography*, that every man has two educations: that which he receives from his teachers and that which he owes to himself; the latter being infinitely the more important. During these five years Milton completed his second education; ranging the whole world of classical[1] antiquity and absorbing the classical genius so thoroughly that the ancients were to him what they afterwards became to Landor, what they have never become to any other English poet in the same degree, even as the very breath of his being; pursuing, too, other interests, such as music, astronomy[2] and the study of Italian literature; and combining these vast and diverse influences into a splendid equipment of hard-won, well-ordered culture. The world has known many greater scholars in the technical, limited sense than Milton, but few men, if any,

---

[1] He was closely familiar too with post-classical writers like Philo and the neo-Platonists; nor must we forget the mediæval element in his learning, due often to Rabbinical teaching.

[2] Science—"natural philosophy", as he terms it—is one of the branches of study advocated in his treatise *On Education*. Of his early interest in astronomy there is a reminiscence in *Paradise Lost*, II. 708–11; where "Milton is not referring to an imaginary comet, but to one which actually did appear when he was a boy of 10 (1618), in the constellation called Ophiuchus. It was of enormous size, the tail being recorded as longer even than that of 1858. It was held responsible by educated and learned men of the day for disasters. Evelyn says in his diary, 'The effects of that comet, 1618, still working in the prodigious revolutions now beginning in Europe, especially in Germany'" (Professor Ray Lankester).

who have mastered more things worth mastering in art, letters and scholarship.[1] It says much for the poet that he was sustained through this period of study, pursued *ohne Hast, ohne Rast*, by the full consciousness that all would be crowned by a masterpiece which should add one more testimony to the belief in that God who ordains the fates of men. It says also a very great deal for the father who suffered his son to follow in this manner the path of learning.

True, Milton gave more than one earnest of his future fame. The dates of the early pieces—*L'Allegro, Il Penseroso, Arcades, Comus* and *Lycidas*—are not all certain; but probably each was composed at Horton before 1638. Four of them have great autobiographic value as an indirect commentary, written from Milton's coign of seclusion, upon the moral crisis through which English life and thought were passing, the clash between the careless hedonism of the Cavalier world and the deepening austerity of Puritanism. In *L'Allegro* the poet holds the balance almost equal between the two opposing tendencies. In *Il Penseroso* it becomes clear to which side his sympathies are leaning. *Comus* is a covert prophecy of the downfall of the Court-party, while *Lycidas* openly "foretells the ruine" of the Established Church. The latter poem is the final utterance of Milton's lyric genius. Here he reaches, in Mr Mark Pattison's words, the high-water mark of English verse; and then—the pity of it—he resigns that place among the *lyrici vates* of which the Roman singer was ambitious, and for nearly twenty years suffers his lyre to hang mute and rusty in the temple of the Muses.

[1] Milton's poems with their undercurrent of perpetual allusion are the best proof of the width of his reading; but interesting supplementary evidence is afforded by the Common-place Book discovered in 1874, and printed by the *Camden Society*, 1876. It contains extracts from about 80 different authors whose works Milton had studied. The entries seem to have been made in the period 1637–46.

The composition of *Lycidas* may be assigned to the year 1637. In the spring of the next year Milton started for Italy. It was natural that he should seek inspiration in the land where many English poets, from Chaucer to Shelley, have found it. Milton remained abroad some fifteen months. Originally he had intended to include Sicily and Greece in his travels, but news of the troubles in England hastened his return. He was brought face to face with the question whether or not he should bear his part in the coming struggle; whether without self-reproach he could lead any longer this life of learning and indifference to the public weal. He decided as we might have expected that he would decide, though some good critics see cause to regret the decision. Milton puts his position very clearly in his *Defensio Secunda*: " I thought it base to be travelling for amusement abroad, while my fellow-citizens were fighting for liberty at home." And later: "I determined to relinquish the other pursuits in which I was engaged, and to transfer the whole force of my talents and my industry to this one important object" (i.e. the vindication of liberty).

The summer of 1639 (July) found Milton back in England. Immediately after his return he wrote the *Epitaphium Damonis*, the beautiful elegy in which he lamented the death of his school friend, Diodati. *Lycidas* was the last of the English lyrics: the *Epitaphium*, which should be studied in close connection with *Lycidas*, the last of the long Latin poems. Thenceforth, for a long spell, the rest was silence, so far as concerned poetry. The period which for all men represents the strength and maturity of manhood, which in the cases of other poets produces the best and most characteristic work, is with Milton a blank. In twenty years he composed no more than a bare handful of Sonnets, and even some of these are infected by the taint of political *animus*. Other interests claimed him—the question of Church-reform, education, marriage, and, above all, politics.

Milton's first treatise upon the government of the Church (*Of Reformation in England*) appeared in 1641. Others followed in quick succession. The abolition of Episcopacy was the watchword of the enemies of the Anglican Church—the *delenda est Carthago* cry of Puritanism, and no one enforced the point with greater eloquence than Milton. During 1641 and 1642 he wrote five pamphlets on the subject. Meanwhile he was studying the principles of education. On his return from Italy he had undertaken the training of his nephews. This led to consideration of the best educational methods; and in the *Tractate of Education*, 1644, Milton assumed the part of educational theorist. In the previous year, May, 1643, he married.[1] The marriage proved unfortunate. Its immediate outcome was the pamphlets on divorce. Clearly he had little leisure for literature proper.

The finest of Milton's prose works, *Areopagitica*, a plea for the free expression of opinion, was published in 1644. In 1645[2] appeared the first collection of his poems. In

[1] His wife (who was only seventeen) was Mary Powell, eldest daughter of Richard Powell, of Forest Hill, a village some little distance from Oxford. She went to stay with her father in July, 1643, and refused to return to Milton; why, it is not certain. She was reconciled to her husband in 1645, bore him four children, and died in 1652, in her twenty-seventh year. No doubt, the scene in *P. L.* x. 909–36, in which Eve begs forgiveness of Adam, reproduced the poet's personal experience, while many passages in *Samson Agonistes* must have been inspired by the same cause.

[2] I.e. old style. The volume was entered on the registers of the Stationers' Company under the date of October 6th, 1645. It was published on Jan. 2, 1645–46, with the following title-page:

"*Poems of Mr. John Milton, both English and Latin, Compos'd at several times. Printed by his true Copies. The Songs were set in Musick by Mr. Henry Lawes Gentleman of the Kings Chappel, and one of His Majesties Private Musick.*

'———*Baccare frontem*
Cingite, ne vati noceat mala lingua futuro.' VIRGIL, *Eclog.* 7.

1649 his advocacy of the anti-royalist cause was recognised by the offer of a post under the newly appointed Council of State. His bold vindication of the trial of Charles I, *The Tenure of Kings*, had appeared earlier in the same year. Milton accepted the offer, becoming Latin[1] Secretary to the Committee of Foreign Affairs. There was nothing distasteful about his duties. He drew up the despatches to foreign governments, translated state-papers, and served as interpreter to foreign envoys. Had his duties stopped here his acceptance of the post would, I think, have proved an unqualified gain. It brought him into contact with the first men in the state, gave him a practical insight into the working of national affairs and the motives of human action; in a word, furnished him with that experience of life which is essential to all poets who aspire to be something more than "the idle singers of an empty day". But unfortunately the secretaryship entailed the necessity of defending at every turn the past course of the revolution and the present policy of the Council. Milton, in fact, held a perpetual brief as advocate for his party. Hence the endless and unedifying controversies into which he drifted; controversies which wasted the most precious years of his

Printed and publish'd according to Order. London, Printed by Ruth Raworth for Humphrey Moseley, and are to be sold at the signe of the Princes Arms in Pauls Churchyard. 1645."

From the prefatory Address to the Reader it is clear that the collection was due to the initiative of the publisher. Milton's own feeling is expressed by the motto, where the words "*vati futuro*" show that, as he judged, his great achievement was yet to come. The volume was divided into two parts, the first containing the English, the second the Latin poems. *Comus* was printed at the close of the former, with a separate title-page to mark its importance. The prominence given to the name of Henry Lawes reflects Milton's friendship.

[1] A Latin Secretary was required because the Council scorned, as Edward Phillips says, "to carry on their affairs in the wheedling, lisping jargon of the cringing French". Milton's salary was £288, in modern money about £900.

life, warped, as some critics think, his nature, and eventually cost him his eyesight.

Between 1649 and 1660 Milton produced no less than eleven pamphlets. Several of these arose out of the publication of the famous *Eikon Basilike*. The book was printed in 1649 and created so extraordinary a sensation that Milton was asked to reply to it; and did so with *Eikonoklastes*. Controversy of this barren type has the inherent disadvantage that once started it may never end. The Royalists commissioned the Leyden professor, Salmasius, to prepare a counterblast, the *Defensio Regia*, and this in turn was met by Milton's *Pro Populo Anglicano Defensio*, 1651, over the preparation of which he lost what little power of eyesight remained.[1] Salmasius retorted, and died before his second *farrago* of scurrilities was issued: Milton was bound to answer, and the *Defensio Secunda* appeared in 1654. Neither of the combatants gained anything by the dispute; while the subsequent development of the controversy in which Milton crushed the Amsterdam pastor and professor, Morus, goes far to prove the contention of Mr Mark Pattison, that it was an evil day when

---

[1] Perhaps this was the saddest part of the episode. Milton tells us in the *Defensio Secunda* that his eyesight was injured by excessive study in boyhood: "from twelve years of age I hardly ever left my studies or went to bed before midnight". Continual reading and writing increased the infirmity, and by 1650 the sight of the left eye had gone. He was warned that he must not use the other for book-work. Unfortunately this was just the time when the Commonwealth stood most in need of his services. If Milton had not written the first *Defence* he might have retained his partial vision, at least for a time. The choice lay between private good and public duty. He repeated in 1650 the sacrifice of 1639. All this is brought out in his *Second Defence*. By the spring of 1652 Milton was quite blind. He was then in his forty-fourth year. Probably the disease from which he suffered was amaurosis. See the *Appendix* on *P. L.* III. 22–26. Throughout *P. L.* and *Samson Agonistes* there are frequent references to his affliction.

the poet left his study at Horton to do battle for the Commonwealth amid the vulgar brawls of the market-place:

> "Not here, O Apollo,
> Were haunts meet for thee."

Fortunately this poetic interregnum in Milton's life was not destined to last much longer. The Restoration came, a blessing in disguise, and in 1660[1] the ruin of Milton's political party and of his personal hopes, the absolute over-throw of the cause for which he had fought for twenty years, left him free. The author of *Lycidas* could once more become a poet.

Much has been written upon this second period, 1639–60. We saw what parting of the ways confronted Milton on his return from Italy. Did he choose aright? Should he have continued upon the path of learned leisure? There are writers who argue that Milton made a mistake. A poet, they say, should keep clear of political strife: fierce controversy can benefit no man: who touches pitch must expect to be, certainly will be, defiled: Milton sacrificed twenty of the best years of his life, doing work which an underling could have done and which was not worth doing: another *Comus* might have been written, a loftier *Lycidas*: that literature should be the poorer by the absence of these possible masterpieces, that the second greatest genius which England has produced should in a way be the "inheritor of unfulfilled renown", is and must be a thing entirely and terribly deplorable. This is the view of the purely literary critic.

There remains the other side of the question. It may fairly be contended that had Milton elected in 1639 to live the scholar's life apart from "the action of men", *Paradise*

---

[1] Milton probably began *Paradise Lost* in 1658; but it was not till the Restoration in 1660 that he definitely resigned all his political hopes, and became quite free to realise his poetical ambition.

Lost, as we have it, or *Samson Agonistes* could never have been written. Knowledge of life and human nature, insight into the problems of men's motives and emotions, grasp of the broader issues of the human tragedy, all these were essential to the author of an epic poem; they could only be obtained through commerce with the world; they would have remained beyond the reach of a recluse. Dryden complained that Milton saw nature through the spectacles of books: we might have had to complain that he saw men through the same medium. Fortunately it is not so: and it is not so because at the age of thirty-two he threw in his fortunes with those of his country; like the diver in Schiller's ballad he took the plunge which was to cost him so dear. The mere man of letters will never move the world. Æschylus fought at Marathon: Shakespeare was practical to the tips of his fingers; a better business man than Goethe there was not within a radius of a hundred miles of Weimar.

This aspect of the question is emphasised by Milton himself. The man, he says, "who would not be frustrate of his hope to write well hereafter in laudable things, ought himself to be a true poem, that is, a composition and pattern of the best and honourablest things; not presuming to sing high praises of heroic men, or famous cities, unless he have in himself the experience and the practice of all that which is praiseworthy".[1] Again, in estimating the qualifications which the writer of an epic such as he contemplated should possess, he is careful to include "insight into all seemly and generous arts and affairs".[2]

Truth usually lies half-way between extremes: perhaps it does so here. No doubt, Milton did gain very greatly by breathing awhile the larger air of public life, even though that air was often tainted by much impurity. No doubt, too, twenty years of contention must have left their mark

[1] *An Apology for Smectymnuus*, P. W. III. 118.
[2] *The Reason of Church Government*, P. W. II. 481.

even on Milton. In one of the very few places where he
"abides our question", Shakespeare writes (*Sonnet* CXI):

"O! for my sake do you with Fortune chide,
The guilty goddess of my harmful deeds,
That did not better for my life provide,
Than public means, which public manners breeds:
Thence comes it that my name receives a brand;
And almost thence my nature is subdued
To what it works in, like the dyer's hand."

Milton's genius was subdued in this way. If we compare
him, the Milton of the great epics and of *Samson Agonistes*,
with Homer or Shakespeare—and none but the greatest
can be his parallel—we find in him a certain want of
humanity, a touch of narrowness. He lacks the large-
heartedness, the genial, generous breadth of Shakespeare;
the sympathy and sense of the *lacrimæ rerum* that even in
Troilus and Cressida or *Timon of Athens* are there for those
who have eyes wherewith to see them. Milton reflects in
some degree the less gracious aspects of Puritanism, its
intolerance, want of humour, one-sided intensity; and it
seems natural to assume that this narrowness was to a great
extent the price he paid for twenty years of ceaseless special
pleading and dispute. The real misfortune of his life lay in
the fact that he fell on evil, angry days when there was no
place for moderate men. He had to be one of two things:
either a controversialist or a student: there was no *via
media*. Probably he chose aright; but we could wish that
the conditions under which he chose had been different.
And he is so great, so majestic in the nobleness of his life,
in the purity of his motives, in the self-sacrifice of his
indomitable devotion to his ideals, that we could wish not
even to seem to pronounce judgment at all.

The last part of Milton's life, 1660–74, passed quietly.
At the age of fifty-two he was thrown back upon poetry,
and could at length discharge his self-imposed obligation.
The early poems he had never regarded as a fulfilment of
the debt due to his Creator. Even when the fire of political

strife burned at its hottest, Milton did not forget the purpose which he had conceived in his boyhood. Of that purpose *Paradise Lost* was the attainment. Begun about 1658, it was finished in 1663, the year of Milton's third[1] marriage; revised from 1663 to 1665; and eventually issued in 1667. Before its publication Milton had commenced (in the autumn of 1665) its sequel *Paradise Regained*, which in turn was closely followed by *Samson Agonistes*. The completion of *Paradise Regained* may be assigned to the year 1666—that of *Samson Agonistes* to 1667. Some time was spent in their revision; and in January, 1671, they were published together, in a single volume.

In 1673 Milton brought out a reprint of the 1645 edition of his *Poems*, adding most of the sonnets[2] written in the

[1] Milton's second marriage took place in the autumn of 1656, i.e. after he had become blind. His wife died in February, 1658. Cf. the *Sonnet*, "Methought I saw my late espoused saint", the pathos of which is heightened by the fact that he had never seen her.

[2] The number of Milton's sonnets is twenty-three (if we exclude the piece "On the New Forcers of Conscience"), five of which were written in Italian, probably during the time of his travels in Italy, 1638, 1639. Ten sonnets were printed in the edition of 1645, the last of them being that entitled (from the *Cambridge* MS.) "To the Lady Margaret Ley". The remaining thirteen were composed between 1645 and 1658. The concluding sonnet, therefore (to the memory of Milton's second wife), immediately preceded his commencement of *Paradise Lost*. Four of these poems (XV, XVI, XVII, XXII) could not, on account of their political tone, be included in the edition of 1673. They were published by Edward Phillips together with his memoir of Milton, 1694 (*Sonnet* XVII having previously appeared in a *Life* of Vane). The sonnet on the "Massacre in Piedmont" is usually considered the finest of the collection, of which Mr Mark Pattison edited a well-known edition, 1883. The sonnet inscribed with a diamond on a window pane in the cottage at Chalfont where the poet stayed in 1665 is (in the judgment of a good critic) Miltonic, if not Milton's (Garnett, *Life of Milton*, p. 175).

interval.[1] The last four years of his life were devoted to
prose works of no particular interest.[2] He continued to
live in London. His third marriage had proved happy,
and he enjoyed something of the renown which was
rightly his. Various well-known men used to visit him—
notably Dryden,[3] who on one of his visits asked and
received permission to dramatise[4] *Paradise Lost*.

Milton died in 1674, November 8th. He was buried in
St Giles' Church, Cripplegate. When we think of him we
have to think of a man who lived a life of very singular
purity and devotion to duty; who for what he conceived to
be his country's good sacrificed—and no one can well
estimate the sacrifice—during twenty years the aim that

[1] The 1673 edition also gave the juvenile piece *On the Death
of a Fair Infant* and *At a Vacation Exercise*, which for some
reason had been omitted from the 1645 edition.

[2] The treatise on *Christian Doctrine* (unpublished during
Milton's lifetime and dating, it is thought, mainly from the
period of his theological treatises) is valuable as throwing much
light on the theological views expressed in the two epic poems
and *Samson Agonistes*. See *Milton Memorial Lectures* (1908),
pp. 109–42. The discovery of the MS. of this treatise in 1823
gave Macaulay an opportunity of writing his famous essay on
Milton, which has been happily described as a Whig counterblast to Johnson's Tory depreciation of the poet.

Milton's *History of Britain*, though not published till 1670,
had been written many years earlier; four of the six books, we
know, were composed between 1646 and 1649.

[3] The lines by Dryden which were printed beneath the
portrait of Milton in Tonson's folio edition of *Paradise Lost*
published in 1688 are too familiar to need quotation; but it is
worth noting that the younger poet had in Milton's lifetime
described the great epic as "one of the most noble, and most
sublime poems which either this age or nation has produced"
(prefatory essay to *The State of Innocence*, 1674). Further,
tradition assigned to Dryden (a Roman Catholic and a Royalist)
the remark, "this fellow (Milton) cuts us all out and the ancients
too".

[4] See Marvell's "Commendatory Verses", 17–30, and the
Notes, pp. 72, 73.

was nearest to his heart and best suited to his genius; who, however, eventually realised his desire of writing a great work *in gloriam Dei*.

PARADISE LOST

We have seen that the dominating idea of Milton's life was his resolve to write a great poem—great in theme, in style, in attainment. To this purpose was he dedicated as a boy: as Hannibal was dedicated, at the altar of patriotism, to the cause of his country's revenge, or Pitt to a life of political ambition. Milton's works—particularly his letters and prose pamphlets—enable us to trace the growth of the idea which was shaping his intellectual destinies; and as every poet is best interpreted by his own words, Milton shall speak for himself.

Two of the earliest indications of his cherished plan are the *Vacation Exercise* and the second *Sonnet*. The *Exercise* commences with an invocation (not without significance, as we shall see) to his "native language", to assist him in giving utterance to the teeming thoughts that knock at the portal of his lips, fain to find an issue thence. The bent of these thoughts is towards the loftiest themes. Might he choose for himself, he would select some "grave subject":

> "Such where the deep transported mind may soar
> Above the wheeling poles, and at Heaven's door
> Look in, and see each blissful deity.
>
> .   .   .   .
> Then sing of secret things that came to pass
> When beldam Nature in her cradle was."

But recognising soon that such matters are inappropriate to the occasion—a College festivity—he arrests the flight of his muse with a grave *descende cælo*, and declines on a lower range of subject, more fitting to the social scene and the audience. This *Exercise* was composed in 1628, in Milton's twentieth year, or, according to his method of dating, *anno ætatis* XIX. It is important as revealing—

firstly, the poet's consciousness of the divine impulse within, for which poetry is the natural outlet; secondly, the elevation of theme with which that poetry must deal. A boy in years, he would like to handle the highest 'arguments', challenging thereby comparison with the *sacri vates* of inspired verse, the elect few whose poetic appeal is to the whole world. A vision of Heaven itself must be unrolled before his steadfast eagle-gaze: he will win a knowledge of the causes of things such as even Virgil, his master, modestly disclaimed. Little wonder, therefore, that, filled with these ambitions, Milton did not shrink, only two years later (1629–30), from attempting to sound the deepest mysteries of Christianity—the Nativity and the Passion of Christ; howbeit, sensible of his immaturity, he left his poem on the latter subject unfinished.[1]

The *Sonnet* to which reference has been made deserves quotation at length:

"How soon hath Time, the subtle thief of youth,
    Stolen on his wing my three-and-twentieth year!
    My hasting days fly on with full career,
    But my late spring no bud or blossom shew'th.
Perhaps my semblance might deceive the truth,
    That I to manhood am arrived so near;
    And inward ripeness doth much less appear,
    That some more timely-happy spirits endu'th.
Yet be it less or more, or soon or slow,
    It shall be still in strictest measure even
    To that same lot, however mean or high,
Toward which Time leads me, and the will of Heaven;
    All is, if I have grace to use it so,
    As ever in my great Task-Master's eye."

[1] A passage in the sixth *Elegy* shows that the *Nativity Ode* (a prelude in some respects to *Paradise Lost*) was begun on Christmas morning, 1629. *The Passion* may have been composed for the following Easter; it breaks off with the notice—"This Subject the Author finding to be above the years he had when he wrote it, and nothing satisfied with what was begun, left it unfinished." Evidently Milton was minded to recur to both subjects; see later.

Mr Mark Pattison justly calls these lines "an inseparable part of Milton's biography": they bring out so clearly the poet's solemn devotion to his self-selected task, and his determination not to essay the execution of that task until the time of complete "inward ripeness" has arrived. The *Sonnet* was one of the last poems composed by Milton during his residence at Cambridge. The date is 1631. From 1632 to 1638 was a period of almost unbroken self-preparation, such as the *Sonnet* foreshadows. Of the intensity of his application to literature a letter written in 1637 (the exact day being Sept. 7, 1637) enables us to judge.

"It is my way", he says to Carlo Diodati, in excuse for remissness as a correspondent, "to suffer no impediment, no love of ease, no avocation whatever, to chill the ardour, to break the continuity, or divert the completion of my literary pursuits. From this and no other reasons it often happens that I do not readily employ my pen in any gratuitous exertions."[1] But these exertions were not sufficient: the probation must last longer. In the same month, on the 23rd, he writes to the same friend, who had made enquiry as to his occupations and plans: "I am sure that you wish me to gratify your curiosity, and to let you know what I have been doing, or am meditating to do. Hear me, my Diodati, and suffer me for a moment to speak without blushing in a more lofty strain. Do you ask what I am meditating? By the help of Heaven, an immortality of fame. But what am I doing? πτεροφυῶ, I am letting my wings grow and preparing to fly; but my Pegasus has not yet feathers enough to soar aloft in the fields of air."[2] Four years later we find a similar admission—"I have neither yet completed to my mind the full circle of my private studies...."[3]

---

[1] *P. W.* III. 492.
[2] *P. W.* III. 495.
[3] *P. W.* II. 476.

This last sentence was written in 1640 (or 1641). Meanwhile his resolution had been confirmed by the friendly and flattering encouragement of Italian *savants*—a stimulus which he records in an oft-cited passage :[1]

"In the private academies[2] of Italy, whither I was favoured to resort, perceiving that some trifles[3] which I had in memory, composed at under twenty or thereabout, (for the manner is, that every one must give some proof of his wit and reading there,) met with acceptance above what was looked for; and other things,[4] which I had shifted in scarcity of books and conveniences to patch up amongst them, were received with written encomiums, which the Italian is not forward to bestow on men of this side the Alps; I began thus far to assent both to them and divers of my friends here at home, and not less to an inward prompting which now grew daily upon me, that by labour and intense study (which I take to be my portion in this life), joined with the strong propensity of nature, I might perhaps leave something so written to aftertimes, as they should not willingly let it die."

It was during this Italian journey (1638–39) that Milton first gave a hint of the particular direction in which this ambition was setting: at least we are vouchsafed a glimpse of the possible subject-matter of the contemplated poem,

[1] *The Reason of Church Government, P. W.* II. 477, 478; a few lines have been quoted in the *Life* of Milton. A passage similar to the concluding sentence might be quoted from the pamphlet *Animadversions*, published the same year (1641) as the *Church Government*; see *P. W.* III. 72.

[2] He refers to literary societies or clubs, of which there were several at Florence, e.g. the Della Crusca, the Svogliati, etc.

[3] I.e. Latin pieces; the *Elegies*, as well as some of the poems included in his *Sylvæ*, were written before he was twenty-one.

[4] Among the Latin poems which date from his Italian journey are the lines *Ad Salsillum*, a few of the *Epigrams*, and *Mansus*. Perhaps, too, the "other things" comprehended those essays in Italian verse which he had the courage to read before a Florentine audience, and they the indulgence to praise.

and there is that on which may be built conjecture as to its style. He had enjoyed at Naples the hospitality of the then famous writer Giovanni Battista Manso, whose courteous reception the young English traveller, *ut ne ingratum se ostenderet*, acknowledged in the piece of Latin hexameters afterwards printed in his *Sylvæ* under the title *Mansus*. In the course of the poem Milton definitely speaks of the remote legends of British history—more especially, the Arthurian legend—as the theme which he might some day treat. "May I", he says, "find such a friend[1] as Manso",

> "*Siquando*[2] *indigenas revocabo in carmina reges,*
> *Arturumque etiam sub terris bella moventem,*
> *Aut dicam invictæ sociali fœdere mensæ*
> *Magnanimos heroas, et* (*O modo spiritus adsit*)
> *Frangam Saxonicas Britonum sub Marte phalanges!*"

This was in 1638. In the next year, after his return to England, he recurs to the project in the *Epitaphium Damonis* (162–71), his account being far more detailed:

> "*Ipse*[3] *ego Dardanias Rutupina per æquora puppes*
> *Dicam, et Pandrasidos regnum vetus Inogeniæ.*
> *Brennumque Arviragumque duces, priscumque Belinum,*
> *Et tandem Armoricos Britonum sub lege colonos;*

[1] I.e., a friend who would pay honour to him as Manso had paid honour to the poet Marini. Manso had helped in the erection of a monument to Marini at Naples; and Milton alludes to this at the beginning of the poem. From Manso he would hear about Tasso.

[2] "If ever I shall revive in verse our native kings, and Arthur levying war in the world below; or tell of the heroic company of the resistless Table Round, and—be the inspiration mine!—break the Saxon bands neath the might of British chivalry" (*Mansus*, 80–4). His Common-place Book has a quaint reference to "Arturs round table".

[3] "I will tell of the Trojan fleet sailing our southern seas, and the ancient realm of Imogen, Pandrasus' daughter, and of Brennus, Arviragus, and Belinus old, and the Armoric settlers subject to British laws. Then will I sing of Iogerne, fatally

Tum gravidam Arturo fatali fraude Iögernen;
Mendaces vultus, assumptaque Gorlöis arma,
Merlini dolus. O, mihi tum si vita supersit,
Tu procul annosa pendebis, fistula, pinu,
Multum oblita mihi, aut patriis mutata Camœnis
Brittonicum strides!"

Here, as before, he first glances at the stories which date
from the very dawn of British myth and romance, and then
passes to the most fascinating of the later cycles of national
legend—the grey traditions that cluster round the hero of
the *Idylls of the King*, the son of mythic Uther. And this
passage, albeit the subject which it indicates was afterwards rejected by Milton, possesses a twofold value for
those who would follow, step by step, the development of
the idea which had as its final issue the composition of
Paradise Lost. For, first, the concluding verses show that
whatever the theme of the poem, whatever the style, the
instrument of expression would be English. Just as Dante
had weighed the merits of the vernacular and Latin and
chosen the former, though the choice imposed on him the
creation of an ideal, transfigured Italian out of the baser
elements of many competing dialects, so Milton—more
fortunate than Dante in that he found an instrument ready
to use—will use that "native language" whose help he had
petitioned in the *Vacation Exercise*. An illustration of his
feeling on this point is furnished by the treatise on *Church
Government*. He says there that his work must make for
"the honour and instruction" of his country: "I applied

pregnant with Arthur—how Uther feigned the features and
assumed the armour of Gorlois, through Merlin's craft. And
you, my pastoral pipe, an life be lent me, shall hang on some
sere pine, forgotten of me; or changed to native notes shall
shrill forth British strains." In the first lines he alludes to the
legend of Brutus and the Trojans landing in England. *Rutu-
pina* = Kentish. The story of Arthur's birth at which he glances
is referred to in the *Idylls of the King*. The general drift of the
last verses is that he will give up Latin for English verse; *strides*
is a future, from *strido* (cf. *Æneid* IV. 689).

myself to that resolution which Ariosto followed...to fix
all the industry and art I could unite to the adorning of my
native tongue; not to make verbal curiosities the end (that
were a toilsome vanity), but to be an interpreter and relater
of the best and sagest things among mine own citizens
throughout this island in the mother dialect. That what the
greatest and choicest wits of Athens, Rome, or modern
Italy, and those Hebrews of old did for their country, I, in
my proportion, with this over and above, of being a
Christian, might do for mine;[1] not caring to be once
named abroad, though perhaps I could attain to that, but
content with these British islands as my world." Here is
a clear announcement of his ambition to take rank as a
great national poet. The note struck is patriotism. He will
produce that which shall set English on a level with the
more favoured Italian, and give his countrymen cause to be
proud of their
                    " dear dear land,
         Dear for her reputation through the world ".[2]

To us indeed it may appear strange that Milton should
have thought it worth while to emphasise what would now
be considered a self-evident necessity: what modern poet,
with a serious conception of his office and duty, would
dream of employing any other language than his own? But
we must remember that in those days the empire of the
classics was unquestioned: scholarship was accorded a
higher dignity than now: the composition of long poems

---

[1] *P. W.* II. 478. Reference has been made so frequently to
this pamphlet on *The Reason of Church Government urged against
Prelaty* (1641), that it may be well to explain that the introduction to the second book is entirely autobiographical. Milton
shows why he embarked on such controversies, how much it
cost him to do so, what hopes he had of returning to poetry,
what was his view of the poet's mission and of his own capacity
to discharge that mission. His prose works contain nothing
more valuable than these ten pages of self-criticism.

[2] *Richard II*, II. i. 57, 58.

in Latin was still a custom honoured in the observance:
and whoso sought to appeal to the "laureate fraternity" of
scholars and men of letters, independently of race and
country, would naturally turn to the *lingua franca* of the
learned. At any rate, the use of English—less known than
either Italian or French—placed a poet at a great disadvantage, so far as concerned acceptance in foreign lands;
and when Milton determined to rely on his *patriæ
Camœnæ*, he foresaw that this would circumscribe his
audience, and that he might have to rest content with the
applause of his own countrymen.

Again, these lines in the *Epitaphium* give us some grounds
of surmise as to the proposed form of his poem. The
historic events—or traditions—epitomised in the passage
were too far separated in point of time, and too devoid of
internal coherence and connection, to admit of dramatic
treatment. Milton evidently contemplated a narrative
poem, and for one who had drunk so deep of the classical
spirit a narrative could scarce have meant aught else than
an epic. Indeed thus much is implied by some sentences
in *The Reason of Church Government*, which represent
him as considering whether to attempt "that epic form
whereof the two poems of Homer, and those other two of
Virgil and Tasso, are a diffuse, and the book of Job a brief
model...or whether those dramatic constitutions, wherein
Sophocles and Euripides reign, shall be found more
doctrinal and exemplary to a nation".[1]

But 'dramatic' introduces a fresh phase; and as the first
period of the history of *Paradise Lost*, or rather of the idea
which finally took shape in that poem, closes with the
Epitaphium (1639), it may not be amiss to summarise the
impressions deduced up to this point from the various
passages which we have quoted from Milton. We have
seen, then, Milton's early resolve; its ambitious scope; his
self-preparation; the encouragement he received in Italy

[1] *P. W.* II. 478, 479.

and from friends at home; his announcement in 1638,
repeated in 1639, that he has discovered a suitable subject
in British fable—more especially, in the legend of the
Coming and Passing of Arthur; his formal farewell to Latin
verse, in favour of his native tongue; his desire to win
recognition as a great national *vates*; and his selection of
the epic style.

In respect of chronology we have reached the year
1639–40. The second period extends from 1640 to 1642.
We shall see that some verses of *Paradise Lost* were written
about 1642: after 1642, up till 1658, we hear no more of the
poem—proof that the idea has been temporarily abandoned
under stress of politics. Therefore 1642 may be regarded
as the ulterior limit of this second period. And it is not,
I think, fanciful to consider that *Paradise Lost* entered on
a fresh stage about 1640, because between that year and
1642 Milton's plans underwent a twofold change by
which the character of the poem was entirely altered.

First, the subject for which he had shown so decided a
bias is discarded: after 1639 no mention is made of King
Arthur. We have no hint of the cause which led Milton to
drop the subject; but it may well have lain in his increasing
republicanism. He could not have treated the theme from
an unfavourable standpoint. The hero of the poem must
have been for him, as for the Milton of our own age, a type
of all kingly grandeur and worth; and it would have gone
sore against the grain with the future apologist for regicide
to exercise his powers in creating a royal figure that would
shed lustre on monarchy, and in a measure plead for the
institution which Milton detested so heartily. Only a
Royalist could have retold the story, making it illustrate
"the divine right of kings", and embodying in the character
of the blameless monarch the Cavalier conception of
Charles I. Perhaps too he was influenced by discovering,
after fuller research, the mythical character of the legend.
So much is rather implied by some remarks in his *History
of Britain*. Milton with his intense earnestness was not the

poet to build a long work on what he had found to be mainly fiction. Be this as it may, Milton rejected the subject, and it finds no place in a list of one hundred possible subjects of his poem.

Secondly, from this period, 1640–2, dates an alteration in the design of the contemplated work. Hitherto his tendency has been towards the epic form: now (1640 or 1641) we find him preferring the dramatic. Shall he imitate Sophocles and Euripides? Shall he transplant to English soil the art of the "lofty grave tragedians" of Greece? The question is answered in a decided affirmative. Had Milton continued the poem of which the opening lines were written in 1642 we should have had—not an epic but—a drama, or possibly a trilogy of dramas, cast in a particular manner, as will be observed presently. This transference of his inclinations from the epic to the dramatic style appears to date from 1641. It is manifested in the Milton MS. at Trinity College.

When the present library of Trinity College, the erection of which was begun during the Mastership of Isaac Barrow, was completed, one of its earliest benefactors was a former member of Trinity, Sir Henry Newton Puckering. Among his gifts was "a thin folio MS. of less than thirty leaves", which had served Milton as a note-book. How it came into the possession of Sir Henry Puckering is not known. He was contemporary with, though junior to, Milton, and may possibly have been one of the admirers who visited the poet in the closing years of his life; or perhaps there was some family connection by means of which the MS. passed into his hands. But if the history of the note-book be obscure, its value is not; for it contains the original drafts of several of his early poems: notably of *Arcades*, *Lycidas* and *Comus*, together with fourteen of the Sonnets, and memoranda relating to his great work. And the bulk of the MS. (forty out of forty-seven written pages) is in Milton's autograph.

It is known that the little volume was rebound in 1736, by which date some of the leaves had got loose, and there is some uncertainty as to the correctness of the order of just the last few pages. But as regards pages 1–42, there seems no reason to doubt that the MS. exists exactly as Milton used it and that we have in all essentials the order in which its contents were entered by him. They cover a long period (1633–58), from *Arcades*, with which the MS. begins, to the last of his Sonnets—"Methought I saw". It is rather more than half way through the MS. that we light on the entries which have so direct a bearing on the history of *Paradise Lost*.

These are notes, written by Milton himself (probably in 1641), and occupying seven pages of the manuscript, on subjects which seemed to him suitable, in varying degrees of appropriateness, for his poem. Some of the entries are very brief—concise jottings down, in two or three words, of any theme that struck him. Others are more detailed: the salient features of some episode in history are selected, and a sketch of the best method of treating them added. In a few instances these sketches are filled in with much minuteness and care: the 'economy' or arrangement of the poem is marked out—the action traced from point to point. But, *Paradise Lost* apart, this has been done in only a few cases—a half dozen, at most. As a rule, the source whence the material of the work might be drawn is indicated. The subjects themselves, numbering just one hundred, fall, in a rough classification, under two headings— Scriptural and British: and by 'British' are meant those which Milton drew from the chronicles of British history prior to the Norman Conquest. The former are the more numerous class: sixty-two being derived from the Bible, of which the Old Testament claims fifty-four. Their character will be best illustrated by quotation of a few typical examples:

> Abram in Ægypt.
> Josuah in Gibeon.   Josu. 10.
> Jonathan rescu'd   Sam. 1. 14.
> Saul in Gilboa   1 Sam. 28. 31.

Gideon Idoloclastes   Jud. 6. 7.
Abimelech the usurper.   Jud. 9.
Samaria liberata[1]   2 Reg. 7.
Asa or Æthiopes.   2 chron. 14. with
the deposing his mother, and burning her Idol.

These are some of the subjects drawn from the New
Testament:

> Christ bound
> Christ crucifi'd
> Christ risen.
> Lazarus   Joan. 11.
> Christus patiens

The Scene in yᵉ garden beginning frō yᵉ comming thither
till Judas betraies & yᵉ officers lead him away yᵉ rest by
message & chorus. his agony may receav noble expressions

Of British subjects[2] there are thirty-three. The last page
is assigned to " Scotch stories or rather brittish of the north
parts ". Among these *Macbeth* is conspicuous. Practically
they may be grouped with the thirty-three, and the combined list is remarkable—first, because it does not include
the Arthurian legend, which had once exercised so powerful a fascination on Milton; secondly, because in its
brevity, as compared with the list of Scriptural subjects, it
suggests his preference for a sacred poem.

Of the Scriptural subjects the story of the Creation and
Fall assumes the most prominent place. Any friend of

---

[1] The title is an obvious allusion to Tasso's *Gerusalemme
Liberata*.

[2] Milton's attitude towards them is illustrated indirectly by
his *History of Britain*. In his paper on " Milton as an Historian "
read before the British Academy recently (Nov. 25, 1908)
Professor Firth says: " It was not only by his treatment of the
mythical period of English history that Milton's interest in the
legendary and anecdotic side of history was revealed. It
appeared in the later books as well as the earlier, and the
introduction of certain episodes, or the space devoted to them,
might often be explained by their inclusion in the list of suggested subjects for his ' British Tragedies '."

Milton glancing through these papers in 1641 could have conjectured, with tolerable certainty, where the poet's final choice would fall. For no less than four of the entries refer to *Paradise Lost*. Three of these stand at the head of the list of sacred themes. In two at least his intention to treat the subject in dramatic form is patent. The two first—mere enumerations of possible *dramatis personæ*—run thus;[1] it will be seen that the longer list is simply an expansion of the other:

the Persons	the Persons
Michael	Moses[2]
Heavenly Love	Justice.[3] Mercie Wisdome
Chorus of Angels	Heavenly Love
Lucifer	Hesperus the Evening Starre
Adam ⎱ with the serpent	Chorus of Angels
Eve ⎰	Lucifer
Conscience	Adam
Death	Eve
Labour ⎫	Conscience[4]
Sicknesse ⎪	Labour ⎫
Discontent ⎬ mutes	Sicknesse ⎪
Ignorance ⎪	Discontent ⎬ mutes
with others ⎭	Ignorance ⎪
Faith	Feare ⎭
Hope	Death
Charity	Faith
	Hope
	Charity

These lists are crossed out; and underneath stands a much fuller sketch, in which the action of the tragedy is

---

[1] Neither is introduced with any title.

[2] Milton first wrote "Michael", as in the other list, but subsituted "Moses".

[3] The epithet *Divine*, qualifying *Justice*, was inserted and then crossed out again. "Wisdome" was added.

[4] After *Conscience* Milton added *Death*, as in the first list; then deleted it, and placed Death among the 'mutes' (*mutæ personæ*, characters who appeared without speaking).

shown, and the division into acts observed. Here, too, we first meet with the title *Paradise Lost*. The scheme is as follows:

Paradise Lost   The Persons

Moses προλογίϛει recounting how he assum'd his true bodie, that it corrupts not because of his with god in the mount declares the like of Enoch and Eliah, besides the purity of yᵉ pl ¹ that certaine pure winds, dues, and clouds præserve it from corruption whence   horts¹ to the sight of god, tells they² cannot se Adam in the state of innocence by reason of thire sin³

Justice ⎫
Mercie   ⎬ debating what should become of man if he fall
Wisdome ⎭

Chorus of Angels sing a hymne of yᵉ creation⁴

Act 2

Heavenly Love
Evening starre
chorus sing the mariage song⁵ and describe Paradice

Act 3

Lucifer contriving Adams ruine
Chorus feares for Adam and relates Lucifers rebellion and fall⁶

Act 4

Adam ⎫
Eve   ⎬ fallen
Conscience cites them to Gods examination⁷
Chorus bewails and tells the good Adā hath lost

----

¹ The margin of the MS. is frayed here.
² *they*, i.e. the imaginary audience to whom the prologue is addressed. Cf. the commencement of *Comus*.
³ After this the first act begins.
⁴ Cf. VII. 253–60, note.
⁵ Cf. IV. 711.
⁶ Cf. bks. V–VI.
⁷ Cf. X. 97 *et seq.*

Act 5

Adam and Eve, driven out of Paradice
    præsented by an angel with[1]

Labour ⎫
greife ⎪
hatred ⎪
Envie ⎪
warre ⎪
famine ⎪   mutes to whome he gives thire names
Pestilence ⎬   likewise winter, heat Tempest[2] &c
sicknesse ⎪
discontent ⎪
Ignorance ⎪
Feare ⎪
Death enterd ⎪
into ye world ⎭

Faith ⎫
Hope ⎬ comfort him and istruct him
Charity ⎭

Chorus breifly concludes

This draft of the tragedy, which occurs on page 35 of the MS., is not deleted; but Milton was still dissatisfied, and later on, page 40, we come to a fourth, and concluding, scheme—which reads thus:

Adam unparadiz'd[3]

The angel Gabriel, either descending or entering,[4] shewing since this globe was created, his frequency as much on earth, as in heavn, describes Paradise. next the Chorus shewing the reason of his[5] comming to keep his watch in Paradise after Lucifers rebellion by command from god, & withall expressing his desire to see, & know more concerning this excellent new creature man. the angel Gabriel as by his name signifying a

---

[1] Cf. bks. XI–XII.   [2] See X. 651, note.

[3] Underneath was written, and crossed out, an alternative title—*Adams Banishment*.

[4] Cf. *Comus*, "The Attendant Spirit descends or enters" (*ad init.*).

[5] *his*, i.e. the chorus's; he makes the chorus now a singular, now a plural, noun.

prince of power tracing[1] paradise with a more free office passes
by the station of y^c chorus & desired by them relates what he
knew of man as the creation of Eve with thire love, & mariage.
after this Lucifer appeares after his overthrow, bemoans himself,
seeks revenge on man the Chorus prepare resistance at his first
approach at last after discourse of enmity on either side he
departs wherat the chorus sings of the battell, & victorie in
heavn against him & his accomplices, as before after the first
act[2] was sung a hymn of the creation. heer[3] again may appear
Lucifer relating, & insulting in what he had don to the destruction of man. man next & Eve having by this time bin seduc't
by the serpent appeares confusedly cover'd with leaves conscience in a shape accuses him, Justice cites him to the place
whither Jehova call'd for him in the mean while the chorus
entertains[4] the stage, & his [sic] inform'd by some angel the
manner of his fall heer[3] the chorus bewailes Adams fall. Adam
then & Eve returne accuse one another but especially Adam
layes the blame to his wife, is stubborn in his offence Justice
appeares reason[5] with him convinces him the[3] chorus admonisheth
Adam, & bids him beware by Lucifers example of impenitence
the Angel is sent to banish them out of paradise but before
causes to passe before his eyes in shapes a mask of all the evills[6]
of this life & world he is humbl'd relents, dispaires. at last
appeares Mercy comforts him promises the Messiah, then calls
in faith, hope, & charity, instructs him he repents gives god the
glory, submitts to his penalty the chorus breifly concludes.
compare this with the former draught.

"It appears plain", says Todd, "that Milton intended to
have marked the division of the Acts in this sketch, as well
as in the preceding. Peck has divided them; and closes the
first Act with Adam and Eve's love." The other Acts may
be supposed to conclude at the following points: Act 2 at
"sung a hymn of the creation"; Act 3 at "inform'd . . . the

[1] passing through; of. *Comus*, 423.
[2] I.e. in the third draft.
[3] Each of these sentences was an after-thought, added below
or in the margin.
[4] occupies.
[5] I.e. reasons; or '*to* reason'.
[6] See XI. 477–93, note.

manner of his fall"; Act 4 at "bids him beware...
impenitence"; Act 5 at "the chorus breifly concludes".

It is in regard to the first Act that this fourth draft, which
Milton bids us "compare with the former", marks a
distinct advance. Milton made Moses the speaker of the
prologue in the third draft because so much of the subject-
matter of *Paradise Lost* is drawn from the Mosaic books of
the Old Testament. But the appearance of a descendant of
Adam, even in a prologue, where much latitude is allowed
by convention, seems an awkward prelude to scenes
coincident with Adam's own creation. It is far more
natural that, before the subject of man's fall is touched
upon at all, we should be told who man is, and that this
first mention of him should come from the supernatural
beings who had, or might have, witnessed the actual
creation of the universe and its inhabitants. The explanation, too, why Moses is able to assume his natural body is
very forced. And altogether this fourth draft exhibits more
of drama, less of spectacle, than its predecessor.

With regard to the subject, therefore, thus much is clear:
as early as 1641–2 Milton has manifested an unmistakeable
preference for the story of the lost Paradise, and the
evidence of the Trinity MSS. coincides with the testimony
of Aubrey and Phillips, who say that the poet did, about
1642, commence the composition of a drama on this theme
—of which drama the opening verses of *Paradise Lost*,
book IV (Satan's address to the sun), formed the exordium.
It is, I think, by no means improbable that some other
portions of the epic are really fragments of this unfinished
work. Milton may have written two or three hundred lines,
have kept them in his desk, and then, years afterward,
when the project was resumed, have made use of them
where opportunity offered. Had the poem, however, been
completed in accordance with his original conception we
should have had a tragedy, not an epic.

Of this there is abundant proof. The third and fourth
sketches, as has been observed, are dramatic. On the first

page of these entries, besides those lists of *dramatis personæ* which we have treated as the first and second sketches, stand the words "*other* Tragedies", followed by the enumeration of several feasible subjects. The list of British subjects is prefaced with the heading—"British Trag." (i.e. tragedies). Wherever Milton has outlined the treatment of any of the Scriptural themes a tragedy is clearly indicated. Twice, indeed, another form is mentioned—the pastoral, and probably a dramatic pastoral was intended.[1] These, however, are exceptions, serving to emphasise his leaning towards tragedy.

But what sort of tragedy? I think we may fairly conclude that, if carried out on the lines laid down in the fourth sketch, *Adam unparadiz'd* would have borne a very marked resemblance to *Samson Agonistes*: it would have conformed, in the main, to the same type—that, namely, of the ancient Greek drama. With the romantic stage of the Elizabethans Milton appears to have felt little sympathy:[2] else he would scarce have written *Il Penseroso*, 101, 102. Nor do I believe that his youthful enthusiasm for Shakespeare remained unmodified:[3] certainly, the condemnation of one important aspect of Shakespearian tragedy in the preface to *Samson Agonistes* is too plain to be misinterpreted. So had Milton been minded to dramatise the story of Macbeth—we have marked its presence in the list of Scottish subjects—his *Macbeth* would have differed *toto cælo* from Shakespeare's. In the same way, his tragedy of *Paradise Lost* would have been wholly un-Shakespearian,

---

[1] These are the two entries in the MS.: "Theristria. a Pastoral out of Ruth"; and—"the sheepshearers in Carmel a Pastoral. 1 Sam. 25". There is but one glance at the epical style; in the list of "British Trag." after mentioning an episode in the life of King Alfred appropriate to dramatic handling, he adds—"A Heroicall Poem may be founded somwhere in Alfreds reigne. especially at his issuing out of Edelingsey on the Danes. whose actions are wel like those of Ulysses".

[2] See *Appendix* to *Samson Agonistes*.

[3] See note on *L'Allegro*, 133, 134.

wholly un-Elizabethan. Nor would it have had any
affinity to the drama of Milton's contemporaries,[1] those
belated Elizabethans bungling with exhausted materials
and forms that had lost all vitality. Tragedy for Milton
could mean but one thing—the tragic stage of the Greeks,
the "dramatic constitutions" of Sophocles and Euripides:
and when we examine these sketches of *Paradise Lost* we
find in them the familiar features of Athenian drama—
certain signs eloquent of the source on which the poet has
drawn.

Let us, for example, glance at the draft of *Adam unparadiz'd*. Milton has kept the 'unities' of place and time.
The scene does not change; it is set in some part of Eden,
and everything represented before the eyes of the audience
occurs at the same spot. But whoso regards the unity of
place must suffer a portion of the action to happen off the
stage—not enacted in the presence of the audience (as in
a modern play where the scene changes), but reported. In
Samson Agonistes Milton employs the traditional device of
the Greek tragedians—he relates the catastrophe by the
mouth of a messenger. So here: the temptation by the
serpent is not represented on the scene: it is described—
partly by Lucifer, "relating, and insulting in what he had
don to the destruction of man"; partly by an angel who
informs the Chorus of the manner of the fall. Again, the
unity of time is observed. The time over which the action
of a tragedy might extend, according to the usual practice
of the Greek dramatists, was twenty-four hours. In
Samson Agonistes the action begins at sunrise and ends at
noon, thus occupying seven or eight hours. In *Adam
unparadiz'd* the action would certainly not exceed the
customary twenty-four hours. Again a Chorus is introduced (sure sign of classical influence), and not only
introduced, but handled exactly as Milton, following his

[1] In the treatise *On Education*, 1644, he speaks of "our common rhymers and play-writers" as "despicable creatures",
P. W. III. 474.

Greek models, has handled it in *Samson Agonistes*: that is
to say, closely identified with the action of the tragedy,
even as Aristotle recommends that it should be. Further,
in the fourth scheme the division into acts is carefully
avoided—an advance this on the third scheme. Similarly,
in *Samson Agonistes* Milton avoids splitting up the play
into scenes and acts, calling attention to the fact in his
preface. Proofs[1] of Milton's classical bias might be multi-
plied from these Milton MSS.; and personally I have no
doubt that when he began the tragedy of which Aubrey
and Phillips speak, he meant to revive in English the
methods and style of his favourite Greek poets. But the
scheme soon had to be abandoned; and not till a quarter of
a century later was it executed in *Samson Agonistes*.[2] With
Milton as with Dante the greatest came last—after long
delay: the life's work of each marked the life's close: and,
the work done, release soon came to each, though to Dante
sooner.[3]

[1] Thus, apart from *P. L.*, the Scriptural themes whereof the
fullest sketches are given, are three tragedies severally entitled
"Abram from Morea, or Isack redeemed—Baptistes" (i.e. on
the subject of John the Baptist and Herod)—and "Sodom
Burning". In each two unities (time and place) are kept, and
a Chorus used. In "Isack redeemed" the incident of the sacrifice is reported, and the description of the character of the hero
Abraham as Milton meant to depict him is simply a paraphrase
on Aristotle's definition of the ideal tragic hero. Most of the
other subjects have a title such as the Greek tragedians employed
—e.g. "Elias Polemistes", "Elisæus Hydrochóos", "Zedechiah
νεοτερίϛων.".

[2] The point is important because it disposes of the notion that
Milton borrowed the idea of writing a tragedy on the classical
model from the play of *Samson* by the Dutch poet Vondel.

[3] "There is at once similarity and difference in the causes
which made each postpone the execution of his undertaking till
a comparatively late period in his life; and a curious parallel
may be observed in the length of time between the first conception and the completion of their monumental works, as well
as in the period that elapsed between the end of their labours
and their death." (Courthope.)

The third period in the genesis of *Paradise Lost* dates from 1658. In that year, according to Aubrey, Milton began the poem as we know it. By then he had gone back to the epic style. He was still Secretary, but his duties were very light, and allowed him to devote himself to poetry. At the Restoration he was in danger, for some time, of his life, and was imprisoned for a few months. But in spite of this interruption, and of his blindness,[1] the epic was finished about 1663. The history of each of his longer poems shows that he was exceedingly careful in revising his works—loth to let them go forth to the world till all that was possible had been done to achieve perfection.[2] It is Aubrey's statement that *Paradise Lost* was completed in 1663; while Milton's friend Thomas Ellwood, the Quaker, describes in a famous passage of his *Autobiography*, how in 1665 the poet placed a manuscript in his hands—"bidding me take it home with me and read it at my leisure, and, when I had so done, return it to him with my judgment thereupon. When I came home, and had set myself to read it, I found

---

[1] According to Edward Phillips, Milton dictated the poem to any one who chanced to be present and was willing to act as amanuensis; afterwards Phillips would go over the MS., correcting errors, under his uncle's direction. The original transcript submitted to the Licenser is extant, and is one of the many literary treasures that have gone to America. It "passed from the possession of the first printer of the poem, Samuel Simmons, to Jacob Tonson [the publisher], and thence to his collateral descendants, remaining in the same family...until 1904", when it was bought by an American collector. (From an article in *The Athenæum* on "*Miltoniana* in America".)

[2] "When we look at his earlier manuscripts, with all their erasures and corrections, we may well wonder what the *Paradise Lost* would have been if he had been able to give it the final touches of a faultless and fastidious hand. When we think of it composed in darkness, preserved in memory, dictated in fragments, it may well seem to us the most astonishing of all the products of high genius guided by unconquerable will" (J. W. Mackail).

it was that excellent poem which he intituled *Paradise Lost*." Ellwood's account may be reconciled with Aubrey's on the reasonable supposition that the interval between 1663 and 1665 was spent in revision. Still, some delay in publishing the poem ensued. On the outbreak of the Plague in 1665 Milton had left London, retiring to Chalfont in Buckinghamshire, where Ellwood had rented a cottage for him. He returned in the next year, 1666; but again there was delay—this time through the great Fire of London which disorganised business. Not till 1667 did *Paradise Lost* appear in print. The agreement (now in the possession of the British Museum) drawn up between Milton and his publisher—by which he received an immediate payment of £5, and retained certain rights over the future sale of the book—is dated April 27, 1667. The date on which *Paradise Lost* was entered in the Stationers' Register is August 20, 1667. No doubt, copies were in circulation in the autumn of this year.

The system of licensing publications, against which Milton had protested so vehemently in his *Areopagitica*, had been revived by the Press Act of 1662 and was now strongly enforced. "By that act", says Dr Masson, "the duty of licensing books of general literature had been assigned to the Secretaries of State, the Archbishop of Canterbury, and the Bishop of London; but it was exceptional for any of those dignitaries to perform the duty in person. It was chiefly performed for them by a staff of under-licencers, paid by fees." Five or six of his chaplains acted so for the Archbishop; and according to tradition one of them, to whom *Paradise Lost* was submitted, hesitated to give his *imprimatur* on account of the lines in the first book about eclipses perplexing monarchs with fear of change (I. 594–9). Milton must have remembered grimly the bitter gibes in his pamphlets, e.g. in the *Animadversions* (1641) against "monkish prohibitions, and expurgatorious indexes", and "proud Imprimaturs not to be obtained without the shallow surview, but not shallow hand of some

mercenary, narrow-souled, and illiterate chaplain". The
wheel had come full circle with a vengeance.

This first edition of *Paradise Lost* raises curious points[1]
of bibliography into which there is no need to enter here;
but we must note three things. The poem was divided into
—not twelve books but—ten. In the earlier copies issued
to the public there were no prose *Arguments*; these (written,
we may suppose, by Milton himself) were printed all
together and inserted at the commencement of each of the
later volumes of this first edition—an awkward arrangement changed in the second edition. Milton prefixed to
the later copies the brief prefatory note on *The Verse*, ex-
plaining why he had used blank verse; and it was preceded
by the address of *The Printer to the Reader*. It seems that
the number of copies printed in the first edition was 1500;
and the statement of another payment made by the
publisher to Milton on account of the sale of the book
shows that by April 26, 1669, i.e. a year and a half after
the date of publication, 1300 copies had been disposed of.

In 1674 the second edition was issued—with several
changes. First, the epic (said to be 670 lines longer than the
Æneid) was divided into twelve books, a more Vergilian
number, by the subdivision of books VII and X. Secondly,
the prose *Arguments* were transferred from the beginning
and prefixed to their respective books. Thirdly, a few
changes were introduced into the text—few of any great

---

[1] For example, no less than nine distinct title-pages of this
edition have been traced. This means that, though the whole
edition was printed in 1667, only a limited number of copies
were bound up and issued in that year. The rest would be kept
in stock, unbound, and published in instalments, as required.
Hence new matter could be inserted (such as the prose *Arguments*), and in each instalment it would be just as easy to bind
up a new title-page as to use the old one. Often the date had
to be changed: and we find that two of these pages bear the
year 1667; four, 1668; and three, 1669. Seven have Milton's
name in full; two, only his initials. Mr Leigh Sotheby collated
them carefully in his book on Milton's autograph, pp. 81–84.

significance. It was to the second edition that the commendatory verses by Samuel Barrow and Andrew Marvell were prefixed. Four years later, 1678, came the third edition, and in 1688 the fourth. This last was the well-known folio published by Tonson; *Paradise Regained* and *Samson Agonistes* were bound up with some copies of it, so that Milton's three great works were obtainable in a single volume. The first annotated edition of *Paradise Lost* was that edited by Patrick Hume in 1695, being the sixth reprint. And during the 18th century editions[1] were numerous. "Milton scholarship",[2] it has been justly said, "was active throughout the whole period."

There is, indeed, little (if any) ground for the view which one so frequently comes across—that *Paradise Lost* met with scant appreciation, and that Milton was neglected by his contemporaries, and without honour in his lifetime. To the general public epic poetry will never appeal, more especially if it be steeped in the classical feeling that pervades *Paradise Lost*; but there must have been a goodly number of scholars and lettered readers to welcome the work—else why these successive editions, appearing at no very lengthy intervals? One thing, doubtless, which prejudiced its popularity was the personal resentment of the Royalist classes at Milton's political actions. They could not forget his long identification with republicanism; and there was much in the poem itself—covert sneers and gibes—which would repel many who were loyal to the Church and the Court. Further, the style of *Paradise Lost* was something very different from the prevailing tone of

---

[1] Pre-eminent among them is Bishop Newton's edition (1749). He was the first editor who took pains to secure accuracy of text, doing, on a smaller scale, for Milton what Theobald did for Shakespeare. His services too in the elucidation of certain aspects (notably the Scriptural) of Milton's learning have never been surpassed.

[2] See Professor Dowden's Tercentenary paper "Milton in the Eighteenth Century (1701–1750)".

the literature then current and popular. Milton was the last of the Elizabethans, a lonely survival lingering on into days when French influence was beginning to dominate English taste. Even the metre of his poem must have sounded strange to ears familiarised to the crisp clearness and epigrammatic ring of the rhymed couplet.[1] Yet, in spite of these obstacles, many whose praise was worth the having were proud of Milton: they felt that he had done honour to his country. He was accorded that which he had sought so earnestly—acceptance as a great national poet; and it is pleasant to read how men of letters and social distinction would pay visits of respect to him, and how the white-winged Fame bore his name and reputation abroad, so that foreigners came to England for the especial purpose of seeing him. And their visits were the prelude of that foreign renown and influence from which he seemed to have cut himself off when he made his native tongue the medium of his great work. "Milton was the first English poet to inspire respect and win fame for our literature on the Continent, and to his poetry was due, to an extent that has not yet been fully recognised, the change which came over European ideas in the eighteenth century with regard to the nature and scope of the epic. *Paradise Lost* was the mainstay of those critics who dared to vindicate, in the face of French classicism, the rights of the imagination over the reason in poetry."[2]

[1] Cf. Marvell's "Commendatory Verses", 45–54.
[2] Professor J. G. Robertson, "Milton's Fame on the Continent", a paper read before the British Academy, Dec. 10, 1908.

Perhaps the strangest and most delightful evidence of Milton's acceptance among foreigners was Mr Maurice Baring's discovery of the popularity of *Paradise Lost*, in a prose translation, amongst the Russian peasantry and private soldiers:

"The schoolmaster said that after all his experience the taste of the peasants in literature baffled him. 'They will not read modern stories', he said. 'When I ask them why they like *Paradise Lost* they point to their heart and say, "It is near to the heart; it speaks; you read, and a sweetness comes to you"'."

There has been much discussion about the 'sources' of *Paradise Lost*, and writers well nigh as countless as Vallombrosa's autumn leaves have been thrust forth from their obscurity to claim the honour of having 'inspired' (as the phrase is) the great epic. Most of these unconscious claimants were, like enough, unknown to Milton; but some of them do seem to stand in a relation which demands recognition.

I should place first the Latin tragedy *Adamus Exul* (1601), written in his youth by the great jurist Hugo Grotius after the model of Seneca. Apart from the question of actual resemblances to *Paradise Lost*, it might fairly be conjectured, if not assumed, that Milton read this tragedy. He knew Grotius personally and knew his works. Describing, in the *Second Defence*, his Italian tour in 1638, Milton mentions his stay in Paris and friendly reception by the English ambassador, and adds: "His lordship gave me a card of introduction to the learned Hugo Grotius, at that time ambassador from the Queen of Sweden to the French court; whose acquaintance I anxiously desired."[1] He quotes the opinions of Grotius with high respect in his treatise on divorce.[2] The alternative titles of the fourth draft of Milton's own contemplated tragedy, viz. *Adam unparadiz'd* and *Adams Banishment*, certainly recall the title *Adamus Exul*; and it may be noted that this draft was sketched in that period (about 1641) of Milton's life to which his meeting with Grotius belongs. Of the likeness between *Paradise Lost* and the *Adamus Exul*, and other works dealing with the same theme, it is impossible to say how much, if not all, is due to identity of subject and (what is no less important) identity of convention as to the machinery proper for its treatment. But I do not think that community of subject accounts entirely for the resemblances between *Paradise Lost* and Grotius's tragedy. The conception of Satan's character and motives unfolded

[1] *P. W.* I. 255.
[2] See chapters XVII, XVIII of *The Doctrine and Discipline*.

in his long introductory speech in the *Adamus*, the general idea of his escaping from Hell and surveying Eden, his invocation of the powers of evil (amongst them Chaos and Night)—these things and some others, such as the Angel's narrative to Adam of the Creation, seem like far-off embryonic dawnings of the splendours of the epic. It should be added that Grotius's other religious plays were known in England. A free rendering of his *Christus Patiens* into rhymed heroics was published in London in 1640 under the title *Christ's Passion*; while his tragedy *Sophompaneas, or Joseph*, appeared in an English version in 1650. And a sidelight may be thrown not merely on the contemporary estimate of Grotius by the exceptionally eulogistic mention of his works in the *Theatrum Poetarum* (1675) of Milton's nephew Edward Phillips. The *Theatrum* is commonly supposed to reflect in some degree Milton's own views[1] and it is significant therefore to find Grotius described as one "whose equal in fame for Wit & Learning, Christendom of late Ages hath rarely produc'd, particularly of so happy a Genius in Poetry, that had his Annals, his Book *De Veritate Christianæ Religionis*...and other his extolled works in Prose, never come to Light, his extant and universally approved Latin Poems, had been sufficient to gain him a Living Name".

It is an easy transition from the *Adamus Exul* to the *Adamo* of the Italian poet Giovanni Battista Andreini (1578–1652), a Florentine, which is said to owe something to Grotius's tragedy. Voltaire, in his *Essai sur la Poésie Epique* written in 1727, related that Milton during his

---

[1] See v. 177, 673, notes. Other touches in the *Theatrum* of Miltonic interest are the accounts of Spenser and Sylvester, and the praise of Henry Lawes in the notice of Waller. One may conjecture, too, that the obscure Erycus Puteanus would not have had his niche but for *Comus*. The *Theatrum* includes also Andreini—but not Vondel. Phillips's account of Milton himself is admirably discreet: and he expressly terms *Paradise Lost* and *Paradise Regained* "Heroic Poems". The relations between uncle and nephew were more than ordinarily close.

residence at Florence saw "a comedy called *Adamo*.[1] . . . The subject of the play was the Fall of Man: the actors, the Devils, the Angels, Adam, Eve, the Serpent, Death, and the Seven Mortal Sins. . . . Milton pierced through the absurdity of that performance to the hidden majesty of the subject; which, being altogether unfit for the stage, yet might be, for the genius of Milton, and his only, the foundation of an epick poem." What authority he had for this legend Voltaire does not say. It is not alluded to by any of Milton's contemporary biographers. It may have been a mere invention by some ill-wisher of the poet, a piece of malicious gossip circulated out of political spite against the great champion of republicanism. But the authenticity of the story is not perhaps very important, for independently there seems to be evidence in the *Adamo* itself that Milton was acquainted with it even before his visit to Italy. One cannot read the scene of the *Adamo* (v. 5) in which the World, personified, tempts Eve with all its pomps and vanities, without being reminded of the scene in *Comus* of the temptation of the Lady. And, as with the *Adamus Exul*, some of the coincidences of incident and treatment between the *Adamo* and *Paradise Lost*, or Milton's early dramatic sketches of the action, seem to constitute a residuum of resemblance after full allowance has been made for the influence of practical identity of theme. Thus the list of characters in the *Adamo* has abstractions like the World, Famine, Labour, Despair, Death: and the appearance of these and kindred evils of life to Adam and Eve (Act IV, scenes 6 and 7) recalls the

[1] It had been printed in 1613 (Milan), and again in 1617. The title-page of the first edition describes the work as "L'Adamo, Sacra Rapresentatione". It is more "a hybrid between a miracle play and an opera" (Courthope) than a "comedy". A translation by Cowper and Hayley was printed in their edition of Milton; and it is in this translation that the work is known to me. The fact that Cowper took the *Adamo* theory seriously is significant.

early drafts of the scheme of *Paradise Lost* and also the
vision shown to Adam in the eleventh (477–99) book of the
poem. Andreini makes Michael drive Adam and Eve out
of Paradise and depicts a final struggle between Michael
and Lucifer. Andreini's representation of the Serpent's
temptation of Eve has been thought to have left some
impression on the parallel scene in *Paradise Lost*. After
the Fall Lucifer summons the spirits of air and fire, earth
and water—a counterpart to *Paradise Regained*, II. 115 *et
seq.* And occasionally a verbal similarity arrests—as where
Lucifer says (IV. 2, end):

> "Let us remain in hell!
> Since there is more content
> To live in liberty, tho' all condemn'd,
> Than, as his vassals, blest"[1]
> > ("*Poi, ch' è maggior contento
> > viver in libertà tutti damnati,
> > che sudditi beati*");

and inveighs (IV. 2):

> "*Ahi luce, ahi luce odiata!*"

or where the Angels describe Man (II. 1):

> "For contemplation of his Maker form'd"
> ("*Per contemplar del suo gran Fabro il merto*").

Leaving the matter for a moment we will pass to the
third claimant, the Dutch poet, Joost van den Vondel. He

---

[1] See I. 263, note; but of course the idea was not peculiar to
any writer. So tradition, literary or theological, may explain the
following similarity, which is at least an interesting illustration
of *P. L.* v. 688, 699. Andreini makes Lucifer (I. 3) address
his followers:

> "I am that Spirit, I, who for your sake
> Collecting dauntless courage, to the north
> Led you far distant from the senseless will
> Of him who boasts to have created heav'n."

The reference occurs again in the *Adamo*, III. 8.

Tradition also may account for another feature common to
the *Adamo*, the *Adamus* and *Paradise Lost*, viz. the long
description of the convulsions and deterioration in the physical
universe after the Fall of Man.

was contemporary with Milton, and the author of a great number of works. Among them were several dramas on Scriptural subjects. With three of them Milton is supposed by some writers to have been acquainted. These are *Lucifer* (1654), a drama on the revolt of the angels and their fall from heaven; *John the Messenger* (1662), and *Adam in Banishment* (1664). In a work published a few years since it was contended that Milton borrowed a good deal from these three poems.

That Milton had heard of Vondel may be conceded. Vondel enjoyed a great reputation; beside which, there was in the 17th century much intercourse between England and Holland, and Milton from his position as Secretary, no less than from his controversies with Salmasius and Morus, must have had his thoughts constantly directed towards the Netherlands. Also, we learn that he had some knowledge of the Dutch language. But it will be observed that the earliest of the poems with which he is thought to have been too conversant, namely *Lucifer*, was not published till after his blindness, while by the time that the last of them, *Adam in Banishment*, appeared, *Paradise Lost* was almost completed. It is impossible that Milton read a line of the works himself; if he knew them at all, it must have been through the assistance of some reader or translator; and considering how many details concerning the last years of Milton's life have survived, it is exceeding curious that this reader or translator should have escaped mention, and that the Vondelian theory should not have been heard of till a century after the poet's death. For there were plenty of people ready to do him an ill-turn and damage his repute; and plagiarism from his Dutch contemporary would have been an excellent cry to raise. As it is, Milton's biographers —and contemporaries—Phillips, Aubrey, Toland, Antony à Wood, are absolutely silent on the subject. Phillips indeed and Toland expressly mention the languages in which Milton used to have works read to him. The list is extensive: it includes Hebrew, Syriac, Greek, Latin, Italian,

Spanish and French: and it does *not* include Dutch. I
think that this fact tells heavily against the hypothesis of
Milton's indebtedness to Vondel. Still, it must be admitted
that critics of eminence accept it.

There remains the so-called Cædmon *Paraphrase*. In
the Bodleian is the manuscript of an Old English metrical
Paraphrase of parts[1] of the Old Testament. This work was
long attributed to the Northumbrian religious writer
Cædmon, of whom Bede speaks. Cædmon lived in the
seventh century. He is supposed to have died about 670.
There is no reason for thinking that he was not the author
of sacred poems, as Bede represents him to have been; but
there is also no possibility of believing that the *Paraphrase*,
as we have it, was written by him. It is a composite work
in which several hands may be traced, and the different
styles belong to a date long subsequent to Cædmon.[2] The
MS. was once in the possession of Archbishop Ussher.
He presented it in 1651 to his secretary, the Teutonic
scholar, Francis Dujon, commonly called Franciscus
Junius. Junius published the MS. at Amsterdam in 1655.
Milton never saw the *Paraphrase* in print, for the same
reason that he never saw Vondel's *Lucifer*. But inasmuch
as Junius had been settled in England since 1620, it is
quite likely that he knew Milton;[3] if so, he may have
mentioned the *Paraphrase*, and even translated[4] parts of it.

[1] Namely *Genesis, Exodus* and *Daniel*. It is the paraphrase of
Genesis that would have concerned Milton most.

[2] See the article by Mr Henry Bradley in the *Dictionary of
National Biography*. There is also a good discussion of the
authorship of the work in the Appendix to Professor Ten
Brink's *Early English Literature*.

[3] This was first pointed out by Sharon Turner; see also
Masson, *Life*, VI. 557.

[4] In a very ingenious paper in *Anglia*, IV. pp. 401–5, Pro-
fessor Wuelcker argues that Milton had not much knowledge of
Anglo-Saxon. In his *History of Britain* he habitually quotes
Latin Chronicles, and in one place virtually admits that an Old
English chronicle was not intelligible to him.

Here, however, as in the previous cases of Andreini and Vondel, we cannot get beyond conjecture, since there is no actual record or external evidence of Milton's acquaintance with the *Paraphrase* or its translator.

These then are the four possible 'sources' of *Paradise Lost* seemingly most deserving of mention; and of them the *Adamus Exul* and the *Adamo* strike me as unquestionably the most important, for various reasons. Milton's acquaintance with them may be referred to the early period when the influence on him of other writers would be greatest. The *Adamus* and the *Adamo* both present some points of resemblance to the early drafts of *Paradise Lost*. With the *Adamus* there is the special consideration of Milton's personal knowledge and admiration of its author. With the *Adamo*, apart from the possibility that Voltaire's story had some basis, there is the consideration of Milton's special devotion to Italian literature. With neither is there, at least not in the same degree as in the case of Vondel's works and the Cædmon *Paraphrase*, the difficulty involved by the poet's blindness. That he knew the *Adamus*[1] and the *Adamo* appears to me, now, hardly an open question. In these and similar works disinterred by the industry of Milton's editors lay the general conception, the theological machinery, the cosmic and supra-cosmic scene of a poem on the Fall of Man. So much is simply a matter of history; and to claim for Milton or any other writer who chose this theme the merit of absolute originality is simply to ignore history. The composition of religious poetry was the great literary activity of the earlier part of the 17th century, and Milton did on the grand scale what others did on the lower. The work of these lesser writers could not be without its influence on him, since no poet can detach himself from the conditions of his age or the associations of

---

[1] As regards the *Adamus Exul* William Lauder had *some* case, but spoilt it by his forgeries; for a sample of his libellous malevolence see I. 261-3, note. Todd (II. 585-9) has an Appendix on "Lauder's Interpolations".

a subject that has become common property and passed
into a convention. But that the qualities which have made
Paradise Lost immortal were due, in the faintest degree, to
any other genius than that of Milton himself: this is a fond
delusion, vainly imagined, without warranty, and altogether
to be cast out.

We must indeed recognise in *Paradise Lost*, the meeting-
point of Renaissance and Reformation, the impress of
four great influences: the Bible, the classics, the Italian
poets, and English literature. Of the Bible Milton possessed a knowledge such as few have had. There are
hundreds of allusions to it: the words of Scripture underlie
some part of the text of every page of *Paradise Lost*; and
apart from verbal reminiscences there is much of the spirit
that pervades that noblest achievement of the English
tongue. Scarcely less powerful was the influence of the
classics. Milton's allusiveness extends over the whole
empire of classical humanity and letters, and to the
scholar his work is full of the exquisite charm of endless
reference to the noblest things that the ancients have
thought and said. That he was deeply versed in Italian
poetry the labours of his early editors have abundantly
proved; and their comparative studies are confirmed by
the frequent mention of Dante,[1] Petrarch, Tasso, Ariosto

---

[1] See Dr Paget Toynbee's *Dante in English Literature*, I. 2,
120, 486, II. 587. Among the points noted are these: Dante
resemblances occur in Milton's early poems before his visit to
Italy; in his Commonplace Book Milton illustrates his views
several times by references to Dante; his rendering of three
lines of the *Inferno* in his treatise *Of Reformation* (see *P. L.* III.
444–97, note) is the first instance of the use of blank verse as a
medium for the translation of Dante and may have suggested
the use of that metre to Cary; Milton was one of the first
English poets to use Dante's *terza rima*—see his translation of
Psalm ii. headed "Done August 8, 1653. Terzetti". Dr
Toynbee also states that Milton's copy (the 3rd ed., Venice,
1529) of the *Convivio* is extant: "Milton has written his name
in the book and the date, 1629. The volume belonged to Heber

and others in his prose works and correspondence. In English literature I imagine that he had read everything worth reading. Without doubt, he was most affected by "our admired Spenser".[1] He was, says Dryden, "the poetical son of Spenser. Milton has acknowledged to me that Spenser was his original." And there was a Spenserian school of poets, mostly Cambridge men, and some of them contemporary with Milton at the University, with whose works he evidently had a considerable acquaintance. Among these the two Fletchers were conspicuous—Giles Fletcher, author of the sacred poems *Christ's Victorie on Earth* and *Christ's Triumph in Heaven*; and Phineas Fletcher, author of *The Purple Island*. The influence of the Fletchers is manifest in Milton's early poems,[2] and it is traceable in *Paradise Lost*. Finally, we must not forget Sylvester. Joshua Sylvester (of whom little is known beyond that he was born in 1563, died in 1618, and diversified the profession of merchant with the making of much rhyme) translated into exceedingly Spenserian verse *The Divine Weeks and Works* of the French poet, Du Bartas.[3] The subject of this very lengthy work is the story of Creation, with the early history of the Jews. The

[the book-collector, half-brother of the bishop], and was sold at his sale in 1834." It contained also the *Sonnets* (1563) of the Italian poet Casa and the marginal markings, if made by Milton, show that he had "read the Sonnets with great attention".

[1] *Animadversions*, P. W. III. 84. On Milton's feeling for Spenser see the note to *Il Penseroso*, 116–20.

[2] See the *Introductions* to *Comus* and *Lycidas*. Phineas Fletcher's *Apollyonists* might also be mentioned (see II. 650, 746, notes). Besides the Fletchers, there was Henry More, the famous "Cambridge Platonist". Milton must have known him at Christ's College.

[3] Sylvester translated a good deal from Du Bartas beside *The Divine Weeks*; and rhymed on his own account. The first collected edition of his translation of *The Divine Weeks* was published in 1605–6, instalments having appeared between 1592 and 1599. Dr Grosart collected Sylvester's works into two bulky volumes.

translation was amazingly popular. Dryden confessed that
he had once preferred Sylvester to Spenser.[1] There is no
doubt that Milton studied *The Divine Weeks* in his youth.
"That Poem hath ever had many great admirers among
us" is the suggestive comment of his nephew Edward
Phillips. It is certainly one of the works[2] whereof account
must be taken in any attempt to estimate the literary
influences that moulded Milton's style.

But a writer may be influenced by others, and not
'plagiarise'; and it is well to remember that from Virgil
downwards the great poets have exercised their royal right
of adapting the words of their forerunners and infusing
into them a fresh charm and suggestion, since in allusion
lies one of the chief delights of literature. It is well, also,
to realise wherein lies the greatness of *Paradise Lost*, and
to understand that all the borrowing in the world could not
contribute a jot to the qualities which have rendered the
epic "a possession for ever". What has made the poem
live is not the story, nobly though that illustrates the eternal
antagonism of righteousness and wrong, and the overthrow of evil; not the construction, though this is sufficiently
architectonic; nor the learning, though this is vast; nor the
characterisation, for which there is little scope: not these
things, though all are factors in the greatness of the poem,

---

[1] Spenser himself admired Du Bartas greatly; see the *Envoy*
addressed to the French poet Bellay at the end of *The Ruines of
Rome*.

In a paper read before the British Academy on some MS.
notes, "dealing mainly with the place of astronomy in poetry",
by Spenser's Cambridge friend Gabriel Harvey, Professor
Gollancz gave the following extract referring to Du Bartas and
Spenser:

"Mr Digges hath the whole Aquarius of Palingenius by
heart, and takes much delight to repeat it often. Mr Spenser
conceives the like pleasure in the fourth day of the first Week
of Bartas which he esteems as the proper profession of Urania."

[2] See some remarks and illustrations in Professor Mackail's
The Springs of Helicon (1909), pp. 195, 196.

and in all Milton rises to the height of his argument—but the incomparable elevation of the style, "the shaping spirit of Imagination", and the mere majesty of the music.

THE STORY OF THE POEM

A sketch of the action of the whole poem, following the sequence of the twelve books, may be useful to those who are acquainted only with parts of *Paradise Lost*:—

I. The scene Hell—the time nine days after the expulsion of Satan and his followers from Heaven. They lie on the burning lake, stupefied. Satan first recovers, rouses Beëlzebub, discusses with him their position, and then makes his way from the lake to a "dreary plain" of dry land. Beëlzebub follows; Satan calls to his comrades to do likewise. Rising on the wing they reach the same firm land. Their numbers and names described. They range themselves in battle-array before Satan, who addresses them. They may still (he says) regain Heaven; or there may be other worlds to win—in particular, a new world, inhabited by new-created beings, of which report had spoken: let these matters be duly conferred of. Straightway, a vast palace—Pandemonium—is made, to serve as council-chamber. Here a council is held; only the great Angels are present.

II. The scene—at first—Pandemonium; the debate begins. Satan invites their counsel—"who can advise may speak". Moloch, Belial and Mammon speak—their several counsels: last Beëlzebub, who reverts to Satan's hint of the new world. Why not ruin it? or make it their own? or win its inhabitants to their side? What better revenge against the Almighty? The plan approved—but who will discover this world? None volunteer: and then Satan offers to undertake the journey. His offer accepted; the council leaving Pandemonium breaks up; the result announced to the rest of the Angels. How they pass the time till his return—some exploring Hell (now more closely described). Meanwhile he reaches Hell-gates, is suffered to pass by

Sin and Death, voyages through Chaos (described), and at last comes within sight of the Universe hung in space (i.e. Chaos). We leave him directing his course towards the World.

III. The scene—at first—Heaven. The Almighty perceives Satan, points him out to the Son, tells what his design is, and its destined success; tells also that Man will be saved ultimately—if he can find a Redeemer. "The Son of God freely offers himself a ransom for Man"; is accepted by the Father, and praised by the Angelic host. Meanwhile —the scene changing—Satan, having reached the outer surface (described) of the Universe, wanders through various regions (described), until, coming to the single opening in the surface, he descends into the inside of the Universe. He arrives at the sphere of the Sun; disguising himself as a young Angel from Heaven, enquires from Uriel, the Sun-spirit, the way to Earth—pretending "desire to behold the new Creation"; is directed by Uriel, descends again, and alights on Mt Niphates.

IV. There, pausing awhile, he gives way to regret that he has rebelled, and rage at his outcast state; passion distorts his face, so that Uriel, watching, now knows him for an evil spirit. Thence, recovering self-control, Satan journeys on towards Eden, the main scene (described); sees Adam and Eve (famous description of them); overhears what they say concerning the Tree of Knowledge, and perceives at once the means whereby to compass their fall. At nightfall he essays to tempt Eve in a dream; is discovered by Gabriel, who, warned by Uriel, has descended to Eden to defend Man. A battle between Satan and Gabriel imminent, but averted. Satan flies.

V. The scene still Eden. A further picture of Adam and Eve—their worship and work. Raphael (the scene having changed for a brief space to Heaven) comes to warn them of their danger, at the bidding of the Almighty—so that Man, if he falls, may fall knowingly, by his own fault. Raphael received and entertained; admonishes Adam;

explains who his enemy is, and why: which leads to an
account of the rebellion in Heaven—its beginning
described.

VI. The scene of the events narrated by Raphael
Heaven. He describes the three days' war in Heaven, at
the end of which Satan and his followers were cast into
Hell. The warning to Adam repeated.

VII. The scene Eden. Raphael describes the Creation
of the World, which is accomplished by the Son of God.

VIII. The scene the same. Adam enquires concerning
the stars and Heavenly bodies; Raphael answers doubt-
fully. Adam recounts his own first experience of Eden—
how the Almighty forbade him to touch the Tree of
Knowledge, under pain of what penalty; how he first saw
Eve. The day declines, and Raphael departs—once more
warning Adam.

IX. The scene the same. "Adam and Eve...go forth to
their labours, which Eve proposes to divide in several
places, each labouring apart." Adam dissuades; she
persisting, he yields. So Satan (in the form of a serpent)
finds her alone and tempts her. She eats of the fruit and
induces Adam to do so. Their sense of sin and shame.

X. The Son of God descends to Eden, and pronounces
doom on Adam and Eve and the Serpent. Meanwhile
Satan, returning to Pandemonium, announces the result of
his journey, and lo! on a sudden he and his followers are
changed to reptiles. Sin and Death now ascend from Hell
to Eden, to claim the World as theirs; but the Almighty
foretells their ultimate overthrow by the Son, and commands the Angels to make changes in the elements and
stars, whereby the Earth becomes less fair. The repentance
of Adam and Eve, who seek comfort in supplication of the
Deity. The scene has changed often.

XI. The Son interceding, the Father sends Michael to
Eden (henceforth the scene) to reveal the future to Adam—
above all, his hope of redemption. After announcing to
Adam his approaching banishment from Eden, Michael

takes him to a high mountain and unrolls before him a vision of the World's history till the Flood.

XII. Then he traces the history of Israel after the Flood, till the coming of Christ, with the subsequent progress of Christianity: ending with renewed promise of redemption. The fiery Cherubim now descend. Michael leads Adam and Eve to the gates of Eden; and they go forth, sad yet consoled with the hope of salvation at the last.

MILTON'S PREFACE ON "THE VERSE" OF *PARADISE LOST*

Milton's attitude towards rhyme reminds us of the condemnations showered on it by Elizabethan critics. Ascham in the *Schoolmaster* (1570) sneers at "our rude beggerly ryming, brought first into Italie by *Gothes* and *Hunnes*, whan all good verses and all good learning to, were destroyed by them... and at last receyued into England by men of excellent wit indeede, but of small learning, and lesse judgement in that behalfe." "Barbarous" is his darling epithet for rhymed verse. Puttenham is of a like mind, waving aside "the rhyming poesie of the barbarians", and Webbe in his *Discourse of English Poetry* (1586) takes up the tale, ridiculing it as "tinkerly verse"—"brutish poesie"—"a great decay of the good order of versifying". Why Milton should have adopted the same position as these Elizabethan critics who approached the question in a spirit of the merest pedantry, and based their objections to rhyme solely on the fact that, as a metrical principle, it was not employed by the ancients, it is not easy to say. He uses rhyme occasionally in *Samson Agonistes*, in spite of his denunciation of it here; and his own early poems are sufficient refutation of the heresy that therein lies "no true musical delight". Moreover, though he appeals to the example of some European poets "of prime note" in support of his view, yet he must have foreseen the obvious and just retort that the weight of "custom" was against him, and that, in particular, the Italian exponents of *versi sciolti* whom he could cite on his side made a poor showing beside those great masters of rhyme—Dante, Ariosto, Tasso[1]—to whom he himself owed so much. His contemptuous dismissal of what "in every country of modern Europe had been adopted as the basis of metrical composition"[2] was a characteristic touch of his resentment of criticism and defiance of authority.

There is a polemical tone in his remarks, as though he were replying to some unnamed antagonist; and I cannot help thinking that this preface was meant to be his contribution to the controversy then raging over the comparative advantages of rhymed and unrhymed metres on the stage. In fact, significant in itself, Milton's opinion becomes doubly so if regarded from the standpoint of his contemporaries. Hardly could they fail to see in it a retort to what Dryden had written in the behalf of rhyme—notably in his *Essay of Dramatic Poesy* (1665), in which the rhymed couplet had been set forth as the best vehicle of dramatic expression. In play after play Dryden had put his theory into practice: others had followed his example: to rhyme or not to rhyme—that had become the great question; and here was Milton brushing the matter on one side as of no moment, with the autocratic dictum that rhyme was a vain and fond thing with which a "sage and serious" poet need have no commerce. His readers must have detected the contemporary application of his words—just as later on they must have interpreted his preface to *Samson Agonistes*, with its pointed eulogy of the Greek stage and its depreciation of Restoration tragedy (and "other common interludes"), as a counterblast to the comparison which Dryden had drawn between the modern and the classical drama, in the interests of the former. There is force too in the suggestion that the association of rhyme with the

---

[1] See, however, p. 67.
[2] Courthope.

amatory Caroline poets (*Lycidas*, 67–9) would not make Milton more favourable to it.

Curiously enough, *Paradise Lost* and *Paradise Regained* both contain a good deal of rhyme. We may compare it with the rare rhymed verse, accidental or designed ("leonine"), in the Latin poets. Cowper noted some instances in his fragment of a commentary on *Paradise Lost*. "Rhyme", he said, "is apt to come uncalled, and to writers of blank verse is often extremely troublesome."[1] Indeed complete absence of rhyme argues some artificiality. To quote Mr Robert Bridges: "Rhyme occurs in *Paradise Lost* (see I. 146, 8, 51; II. 220, 1; IV. 24–7), but only as a natural richness among the varieties of speech; and it would seem that it cannot be forbidden in a long poem but by the scrupulosity which betrays art." Possibly, however, the amount of rhyme in the two epics exceeds what Milton would have desired. It illustrates, I think, the terrible difficulty of revision imposed by his blindness. Yet such is the spell of the rhythm of his verse that one may be unconscious of the rhyme till its presence is pointed out. Of consecutive rhymed lines, some being actual rhymed couplets, the following passages are examples. *Paradise Lost*, II. 220, 221; IV. 956, 957; VI. 709, 710; IX. 105, 106, 477, 478; XI. 230, 231, 597, 598, 671, 672; *Paradise Regained*, III. 214, 215; IV. 591, 592. In II. 893, 894, a slight difference of pronunciation, indicated by Milton's spelling, may account for what appears to the eye as a couplet. In V. 167, 168, 274, 275, IX. 191, 192, the assonance has the effect of rhyme. Of course, the most frequent rhyme is that which comes with an interval of one or two intervening lines, as in two out of the three passages remarked by Mr Bridges. Other examples[2] are: *Paradise Lost*, I. 274, 276, 711, 713 764, 767; II. 390, 393,

---

[1] "The blank verse Italians have often done this [i.e. rhymed]: in fact, it is excessively difficult to prevent in Italian" (Saintsbury).

[2] The list is illustrative, not exhaustive.

942, 944; III. 140, 142, 168, 170; IV. 222, 224, 288, 290, 678, 680; V. 160, 162, 383, 385, 857, 859; VI. 14, 16, 161, 163, 174, 176; VIII. 1, 3, 171, 173, 229, 231; IX. 590, 591, 606, 608; XI. 201, 204, 206, 637, 639, 740, 741; XII. 353, 355, 366, 368; *Paradise Regained*, II. 206, 208, 245, 247, 250; IV. 25, 27, 145, 147, 222, 224. As remarked before, I cannot help thinking that a portion of this rhyme represents Milton's inability to focus the full measure of his fastidious taste[1] on the revision of his work.

Superfluous as it may seem to us that he should justify his adoption of blank verse—wherein his surpassing skill is the best of all justifications—we have cause to be grateful to the "stumblings" of the unlettered which led him to write this preface, since it happily defines the qualities for which the metre of *Paradise Lost* is remarkable.

The distinguishing characteristic of Milton's blank verse is his use of what Mr Saintsbury calls the verse-paragraph. Blank verse is exposed to two dangers: it may be formal and stiff by being circumscribed in single lines or couplets; or diffuse and formless through the sense and rhythm being carried on beyond the couplet. In its earlier stages, exemplified by works like *Gorboduc*, the metre suffered from the former tendency. It either closed with a strong pause at the end of every line, or just struggled to the climax of the couplet. Further it never extended until Marlowe took the "drumming decasyllabon" into his hands, broke up the fetters of the couplet-form, and by the process of overflow carried on the rhythm from verse to verse according as the sense required. It is in his plays that we first get verse in which variety of cadence and pause and beat takes the place of rhyme. Milton entered on the heritage that Marlowe and Shakespeare bequeathed, and brought blank verse to its highest pitch of perfection as an instrument of narration.

[1] It would have resented surely the substitution of *Chersonese* in most modern texts for the *Chersoness* of the original editions in *Paradise Regained*, IV. 74. See the termination of the previous line.

Briefly, that perfection lies herein: if we examine a page of *Paradise Lost* we find that what the poet has to say is, for the most part, conveyed, not in single lines, nor in rigid couplets—but in flexible combinations of verses, which wait upon his meaning, not twisting or constraining the sense, but suffering it to be "variously drawn out", so that the thought is merged in its expression.

These combinations, or paragraphs, are informed by a perfect internal concent and rhythm[1]—held together by a chain of harmony. With a writer less sensitive to sound this free method of versifying would result in mere chaos. But Milton's ear is so delicate, that he steers unfaltering through the long, involved passages, distributing the pauses and rests and alliterative balance with a cunning which knits the paragraph into a coherent, regulated whole. He combines, in fact, the two essential qualities of blank verse— freedom and form: the freedom that admits variety of effect, without which a long narrative becomes intolerably monotonous; and the form which saves an unrhymed measure from drifting into that which is nearer to bad prose than to good verse. And restoration of form was precisely what the metre needed. With the later Jacobean and Caroline dramatists metrical freedom had turned to "licence and slipshodness...then comes Milton,...takes non-dramatic blank verse in hand once for all, and introduces into it the order, proportion, and finish which dramatic blank verse had then lost".[2] Milton in fact was the re-creator of blank verse, "the first to establish this peculiarly English form of metre in non-dramatic poetry".[2] Nor was he unconscious of the character of his achievement. Here, in the last lines of his preface, he congratulates himself upon "an example set"; and many years

[1] Cf. Professor Mackail's fine metaphor for it—"the planetary wheeling of the long period"—"that continuous planetary movement" (Lecture II on Milton in *The Springs of Helicon*, pp. 156, 196).

[2] Saintsbury, *History of English Prosody*, II. 208, 224.

before, in the grand passage apostrophising the Divine
Goodness at the end of the treatise *Of Reformation*, he had
written, with obvious reference to the great design that
ruled his whole life: "Then, amidst the hymns and hal-
lelujahs of saints, some one may perhaps be heard offering
at high strains in new and lofty measure to sing and
celebrate thy divine mercies and marvellous judgments in
this land throughout all ages."[1] It were hard to frame an
apter summary of the metre of *Paradise Lost* than "new
and lofty".

As he lays such stress upon the internal economy and
balance of his verse-paragraphs, much must depend on the
pause or rest which in English prosody answers, to some
extent, to the classical *cæsura*. Dr Masson notes that
Milton's favourite pause is at the end of the third foot.
These are typical specimens:

> "I, at first, with two fair gifts
> Created him endowed | —with happiness
> And immortality; | that fondly lost,
> This other served but to eternize woe,
> Till I provided death: | so death becomes
> His final remedy" | (XI. 57–62).

Next in frequency comes the pause after the second
foot; cf.
> "ere fallen
> From innocence" | (XI. 29, 30).

"Made one with me, | as I with thee am one" (XI. 44).

Scarcely need we say that in this, as in everything else,
Milton never forgets that variety of effect is essential.

It remains to note two other remarks made by Milton.
One of the elements, he says, of "true musical delight" is
"fit quantity of syllables". By this, I think, he meant that
every word should bear its natural accent, i.e. that a word
should not be forced by the exigence of the metre to bear
an accent alien to it. Rather, a poet should be careful to

---

[1] *P. W.* II. 418.

"span words with just note and accent",[1] so that each stress should fall naturally, and the "fit quantity" of the component parts of a line not be violated. Considering the length of *Paradise Lost*, it is marvellous how he maintains an unfaltering appropriateness of accent. But another interpretation of his words is possible, namely that by "fit quantity of syllables" he meant "that blank verse might be extended beyond the usual number of ten syllables when its sense and feeling so required".[2] Taken in this way, "quantity" would have reference to the trisyllabic element in his verse by which the number of syllables in a line is increased, and perhaps more obviously to the hypermetrical element.

One peculiarity of the metre of *Paradise Lost*, pointed out by Coleridge, is the rarity of verses with an extra syllable (or two extra syllables) at the close. Shakespeare, of course, uses them freely—especially in his later plays, and the percentage of them in *Comus* and *Samson Agonistes* is high. But in *Paradise Lost* Milton avoids them. There are several varieties of this extra-syllable verse—e.g. lines (i) where the supernumerary syllable comes at the close; (ii) where it comes in the course of the line, particularly after the second foot; (iii) where there are two extra syllables at the end, as in the line, " Like one | that means | his pro|per harm, | in mánacles" (*Coriolanus*, I. 9. 57); and (iv) where there are two extra syllables in the middle, as in *Coriolanus*, I. 1. 230, "Our must|y super-fluity|. See our | best elders". In *Comus* there are examples of all four varieties: in *Paradise Lost* of only two[3]—(i) and (iii). This paucity is an illustration of what

---

[1] *Sonnet* to Henry Lawes.

[2] Courthope, *History of English Poetry*, III. 428. Personally I think that in a specifically metrical context "quantity" conveys the notion "long" or "short", i.e. with or without accent (stress).

[3] In most of the cases of *one* extra syllable it is a present participle that is affected. I believe that the cases with *two* such

must be recognised as the great metrical feature of the epic—that its metre is mainly iambic, and consequently decasyllabic in character. Such verse has a slower, statelier movement, and is therefore appropriate to a narrative poem that deals with the loftiest themes in an elevated, solemn style. Verse, on the other hand, that admits the supernumerary syllable at the close of the line tends towards a conversational rapidity of rhythm which makes it suitable for the purposes of the dramatist. It is typical of Milton's "inevitable", almost infallible, art that he should vary his style so precisely to fit the several characteristics and requirements of the drama and of epic narration. Such variation illustrates "a quality for which he seldom or never gets the full credit due to him, a dramatic sense of extreme delicacy. With him, as with Sophocles, this quality is so fine that it may easily elude observation."[1]

Again, another element of the pleasure offered by poetry lies in "apt numbers". Here Milton referred to that adaptation of expression to subject whereby the sound becomes an echo to the sense. This adaptation is shown in its simplest form by the suggestion of specific effects such as movement or sound.[2] But it dominates the whole relation of the manner to the matter. No one has understood the art of blending the thought with its expression better than Milton. "What other poets effect," says Dr

syllables are—in Milton—confined to words like *society*; cf. *P.R.* I. 302, "Such solitude before choicest soci*ety*". So in *P. L.* VIII. 216. Of course in these cases an "Alexandrine" solves the difficulty.

[1] *The Springs of Helicon*, p. 175 (see also p. 178).

[2] Cf. e.g. I. 742–6, 768, II. 947–50, 1021, 1022, VII. 495 (note), X. 521–8 (note). So in II. 641 we get the sense of vast space; in II. 879–83 of combined movement and jarring noise; in II. 890–906 of confusion; in IV. 181 (note) of scornful laughter; in VII. 480 of length. A very elaborate example (admirably analysed in Mayor's *Modern English Metre*, pp. 99–106) is the description of the march of the fallen angels in I. 549–62.

Guest,[1] "as it were by chance, Milton achieved by the aid of science and art; he studied the aptness of his numbers, and diligently tutored an ear which nature had gifted with the most delicate sensibility. In the flow of his rhythm, in the quality of his letter sounds, in the disposition of his pauses, his verse almost ever fits the subject, and so insensibly does poetry blend with this—the last beauty of exquisite versification—that the reader may sometimes doubt whether it be the thought itself, or merely the happiness of its expression, which is the source of a gratification so deeply felt."

We have seen that Milton may have had in view the scansion of his verse when he referred to the "fit quantity of syllables". That scansion has as its basic principle the "pure iambic"—*carmen iambicum*—so much canvassed by Elizabethan metricists. This stately, self-contained line of five feet in rising rhythm—"O Prince, O chief of many throned powers—" lies at the centre of the prosody of *Paradise Lost*. So much is patent; nor are the main means by which it is varied obscure. By letting the lines run on so that the rhythm of the unit of five feet passes into the richer harmony of groups of units Milton gives us the "verse-paragraph". And by substituting each of the possible variations of the disyllabic foot—namely, the trochee (or inversion of rhythm), the spondee and the pyrrhic—he tempers the monotony of a single-foot measure to "stops of various quills". But these foot-modifications had become part of the machinery of blank verse as developed since the pioneer days. There is nothing specifically Miltonic about the use of them in *Paradise Lost*, except possibly as regards the spondee. Cowper was inclined to think that "the grand secret to which his [Milton's] verse is principally indebted for its stately movement" is the frequent employment of spondaic feet: "the more long syllables there are in a verse, the more the line of it is pro-

[1] *English Rhythms*, p. 530.

tracted, and consequently the pace, with which it moves, is the more majestic". That Milton's use of the trochee (or rare double trochee) was due to the partiality of the Italians for this foot seems a needless assumption, the trochee having been firmly established by Marlowe. And "pyrrhic" is merely a rather pedantic-sounding term for a quite ordinary feature of blank verse—namely, the occurrence of a foot with a weak stress. Dr Abbott estimates that of Shakespeare's lines "rather less than one of three has the full number of five emphatic accents". I doubt whether the instances are so frequent in Milton; but they are sufficiently common to make it desirable to remember that five stresses are not indispensable—rather that for variety's sake it is necessary that one or more should occasionally be remitted. Taken as a whole, the obviously disyllabic element of Milton's poetry does not present much difficulty: the crux lies in the less obviously trisyllabic strata.

This is a subject on which irreconcilable opinions are held; the Miltonic blank verse described by Dr Masson is simply a different thing from the Miltonic blank verse described by Mr Bridges; and the essential truth seems to me to lie very much nearer to the views of the latter critic. I think that Milton himself would have been astonished at the elaborate trisyllabic apparatus—bacchics and amphibrachs and cretics rare—with which the verse of *Paradise Lost* has been credited. The base-principle of the slow-moving, majestic iambic decasyllable is lost in the mazes of so complex a system. On the other hand, to attempt to ban the trisyllabic foot altogether from his metre involves impossible twistings and distortions. We shall not be far astray if we steer a middle course and admit the anapæst ("the foot-of-all-work of English prosody") and (to a much less important share) the dactyl and the tribrach.[1] These may be taken to represent collectively "the trisyl-

[1] See Saintsbury, *A History of English Prosody*, I. 403, II. 259, 260.

labic foot, which was inherent in the nature of the [English] language, and had been recognised by long poetical usage ".[1] It reproduces "the swift triple rhythm"[1] of Old English poetry, while the iambic element corresponds with the typical movement of the Greek senarius. And in the verse of *Paradise Lost* it is the iambic movement that prevails, especially perhaps in the first six books, which are cast more in the typically grand Miltonic manner than the second half of the poem, where the less impressive and less coherent interest of the subject is reflected in the style. But the measure of this iambic predominance depends on the degree to which the principle of elision of vowels applies.

"Elision" comprehends not merely the case where a vowel must be dropped altogether in pronunciation, but those more numerous cases where the metre indicates, or seems to indicate, that a vowel has *something* less than its normal quantitative value, so that it is either slurred or made almost to coalesce with a preceding or succeeding sound. Such elision resolves itself practically into cases of the open vowel and the vowel (or double vowel) followed by a liquid. Elision of the former type belongs to poetic usage, of the latter to the currency of everyday speech; and each is permissive, not obligatory. Moreover, elision is a matter of scansion, not necessarily of pronunciation and reading. It is, I think, perfectly true to say that "Milton came to scan his verses one way, and read them another". But is it not true of all poetic elision? Who knows what precisely happened to the elided vowels of Greek and Latin verse? Metrically their suppression

---

[1] Courthope. Compare also Mayor (*Modern English Metre*, p. 15): "Anapaestic rhythm was familiar to the Elizabethan poets, not merely from its use by older writers, such as the author of *Piers Ploughman*, but from the later 'tumbling verse' as used by Skelton and Udall." And again (p. 44): "Trisyllabic rhythm is a marked feature of the Old English alliterative verse, and of the 'tumbling measure' which followed it."

may have been absolute, as it is (I am told) in Greek MSS.:
but in actual declamation? Similarly, though I cannot
doubt that Milton scanned "th'⌢Aonian mount" and
"th'⌢oblivious pool", yet I should not like to say that he
read the words so. Nor should I like to have to determine
whether in scansion he extended this principle of the
elision of the open vowel beyond monosyllables like *the* and
to and the terminal *y* which slides so easily into a vowel at
the beginning of the next word. Thus it satisfies my "gross
unpurged ear" to scan "Who highly thus t'⌢entitle me
vouchsaf'st" (x. 170); but to wrest an iambus out of the
second foot of the line "Virtue in her shape how lovely;
saw and pined" (IV. 848) by eliding the double vowel *ue*
("Vir*tue* in | her shape") seems a needless violence, when
the easy access of the anapæst ("Virtue | in her shape")
solves all. And so with many another line.

Some light is thrown on this difficult question of Milton's
elisions by the Cambridge autographs of his earlier poems.
The evidence, indeed, is not conclusive because the MSS.
are not consistent in giving always an elided form where
the metre requires one as an alternative to a trisyllabic
scansion. But one cannot help drawing some inference
from elisions like "Temper'd to th' oaten flute", and elided
forms such as *watrie—westring—batning—wandring—
toured*, and the many contractions of the inflections of
verbs, such as *honour'st—tun'st—forc't—nur'st—stoopt—
stolne—dan'ct*.[1] With some of these examples before us, it
is not hard to conjecture how Milton would have scanned,
say, *Paradise Lost*, XI. 779, "Wandering that watery desert;
I had hope". Similarly when we come across lines of the
epic in which *Heaven* appears to be equivalent to a monosyllable, it is apposite to remember that his autograph has
heavn in the prose draft of *Adam unparadiz'd* (line 2).
And *faln* in the prose draft of *Isaac redeemd* serves as a

[1] Cf. *Lycidas*, 4, 12, 23, 29, 31, 33; *Arcades*, 21; *Comus*, 39;
Sonnets II and XIII.

metrical gloss on i. 84, "If thou beest he—but Oh how fallen! how changed!" The drift of such elisions and contractions is obviously to diminish the trisyllabic element, and maintain that iambic rhythm which was ever present[1] to Milton's ear and ever wafting the proud full sail of his verse.

[1] Two groups of exceptions to the general movement of his lines have been remarked, viz. passages where he indulges his taste for sonorous proper names, and passages "where he follows the Authorised Version of the Bible—especially where the speaker is the Deity".

COMMENDATORY VERSES

IN PARADISUM AMISSAM SUMMI POETÆ
JOHANNIS MILTONI

QUI legis Amissam Paradisum, grandia magni
    Carmina Miltoni, quid nisi cuncta legis?
Res cunctas, et cunctarum primordia rerum,
    Et fata, et fines, continet iste liber.
Intima panduntur magni penetralia mundi,
    Scribitur et toto quicquid in orbe latet;
Terræque, tractusque maris, cœlumque profundum,
    Sulphureumque Erebi flammivomumque specus;
Quæque colunt terras, pontumque, et Tartara cæca,
    Quæque colunt summi lucida regna poli;   10
Et quodcunque ullis conclusum est finibus usquam;
    Et sine fine Chaos, et sine fine Deus;
Et sine fine magis, si quid magis est sine fine,
    In Christo erga homines conciliatus amor.
Hæc qui speraret quis crederet esse futurum?
    Et tamen hæc hodie terra Britanna legit.
O quantos in bella duces, quæ protulit arma!
    Quæ canit, et quanta, prælia dira tuba!
Cœlestes acies, atque in certamine cœlum!
    Et quæ cœlestes pugna deceret agros!   20
Quantus in ætheriis tollit se Lucifer armis,
    Atque ipso graditur vix Michaele minor!
Quantis et quam funestis concurritur iris,
    Dum ferus hic stellas protegit, ille rapit!
Dum vulsos montes ceu tela reciproca torquent,
    Et non mortali desuper igne pluunt:
Stat dubius cui se parti concedat Olympus,
    Et metuit pugnæ non superesse suæ
At simul in cœlis Messiæ insignia fulgent,
    Et currus animes, armaque digna Deo,   30

Horrendumque rotæ strident, et sæva rotarum
   Erumpunt torvis fulgura luminibus,
Et flammæ vibrant, et vera tonitrua rauco
   Admistis flammis insonuere polo,
Excidit attonitis mens omnis, et impetus omnis,
   Et cassis dextris irrita tela cadunt;
Ad pœnas fugiunt, et, ceu foret Orcus asylum,
   Infernis certant condere se tenebris.
Cedite, Romani Scriptores; cedite, Graii;
   Et quos fama recens vel celebravit anus: 40
Hæc quicunque leget tantum cecinisse putabit
   Mæonidem ranas, Virgilium culices.

                                      S. B., M.D.

ON PARADISE LOST

WHEN I beheld the Poet blind, yet bold,
In slender book his vast design unfold,
Messiah crowned, God's reconciled decree,
Rebelling Angels, the Forbidden Tree,
Heaven, Hell, Earth, Chaos, all; the argument
Held me a while misdoubting his intent,
That he would ruin (for I saw him strong)
The sacred truths to fable and old song
(So Samson groped the temple's posts in spite),
The world o'erwhelming to revenge his sight.   10

   Yet as I read, soon growing less severe,
I liked his project, the success did fear;
Through that wide field how he his way should find
O'er which lame Faith leads Understanding blind;
Lest he perplexed the things he would explain,
And what was easy he should render vain.

   Or, if a work so infinite he spanned,
Jealous I was that some less skilful hand
(Such as disquiet always what is well,
And by ill imitating would excel)   20
Might hence presume the whole Creation's day
To change in scenes, and show it in a play.

Pardon me, mighty Poet; nor despise
My causeless, yet not impious, surmise.
But I am now convinced, and none will dare
Within thy labours to pretend a share.
Thou hast not missed one thought that could be fit,
And all that was improper dost omit;
So that no room is here for writers left,
But to detect their ignorance or theft.   30

That majesty which through thy work doth reign
Draws the devout, deterring the profane.
And things divine thou treat'st of in such state
As them preserves, and thee, inviolate.
At once delight and horror on us seize;
Thou sing'st with so much gravity and ease,
And above human flight dost soar aloft
With plume so strong, so equal, and so soft.
The bird named from that Paradise you sing
So never flags, but always keeps on wing.   40

Where could'st thou words of such a compass find?
Whence furnish such a vast expense of mind?
Just Heaven, thee like Tiresias to requite,
Rewards with prophecy thy loss of sight.

Well might'st thou scorn thy readers to allure
With tinkling rime, of thy own sense secure;
While the Town-Bayes writes all the while and spells,
And, like a pack-horse, tires without his bells.
Their fancies like our bushy points appear;
The poets tag them, we for fashion wear.   50
I too, transported by the mode, offend,
And while I meant to praise thee, must commend.
Thy verse created like thy theme sublime,
In number, weight, and measure, needs not rime.

A. M.

THE VERSE.[1]

The measure is English heroic verse, without rime, as that of Homer in Greek, and of Virgil in Latin; rime being no necessary adjunct or true ornament of poem or good verse, in longer works especially, but the invention of a barbarous age, to set off wretched matter and lame metre; graced indeed since by the use of some famous modern poets, carried away by custom, but much to their own vexation, hindrance, and constraint to express many things otherwise, and for the most part worse, than else they would have expressed them. Not without cause, therefore, some both Italian and Spanish poets of prime note have rejected rime both in longer and shorter works, as have also, long since, our best English tragedies; as a thing of itself, to all judicious ears, trivial and of no true musical delight; which consists only in apt numbers, fit quantity of syllables, and the sense variously drawn out from one verse into another, not in the jingling sound of like endings, a fault avoided by the learned ancients both in poetry and all good oratory. This neglect then of rime so little is to be taken for a defect, though it may seem so perhaps to vulgar readers, that it rather is to be esteemed an example set, the first in English, of ancient liberty recovered to heroic poem from the troublesome and modern bondage of riming.

[1] Preceded by some remarks from the publisher:

The Printer to the Reader.

Courteous Reader, there was no Argument at first intended to the book; but for the satisfaction of many that have desired it, I have procured it, and withal a reason of that which stumbled many others, why the poem rimes not.—*S. Simmons.*

The portrayal of Satan is paradoxical.

PARADISE LOST

BOOK I

Main Themes:
Political views.
Good vs evil
Leadership vs rebellion.
Authority.
Stability.
Courage
Weakness
Sin
Valour (bravery)
Strength
Pride.

Look for antithesis
(means an emphatic
contrast. Stark.

Key themes for oral:
- Power.
- wealth.
- Manipulation.
- Meretricious → things look better than they are.
- Satan is always offering what he can't provide.

♡
Clarty Clarkey Babs Lush (long story). Ben = Slut

Milton was a rebel, very intellectual. Written in 1667, in King Charles II reign.

THE ARGUMENT

This First Book proposes, first in brief, the whole subject, Man's disobedience, and the loss thereupon of Paradise, wherein he was placed: then touches the prime cause of his fall, the Serpent, or rather Satan in the Serpent; who revolting from God, and drawing to his side many legions of Angels, was by the command of God driven out of Heaven with all his crew into the great Deep. Which action passed over, the Poem hastes into the midst of things; presenting Satan with his Angels now fallen into Hell, described here, not in the Centre (for Heaven and Earth may be supposed as yet not made, certainly not yet accursed) but in a place of utter darkness, fitliest called Chaos: here Satan with his Angels lying on the burning lake, thunderstruck and astonished, after a certain space recovers, as from confusion; calls up him who, next in order and dignity, lay by him; they confer of their miserable fall. Satan awakens all his legions, who lay till then in the same manner confounded; they rise: their numbers, array of battle, their chief leaders named, according to the idols known afterwards in Canaan and the countries adjoining. To these Satan directs his speech; comforts them with hope yet of regaining Heaven; but tells them lastly of a new world and new kind of creature to be created, according to an ancient prophecy or report in Heaven; for that Angels were long before this visible creation was the opinion of many ancient Fathers. To find out the truth of this prophecy, and what to determine thereon, he refers to a full council. What his associates thence attempt. Pandemonium, the palace of Satan, rises, suddenly built out of the Deep: the infernal Peers there sit in council.

Satan — Samuel, Son of Morning, like the morning star → we should follow Satan to give guide is evil nature?

Opens with a celestial song.
References Genesis.
Lots of caesura.

PARADISE LOST

BOOK I

Adam — _Mountain where Mosis got his 10 Commandments._

Of Man's first disobedience, and the fruit
Of that forbidden Tree, whose mortal taste → _Creates a bond with the reader._
Brought death into the world, and all our woe,
With loss of Eden, till one greater Man
Restore us, and regain the blissful seat,
Sing, Heavenly Muse, that on the secret top
Of Oreb, or of Sinai, didst inspire
That shepherd, who first taught the chosen seed
In the beginning how the Heavens and Earth
Rose out of Chaos: or, if Sion hill   10
Delight thee more, and Siloa's brook that flowed
Fast by the oracle of God, I thence → _Asking for help._
Invoke thy aid to my adventurous song,
That with no middle flight intends to soar
Above the Aonian mount, while it pursues
Things unattempted yet in prose or rhyme.
And chiefly thou, O Spirit, that dost prefer
Before all temples the upright heart and pure,
Instruct me, for thou know'st; thou from the first
Wast present, and, with mighty wings outspread,   20
Dove-like sat'st brooding on the vast Abyss, → _First instance of dark vs light._
And mad'st it pregnant: what in me is dark
Illumine, what is low raise and support;
That to the highth of this great argument → _As a poet, his purpose is to explain God's thoughts to Man._
I may assert Eternal Providence,
And justify the ways of God to men.
   Say first (for Heaven hides nothing from thy view,
Nor the deep tract of Hell) say first what cause
Moved our grand parents, in that happy state,
Favoured of Heaven so highly, to fall off   30
→ _Small preview of what the poem is going to include → limited suspense._
Sneak peek for what to come.

PARADISE LOST

From their Creator, and transgress his will
For one restraint, lords of the world besides.
Who first seduced them to that foul revolt?
The infernal Serpent; he it was, whose guile,
Stirred up with envy and revenge, deceived
The Mother of Mankind, what time his pride
Had cast him out from Heaven, with all his host
Of rebel Angels, by whose aid, aspiring
To set himself in glory above his peers,
He trusted to have equalled the Most High,
If he opposed; and with ambitious aim
Against the throne and monarchy of God
Raised impious war in Heaven and battle proud,
With vain attempt. Him the Almighty Power
Hurled headlong flaming from the ethereal sky,
With hideous ruin and combustion, down
To bottomless perdition; there to dwell
In adamantine chains and penal fire,
Who durst defy the Omnipotent to arms.
Nine times the space that measures day and night   50
To mortal men, he with his horrid crew
Lay vanquished, rolling in the fiery gulf,
Confounded though immortal. But his doom
Reserved him to more wrath; for now the thought
Both of lost happiness and lasting pain
Torments him; round he throws his baleful eyes,
That witnessed huge affliction and dismay,
Mixed with obdurate pride and steadfast hate.
At once, as far as Angels ken, he views
The dismal situation waste and wild: 60
A dungeon horrible, on all sides round,
As one great furnace flamed; yet from those flames
No light, but rather darkness visible
Served only to discover sights of woe,
Regions of sorrow, doleful shades, where peace

And rest can never dwell, hope never comes
That comes to all; but torture without end
Still urges, and a fiery deluge, fed
With ever-burning sulphur unconsumed.
Such place Eternal Justice had prepared
For those rebellious; here their prison ordained
In utter darkness, and their portion set,
As far removed from God and light of Heaven
As from the centre thrice to the utmost pole.
Oh how unlike the place from whence they fell!
There the companions of his fall, o'erwhelmed
With floods and whirlwinds of tempestuous fire,
He soon discerns; and, weltering by his side,
One next himself in power, and next in crime,
Long after known in Palestine, and named
Beëlzebub. To whom the Arch-Enemy,
And thence in Heaven called Satan, with bold words
Breaking the horrid silence, thus began:
"If thou beest he—but Oh how fallen! how changed
From him, who in the happy realms of light,
Clothed with transcendent brightness, didst outshine
Myriads, though bright! if he whom mutual league,
United thoughts and counsels, equal hope
And hazard in the glorious enterprise,
Joined with me once, now misery hath joined
In equal ruin: into what pit thou seest
From what highth fallen, so much the stronger proved
He with his thunder; and till then who knew
The force of those dire arms? Yet not for those,
Nor what the potent victor in his rage
Can else inflict, do I repent, or change,
Though changed in outward lustre, that fixed mind,
And high disdain from sense of injured merit,
That with the Mightiest raised me to contend,
And to the fierce contention brought along

80

100

Handwritten annotations:

Satan's tragic flaw is pride, he is the anti-hero.
Satan is presented with human qualities.
sympathy for the devil. It's his pride that is keeping him going.

→ Antithesis.
→ Emphasis.
→ Always miserable.
Further emphasising how different heaven

Light vs darkness, both mentally & between heaven & hell.

→ Satan is offering support to him.
→ Emphasising.
Beelzebub is sad.

→ Describing Beelzebub.
Emphasis at the start

→ Talking about overthrowing Heaven but losing.

→ God controls all the elements. OR he is painted negatively.
→ Caesura
→ Contrast of them being friends now with misery.

Paradoxical, injure = bad. merit = good.

(left margin) Zone of two ones (what he calls hell) Anywhere they are (their own mind)

(left margin) Emphasises the contrast

1st speech

→ Evil can take many forms but the core is still the same.

(bottom left) Still has fighting breath, refuses to give up.

Innumerable force of Spirits armed,
That durst dislike his reign, and, me preferring,
His utmost power with adverse power opposed
In dubious battle on the plains of Heaven,
And shook his throne. What though the field be lost?
All is not lost: the unconquerable will,
And study of revenge, immortal hate,
And courage never to submit or yield:
And what is else not to be overcome?
That glory never shall his wrath or might
Extort from me. To bow and sue for grace   110
With suppliant knee, and deify his power
Who, from the terror of this arm, so late
Doubted his empire—that were low indeed;
That were an ignominy and shame beneath
This downfall; since by fate the strength of gods
And this empyreal substance cannot fail;
Since, through experience of this great event,
In arms not worse, in foresight much advanced,
We may with more successful hope resolve
To wage by force or guile eternal war,
Irreconcilable to our grand foe,
Who now triumphs, and in the excess of joy
Sole reigning holds the tyranny of Heaven."
    So spake the apostate Angel, though in pain,
Vaunting aloud, but racked with deep despair;
And him thus answered soon his bold compeer:
    "O Prince, O Chief of many thronèd powers,
That led the embattled Seraphim to war
Under thy conduct, and, in dreadful deeds   130
Fearless, endangered Heaven's perpetual King,
And put to proof his high supremacy,
Whether upheld by strength, or chance, or fate!
Too well I see and rue the dire event
That with sad overthrow and foul defeat

Hath lost us Heaven, and all this mighty host
In horrible destruction laid thus low,
As far as gods and Heavenly essences
Can perish: for the mind and spirit remains
Invincible, and vigour soon returns,
Though all our glory extinct, and happy state
Here swallowed up in endless misery.
But what if he our conqueror (whom I now
Of force believe almighty, since no less
Than such could have o'erpowered such force as ours)
Have left us this our spirit and strength entire,
Strongly to suffer and support our pains,
That we may so suffice his vengeful ire;
Or do him mightier service, as his thralls
By right of war, whate'er his business be,
Here in the heart of Hell to work in fire,
Or do his errands in the gloomy deep?
What can it then avail, though yet we feel
Strength undiminished, or eternal being
To undergo eternal punishment?"
    Whereto with speedy words the Arch-Fiend replied:
"Fallen Cherub, to be weak is miserable,
Doing or suffering: but of this be sure,
To do aught good never will be our task,
But ever to do ill our sole delight,
As being the contrary to his high will
Whom we resist. If then his providence
Out of our evil seek to bring forth good,
Our labour must be to pervert that end,
And out of good still to find means of evil;
Which oft times may succeed, so as perhaps
Shall grieve him, if I fail not, and disturb
His inmost counsels from their destined aim.
But see! the angry victor hath recalled
His ministers of vengeance and pursuit
Back to the gates of Heaven: the sulphurous hail,

149

150

160

170

Shot after us in storm, o'erblown hath laid
The fiery surge that from the precipice
Of Heaven received us falling; and the thunder,
Winged with red lightning and impetuous rage,
Perhaps hath spent his shafts, and ceases now
To bellow through the vast and boundless deep.
Let us not slip the occasion, whether scorn
Or satiate fury yield it from our foe.
Seest thou yon dreary plain, forlorn and wild,   180
The seat of desolation, void of light,
Save what the glimmering of these livid flames
Casts pale and dreadful? Thither let us tend
From off the tossing of these fiery waves;
There rest, if any rest can harbour there;
And, re-assembling our afflicted powers,
Consult how we may henceforth most offend
Our enemy, our own loss how repair,
How overcome this dire calamity,
What reinforcement we may gain from hope,   190
If not what resolution from despair."
    Thus Satan, talking to his nearest mate,
With head uplift above the wave, and eyes
That sparkling blazed; his other parts besides,
Prone on the flood, extended long and large,
Lay floating many a rood, in bulk as huge
As whom the fables name of monstrous size,
Titanian, or Earth-born, that warred on Jove,
Briareos or Typhon, whom the den
By ancient Tarsus held, or that sea-beast   200
Leviathan, which God of all his works
Created hugest that swim the ocean-stream.
Him, haply, slumbering on the Norway foam,
The pilot of some small night-foundered skiff
Deeming some island, oft, as seamen tell,
With fixed anchor in his scaly rind,

Moors by his side under the lee, while night
Invests the sea, and wished morn delays:
So stretched out huge in length the Arch-Fiend lay,
Chained on the burning lake; nor ever thence 210
Had risen or heaved his head, but that the will
And high permission of all-ruling Heaven
Left him at large to his own dark designs,
That with reiterated crimes he might
Heap on himself damnation, while he sought
Evil to others, and enraged might see
How all his malice served but to bring forth
Infinite goodness, grace and mercy shewn
On Man by him seduced, but on himself
Treble confusion, wrath and vengeance poured. 220
　　Forthwith upright he rears from off the pool
His mighty stature; on each hand the flames
Driven backward slope their pointing spires, and, rolled
In billows, leave i' the midst a horrid vale.
Then with expanded wings he steers his flight
Aloft, incumbent on the dusky air,
That felt unusual weight; till on dry land
He lights—if it were land that ever burned
With solid, as the lake with liquid fire,
And such appeared in hue, as when the force 230
Of subterranean wind transports a hill
Torn from Pelorus, or the shattered side
Of thundering Ætna, whose combustible
And fuelled entrails thence conceiving fire,
Sublimed with mineral fury, aid the winds,
And leave a singed bottom all involved
With stench and smoke: such resting found the sole
Of unblest feet. Him followed his next mate,
Both glorying to have scaped the Stygian flood
As gods, and by their own recovered strength, 240
Not by the sufferance of supernal power.

"Is this the region, this the soil, the clime,"
Said then the lost Archangel, "this the seat
That we must change for Heaven? this mournful gloom
For that celestial light? Be it so, since he
Who now is sovran can dispose and bid
What shall be right: farthest from him is best,
Whom reason hath equalled, force hath made supreme
Above his equals. Farewell, happy fields,
Where joy for ever dwells! Hail, horrors! hail,
Infernal world! and thou, profoundest Hell,
Receive thy new possessor, one who brings
A mind not to be changed by place or time.
The mind is its own place, and in itself
Can make a Heaven of Hell, a Hell of Heaven.
What matter where, if I be still the same,
And what I should be, all but less than he
Whom thunder hath made greater? Here at least
We shall be free; the Almighty hath not built
Here for his envy, will not drive us hence:
Here we may reign secure, and in my choice
To reign is worth ambition, though in Hell:
Better to reign in Hell, than serve in Heaven.
But wherefore let we then our faithful friends,
The associates and co-partners of our loss,
Lie thus astonished on the oblivious pool,
And call them not to share with us their part
In this unhappy mansion, or once more
With rallied arms to try what may be yet
Regained in Heaven, or what more lost in Hell?"
So Satan spake; and him Beëlzebub
Thus answered: "Leader of those armies bright
Which but the Omnipotent none could have foiled,
If once they hear that voice, their liveliest pledge
Of hope in fears and dangers—heard so oft
In worst extremes, and on the perilous edge

Handwritten annotations:

Hell = bad, but Satan is welcoming it. Milton is highlighting that bad = power. However he's very motivating to do the bad things. Renouncing heaven, "goodness".

He is lost, has no idea what to do but still sits on his throne of power.

Contrasting heaven & hell. Emphatic imagery. Light & dark contrasts.

Caesura.

→ Semantic field of n...
→ Say go... to... embrace th... bad.

→ Triplet Alliteration
→ Satan aware
→ Taking co... manipulati... his fallen ange...
→ Satan wa... to be God.
→ Possessive controlling
→ Syntactical parallelism.

→ Caesura emph...
the sentence, i... idolised as a ru... of hell. 260

→ Sends out a greedy messa...
→ Other ange... have been br... to just accept it.
→ Two outcomes go back to hea... or reign in h... rhetorical ques...

270 → Best, he's going to s... Satan

Mocking remark →
Exclamatory remark → All about himself.
Metaphor →
Take note → Hell in it together.
Metaphor Juxtaposition alluding to new pandemonium foreshadowing

→ Bad morals, doing the bad in nice ways.

Of battle when it raged, in all assaults
Their surest signal—they will soon resume
New courage and revive, though now they lie
Grovelling and prostrate on yon lake of fire,   280
As we erewhile, astounded and amazed—
No wonder, fallen such a pernicious highth!''
    He scarce had ceased when the superior Fiend
Was moving toward the shore; his ponderous shield,
Ethereal temper, massy, large, and round,
Behind him cast. The broad circumference
Hung on his shoulders like the moon, whose orb
Through optic glass the Tuscan artist views
At evening from the top of Fesolè,
Or in Valdarno, to descry new lands,   290
Rivers, or mountains, in her spotty globe.
His spear—to equal which the tallest pine
Hewn on Norwegian hills, to be the mast
Of some great ammiral, were but a wand—
He walked with, to support uneasy steps
Over the burning marle, not like those steps
On Heaven's azure; and the torrid clime
Smote on him sore besides, vaulted with fire.
Nathless he so endured, till on the beach
Of that inflamèd sea he stood, and called   300
His legions, Angel forms, who lay entranced,
Thick as autumnal leaves that strow the brooks
In Vallombrosa, where the Etrurian shades
High over-arched embower; or scattered sedge
Afloat, when with fierce winds Orion armed
Hath vexed the Red-Sea coast, whose waves o'erthrew
Busiris and his Memphian chivalry,
While with perfidious hatred they pursued
The sojourners of Goshen, who beheld
From the safe shore their floating carcases   310
And broken chariot-wheels: so thick bestrown,

Abject and lost, lay these covering the flood,
Under amazement of their hideous change.
He called so loud that all the hollow deep
Of Hell resounded: "Princes, Potentates,
Warriors, the flower of Heaven, once yours, now lost,
If such astonishment as this can seize
Eternal Spirits: or have ye chosen this place
After the toil of battle to repose
Your wearied virtue, for the ease you find   320
To slumber here, as in the vales of Heaven?
Or in this abject posture have ye sworn
To adore the conqueror, who now beholds
Cherub and Seraph rolling in the flood
With scattered arms and ensigns, till anon
His swift pursuers from Heaven-gates discern
The advantage, and descending tread us down
Thus drooping, or with linked thunderbolts
Transfix us to the bottom of this gulf?
Awake, arise, or be for ever fallen!"   330
    They heard, and were abashed, and up they sprung
Upon the wing, as when men wont to watch
On duty, sleeping found by whom they dread,
Rouse and bestir themselves ere well awake.
Nor did they not perceive the evil plight
In which they were, or the fierce pains not feel;
Yet to their General's voice they soon obeyed
Innumerable. As when the potent rod
Of Amram's son, in Egypt's evil day,
Waved round the coast, up called a pitchy cloud   340
Of locusts, warping on the eastern wind,
That o'er the realm of impious Pharaoh hung
Like night, and darkened all the land of Nile:
So numberless were those bad Angels seen
Hovering on wing under the cope of Hell,
'Twixt upper, nether, and surrounding fires;

Till, as a signal given, the uplifted spear
Of their great Sultan waving to direct
Their course, in even balance down they light
On the firm brimstone, and fill all the plain: 350
A multitude, like which the populous North
Poured never from her frozen loins, to pass
Rhene or the Danaw, when her barbarous sons
Came like a deluge on the South, and spread
Beneath Gibraltar to the Libyan sands.
Forthwith, from every squadron and each band,
The heads and leaders thither haste where stood
Their great Commander; godlike shapes, and forms
Excelling human, princely dignities,
And powers that erst in Heaven sat on thrones; 360
Though of their names in Heavenly records now
Be no memorial, blotted out and rased
By their rebellion from the Books of Life.
Nor had they yet among the sons of Eve
Got them new names, till, wandering o'er the Earth,
Through God's high sufferance for the trial of Man,
By falsities and lies the greatest part
Of Mankind they corrupted to forsake
God their Creator, and the invisible
Glory of him that made them to transform 370
Oft to the image of a brute, adorned
With gay religions full of pomp and gold,
And devils to adore for deities.
Then were they known to men by various names,
And various idols through the heathen world.
   Say, Muse, their names then known, who first, who last,
Roused from the slumber on that fiery couch,
At their great Emperor's call, as next in worth
Came singly where he stood on the bare strand,
While the promiscuous crowd stood yet aloof. 380
   The chief were those who, from the pit of Hell

Roaming to seek their prey on Earth, durst fix
Their seats long after next the seat of God,
Their altars by his altar, gods adored
Among the nations round, and durst abide
Jehovah thundering out of Sion, throned
Between the Cherubim; yea, often placed
Within his sanctuary itself their shrines,
Abominations; and with cursed things
His holy rites and solemn feasts profaned,   390
And with their darkness durst affront his light.
First, Moloch, horrid king, besmeared with blood
Of human sacrifice, and parents' tears,
Though, for the noise of drums and timbrels loud,
Their children's cries unheard, that passed through fire
To his grim idol. Him the Ammonite
Worshiped in Rabba and her watery plain,
In Argob and in Basan, to the stream
Of utmost Arnon. Nor content with such
Audacious neighbourhood, the wisest heart   400
Of Solomon he led by fraud to build
His temple right against the temple of God
On that opprobrious hill, and made his grove
The pleasant valley of Hinnom, Tophet thence
And black Gehenna called, the type of Hell.
Next Chemos, the obscene dread of Moab's sons,
From Aroer to Nebo, and the wild
Of southmost Abarim; in Hesebon
And Horonaim, Seon's realm, beyond
The flowery dale of Sibma clad with vines,   410
And Elealè to the Asphaltic pool.
Peor his other name, when he enticed
Israel in Sittim, on their march from Nile,
To do him wanton rites, which cost them woe.
Yet thence his lustful orgies he enlarged
Even to that hill of scandal, by the grove

Of Moloch homicide, lust hard by hate;
Till good Josiah drove them thence to Hell.
With these came they who, from the bordering flood
Of old Euphrates to the brook that parts   420
Egypt from Syrian ground, had general names
Of Baalim and Ashtaroth—those male,
These feminine. For Spirits, when they please,
Can either sex assume, or both; so soft
And uncompounded is their essence pure,
Not tied or manacled with joint or limb,
Nor founded on the brittle strength of bones,
Like cumbrous flesh; but, in what shape they choose,
Dilated or condensed, bright or obscure,
Can execute their aery purposes,   430
And works of love or enmity fulfil.
For those the race of Israel oft forsook
Their living Strength, and unfrequented left
His righteous altar, bowing lowly down
To bestial gods; for which their heads as low
Bowed down in battle, sunk before the spear
Of despicable foes. With these in troop
Came Astoreth, whom the Phœnicians called
Astarte, Queen of Heaven, with crescent horns;
To whose bright image nightly by the moon   440
Sidonian virgins paid their vows and songs;
In Sion also not unsung, where stood
Her temple on the offensive mountain, built
By that uxorious king whose heart, though large,
Beguiled by fair idolatresses, fell
To idols foul. Thammuz came next behind,
Whose annual wound in Lebanon allured
The Syrian damsels to lament his fate
In amorous ditties all a summer's day
While smooth Adonis from his native rock   450
Ran purple to the sea, supposed with blood

Of Thammuz yearly wounded: the love-tale
Infected Sion's daughters with like heat,
Whose wanton passions in the sacred porch
Ezekiel saw, when, by the vision led,
His eye surveyed the dark idolatries
Of alienated Judah. Next came one
Who mourned in earnest, when the captive ark
Maimed his brute image, head and hands lopt off
In his own temple, on the grunsel-edge,   460
Where he fell flat, and shamed his worshipers:
Dagon his name, sea-monster, upward man
And downward fish; yet had his temple high
Reared in Azotus, dreaded through the coast
Of Palestine, in Gath and Ascalon,
And Accaron and Gaza's frontier bounds.
Him followed Rimmon, whose delightful seat
Was fair Damascus, on the fertile banks
Of Abbana and Pharphar, lucid streams.
He also against the house of God was bold: 470
A leper once he lost and gained a king,
Ahaz, his sottish conqueror, whom he drew
God's altar to disparage and displace
For one of Syrian mode, whereon to burn
His odious offerings, and adore the gods
Whom he had vanquished. After these appeared
A crew who, under names of old renown,
Osiris, Isis, Orus, and their train,
With monstrous shapes and sorceries abused
Fanatic Egypt and her priests, to seek   480
Their wandering gods disguised in brutish forms
Rather than human. Nor did Israel scape
The infection, when their borrowed gold composed
The calf in Oreb; and the rebel king
Doubled that sin in Bethel and in Dan,
Likening his Maker to the grazed ox—

Jehovah, who, in one night, when he passed
From Egypt marching, equalled with one stroke
Both her first-born and all her bleating gods.
Belial came last, than whom a Spirit more lewd   490
Fell not from Heaven, or more gross to love
Vice for itself. To him no temple stood
Or altar smoked; yet who more oft than he
In temples and at altars, when the priest
Turns atheist, as did Eli's sons, who filled
With lust and violence the house of God?
In courts and palaces he also reigns,
And in luxurious cities, where the noise
Of riot ascends above their loftiest towers,
And injury and outrage; and when night   500
Darkens the streets, then wander forth the sons
Of Belial, flown with insolence and wine.
Witness the streets of Sodom, and that night
In Gibeah, when the hospitable door
Exposed a matron, to avoid worse rape.
    These were the prime in order and in might;
The rest were long to tell, though far renowned,
The Ionian gods—of Javan's issue held
Gods, yet confessed later than Heaven and Earth,
Their boasted parents: Titan, Heaven's first-born,   510
With his enormous brood, and birthright seized
By younger Saturn; he from mightier Jove,
His own and Rhea's son, like measure found;
So Jove usurping reigned. These, first in Crete
And Ida known, thence on the snowy top
Of cold Olympus ruled the middle air,
Their highest Heaven; or on the Delphian cliff,
Or in Dodona, and through all the bounds
Of Doric land; or who with Saturn old
Fled over Adria to the Hesperian fields,   520
And o'er the Celtic roamed the utmost isles.

All these and more came flocking; but with looks
Downcast and damp, yet such wherein appeared
Obscure some glimpse of joy, to have found their Chief
Not in despair, to have found themselves not lost
In loss itself; which on his countenance cast
Like doubtful hue. But he, his wonted pride
Soon recollecting, with high words, that bore
Semblance of worth, not substance, gently raised
Their fainting courage, and dispelled their fears: 530
Then straight commands that, at the warlike sound
Of trumpets loud and clarions, be upreared
His mighty standard. That proud honour claimed
Azazel as his right, a Cherub tall:
Who forthwith from the glittering staff unfurled
The imperial ensign, which, full high advanced,
Shone like a meteor streaming to the wind,
With gems and golden lustre rich emblazed,
Seraphic arms and trophies; all the while
Sonorous metal blowing martial sounds: 540
At which the universal host up-sent
A shout that tore Hell's concave, and beyond
Frighted the reign of Chaos and old Night.
All in a moment through the gloom were seen
Ten thousand banners rise into the air,
With orient colours waving; with them rose
A forest huge of spears; and thronging helms
Appeared, and serried shields in thick array
Of depth immeasurable. Anon they move
In perfect phalanx to the Dorian mood   550
Of flutes and soft recorders; such as raised
To highth of noblest temper heroes old
Arming to battle, and instead of rage
Deliberate valour breathed, firm and unmoved
With dread of death to flight or foul retreat;
Nor wanting power to mitigate and swage,

With solemn touches, troubled thoughts, and chase
Anguish and doubt and fear and sorrow and pain
From mortal or immortal minds. Thus they,
Breathing united force with fixed thought,   560
Moved on in silence to soft pipes that charmed
Their painful steps o'er the burnt soil; and now
Advanced in view they stand, a horrid front
Of dreadful length and dazzling arms, in guise
Of warriors old, with ordered spear and shield,
Awaiting what command their mighty Chief
Had to impose. He through the armed files
Darts his experienced eye, and soon traverse
The whole battalion views—their order due,
Their visages and stature as of gods;   570
Their number last he sums. And now his heart
Distends with pride, and hardening in his strength
Glories; for never, since created Man,
Met such embodied force as, named with these,
Could merit more than that small infantry
Warred on by cranes: though all the giant brood
Of Phlegra with the heroic race were joined
That fought at Thebes and Ilium, on each side
Mixed with auxiliar gods; and what resounds
In fable or romance of Uther's son,   580
Begirt with British and Armoric knights;
And all who since, baptized or infidel,
Jousted in Aspramont, or Montalban,
Damasco, or Marocco, or Trebisond;
Or whom Biserta sent from Afric shore
When Charlemain with all his peerage fell
By Fontarabbia. Thus far these beyond
Compare of mortal prowess, yet observed
Their dread Commander. He, above the rest
In shape and gesture proudly eminent,   590
Stood like a tower: his form had yet not lost

All her original brightness, nor appeared
Less than Archangel ruined, and the excess
Of glory obscured: as when the sun new-risen
Looks through the horizontal misty air
Shorn of his beams, or from behind the moon,
In dim eclipse, disastrous twilight sheds
On half the nations, and with fear of change
Perplexes monarchs. Darkened so, yet shone
Above them all the Archangel; but his face   600
Deep scars of thunder had intrenched, and care
Sat on his faded cheek, but under brows
Of dauntless courage, and considerate pride
Waiting revenge. Cruel his eye, but cast
Signs of remorse and passion, to behold
The fellows of his crime, the followers rather
(Far other once beheld in bliss), condemned
For ever now to have their lot in pain;
Millions of Spirits for his fault amerced
Of Heaven, and from eternal splendours flung   610
For his revolt; yet faithful how they stood,
Their glory withered: as, when Heaven's fire
Hath scathed the forest oaks or mountain pines,
With singed top their stately growth, though bare,
Stands on the blasted heath. He now prepared
To speak; whereat their doubled ranks they bend
From wing to wing, and half enclose him round
With all his peers: attention held them mute.
Thrice he assayed, and thrice, in spite of scorn,
Tears, such as Angels weep, burst forth: at last   620
Words interwove with sighs found out their way:
    "O myriads of immortal Spirits! O Powers
Matchless, but with the Almighty!—and that strife
Was not inglorious, though the event was dire,
As this place testifies, and this dire change,
Hateful to utter. But what power of mind,

Foreseeing or presaging, from the depth
Of knowledge past or present, could have feared
How such united force of gods, how such
As stood like these, could ever know repulse? 630
For who can yet believe, though after loss,
That all these puissant legions, whose exile
Hath emptied Heaven, shall fail to re-ascend,
Self-raised, and re-possess their native seat?
For me, be witness all the host of Heaven,
If counsels different, or danger shunned
By me, have lost our hopes. But he who reigns
Monarch in Heaven, till then as one secure
Sat on his throne, upheld by old repute,
Consent or custom, and his regal state 640
Put forth at full, but still his strength concealed,
Which tempted our attempt, and wrought our fall.
Henceforth his might we know, and know our own,
So as not either to provoke, or dread
New war, provoked; our better part remains
To work in close design, by fraud or guile,
What force effected not; that he no less
At length from us may find, who overcomes
By force hath overcome but half his foe.
Space may produce new worlds; whereof so rife 650
There went a fame in Heaven that he ere long
Intended to create, and therein plant
A generation whom his choice regard
Should favour equal to the Sons of Heaven.
Thither, if but to pry, shall be perhaps
Our first eruption, thither or elsewhere;
For this infernal pit shall never hold
Celestial Spirits in bondage, nor the Abyss
Long under darkness cover. But these thoughts
Full counsel must mature. Peace is despaired, 660
For who can think submission? War, then, war

Open or understood, must be resolved."
  He spake; and, to confirm his words, out-flew
Millions of flaming swords, drawn from the thighs
Of mighty Cherubim; the sudden blaze
Far round illumined Hell. Highly they raged
Against the Highest, and fierce with grasped arms
Clashed on their sounding shields the din of war,
Hurling defiance toward the vault of Heaven.
  There stood a hill not far, whose grisly top   670
Belched fire and rolling smoke; the rest entire
Shone with a glossy scurf, undoubted sign
That in his womb was hid metallic ore,
The work of sulphur. Thither, winged with speed,
A numerous brigad hastened: as when bands
Of pioners, with spade and pickaxe armed,
Forerun the royal camp, to trench a field,
Or cast a rampart. Mammon led them on,
Mammon, the least erected Spirit that fell
From Heaven, for even in Heaven his looks and thoughts   680
Were always downward bent, admiring more
The riches of Heaven's pavement, trodden gold,
Than aught divine or holy else enjoyed
In vision beatific. By him first
Men also, and by his suggestion taught,
Ransacked the centre, and with impious hands
Rifled the bowels of their mother Earth
For treasures better hid. Soon had his crew
Opened into the hill a spacious wound,
And digged out ribs of gold. Let none admire
That riches grow in Hell; that soil may best
Deserve the precious bane. And here let those
Who boast in mortal things, and wondering tell
Of Babel, and the works of Memphian kings,
Learn how their greatest monuments of fame,
And strength, and art, are easily outdone

By Spirits reprobate, and in an hour
What in an age they, with incessant toil
And hands innumerable, scarce perform.
Nigh on the plain, in many cells prepared,   700
That underneath had veins of liquid fire
Sluiced from the lake, a second multitude
With wondrous art founded the massy ore,
Severing each kind, and scummed the bullion-dross.
A third as soon had formed within the ground
A various mould, and from the boiling cells
By strange conveyance filled each hollow nook:
As in an organ, from one blast of wind,
To many a row of pipes the sound-board breathes.
Anon out of the earth a fabric huge   710
Rose like an exhalation, with the sound
Of dulcet symphonies and voices sweet,
Built like a temple, where pilasters round
Were set, and Doric pillars overlaid
With golden architrave; nor did there want
Cornice or frieze, with bossy sculptures graven;
The roof was fretted gold. Not Babylon,
Nor great Alcairo, such magnificence
Equalled in all their glories, to enshrine
Belus or Serapis their gods, or seat   720
Their kings, when Egypt with Assyria strove
In wealth and luxury. The ascending pile
Stood fixed her stately highth, and straight the doors,
Opening their brazen folds, discover, wide
Within, her ample spaces o'er the smooth
And level pavement: from the arched roof,
Pendent by subtle magic, many a row
Of starry lamps and blazing cressets, fed
With naphtha and asphaltus, yielded light
As from a sky. The hasty multitude   730
Admiring entered, and the work some praise,

And some the architect: his hand was known
In Heaven by many a towered structure high,
Where sceptred Angels held their residence,
And sat as princes, whom the supreme King
Exalted to such power, and gave to rule,
Each in his Hierarchy, the Orders bright.
Nor was his name unheard or unadored
In ancient Greece; and in Ausonian land
Men called him Mulciber; and how he fell   740
From Heaven they fabled, thrown by angry Jove
Sheer o'er the crystal battlements: from morn
To noon he fell, from noon to dewy eve,
A summer's day; and with the setting sun
Dropt from the zenith, like a falling star,
On Lemnos, the Ægæan isle. Thus they relate,
Erring; for he with this rebellious rout
Fell long before; nor aught availed him now
To have built in Heaven high towers; nor did he scape
By all his engines, but was headlong sent   750
With his industrious crew to build in Hell.
    Meanwhile the winged haralds, by command
Of sovran power, with awful ceremony
And trumpet's sound, throughout the host proclaim
A solemn council forthwith to be held
At Pandemonium, the high capital
Of Satan and his peers. Their summons called
From every band and squared regiment
By place or choice the worthiest; they anon
With hundreds and with thousands trooping came   760
Attended. All access was thronged, the gates
And porches wide, but chief the spacious hall
(Though like a covered field, where champions bold
Wont ride in armed, and at the Soldan's chair
Defied the best of Panim chivalry
To mortal combat, or career with lance)

Thick swarmed, both on the ground and in the air,
Brushed with the hiss of rustling wings. As bees
In spring-time, when the Sun with Taurus rides,
Pour forth their populous youth about the hive   770
In clusters; they among fresh dews and flowers
Fly to and fro, or on the smoothed plank,
The suburb of their straw-built citadel,
New rubbed with balm, expatiate and confer
Their state-affairs. So thick the aery crowd
Swarmed and were straitened; till, the signal given,
Behold a wonder! they but now who seemed
In bigness to surpass Earth's giant sons,
Now less than smallest dwarfs, in narrow room
Throng numberless, like that pygmean race   780
Beyond the Indian mount; or faery elves,
Whose midnight revels, by a forest-side
Or fountain, some belated peasant sees,
Or dreams he sees, while overhead the moon
Sits arbitress, and nearer to the Earth
Wheels her pale course; they, on their mirth and dance
Intent, with jocund music charm his ear;
At once with joy and fear his heart rebounds.
Thus incorporeal Spirits to smallest forms
Reduced their shapes immense, and were at large,   790
Though without number still, amidst the hall
Of that infernal court. But far within,
And in their own dimensions like themselves,
The great Seraphic Lords and Cherubim
In close recess and secret conclave sat,
A thousand demi-gods on golden seats,
Frequent and full. After short silence then,
And summons read, the great consult began.

PARADISE LOST

BOOK II

THE ARGUMENT

The consultation begun, Satan debates whether another battle be to be hazarded for the recovery of Heaven: some advise it, others dissuade. A third proposal is preferred, mentioned before by Satan, to search the truth of that prophecy or tradition in Heaven concerning another world, and another kind of creature, equal, or not much inferior, to themselves, about this time to be created. Their doubt who shall be sent on this difficult search: Satan, their chief, undertakes alone the voyage; is honoured and applauded. The council thus ended, the rest betake them several ways and to several employments, as their inclinations lead them, to entertain the time till Satan return. He passes on his journey to Hell-gates, finds them shut, and who sat there to guard them; by whom at length they are opened, and discover to him the great gulf between Hell and Heaven; with what difficulty he passes through, directed by Chaos, the Power of that place, to the sight of this new world which he sought.

PARADISE LOST

BOOK II

HIGH on a throne of royal state, which far
Outshone the wealth of Ormus and of Ind,
Or where the gorgeous East with richest hand
Showers on her kings barbaric pearl and gold,
Satan exalted sat, by merit raised
To that bad eminence; and, from despair
Thus high uplifted beyond hope, aspires
Beyond thus high, insatiate to pursue
Vain war with Heaven; and, by success untaught,
His proud imaginations thus displayed: 10
    "Powers and Dominions, Deities of Heaven!
For since no deep within her gulf can hold
Immortal vigour, though oppressed and fallen,
I give not Heaven for lost: from this descent
Celestial Virtues rising will appear
More glorious and more dread than from no fall,
And trust themselves to fear no second fate.
Me though just right, and the fixed laws of Heaven,
Did first create your leader, next, free choice,
With what besides, in counsel or in fight,   20
Hath been achieved of merit, yet this loss,
Thus far at least recovered, hath much more
Established in a safe unenvied throne,
Yielded with full consent. The happier state
In Heaven, which follows dignity, might draw
Envy from each inferior; but who here
Will envy whom the highest place exposes
Foremost to stand against the Thunderer's aim
Your bulwark, and condemns to greatest share
Of endless pain? Where there is then no good   30

For which to strive, no strife can grow up there
From faction; for none sure will claim in Hell
Precedence, none whose portion is so small
Of present pain that with ambitious mind
Will covet more. With this advantage then
To union, and firm faith, and firm accord,
More than can be in Heaven, we now return
To claim our just inheritance of old,
Surer to prosper than prosperity
Could have assured us; and by what best way,   40
Whether of open war or covert guile,
We now debate; who can advise may speak."
  He ceased; and next him Moloch, sceptred king,
Stood up, the strongest and the fiercest Spirit
That fought in Heaven, now fiercer by despair.
His trust was with the Eternal to be deemed
Equal in strength, and rather than be less
Cared not to be at all; with that care lost
Went all his fear: of God, or Hell, or worse,
He recked not, and these words thereafter spake: 50
  "My sentence is for open war: of wiles,
More unexpert, I boast not: them let those
Contrive who need, or when they need, not now.
For while they sit contriving, shall the rest,
Millions that stand in arms, and longing wait
The signal to ascend, sit lingering here
Heaven's fugitives, and for their dwelling-place
Accept this dark opprobrious den of shame,
The prison of his tyranny who reigns
By our delay? No! let us rather choose,   60
Armed with Hell-flames and fury, all at once
O'er Heaven's high towers to force resistless way,
Turning our tortures into horrid arms
Against the Torturer; when to meet the noise
Of his almighty engine he shall hear

Infernal thunder, and for lightning see
Black fire and horror shot with equal rage
Among his Angels, and his throne itself
Mixed with Tartarean sulphur and strange fire,
His own invented torments. But perhaps   70
The way seems difficult and steep to scale
With upright wing against a higher foe.
Let such bethink them, if the sleepy drench
Of that forgetful lake benumb not still,
That in our proper motion we ascend
Up to our native seat; descent and fall
To us is adverse. Who but felt of late,
When the fierce foe hung on our broken rear
Insulting, and pursued us through the deep,
With what compulsion and laborious flight   80
We sunk thus low? The ascent is easy then;
The event is feared: should we again provoke
Our stronger, some worse way his wrath may find
To our destruction—if there be in Hell
Fear to be worse destroyed! What can be worse
Than to dwell here, driven out from bliss, condemned
In this abhorrèd deep to utter woe;
Where pain of unextinguishable fire
Must exercise us without hope of end,
The vassals of his anger, when the scourge   90
Inexorably, and the torturing hour,
Calls us to penance? More destroyed than thus,
We should be quite abolished, and expire.
What fear we then? what doubt we to incense
His utmost ire? which, to the highth enraged,
Will either quite consume us, and reduce
To nothing this essential—happier far
Than miserable to have eternal being!—
Or if our substance be indeed divine,
And cannot cease to be, we are at worst   100

On this side nothing; and by proof we feel
Our power sufficient to disturb his Heaven,
And with perpetual inroads to alarm,
Though inaccessible, his fatal throne:
Which, if not victory, is yet revenge."
  He ended frowning, and his look denounced
Desperate revenge, and battle dangerous
To less than gods. On the other side up rose
Belial, in act more graceful and humane;
A fairer person lost not Heaven; he seemed   110
For dignity composed, and high exploit.
But all was false and hollow; though his tongue
Dropt manna, and could make the worse appear
The better reason, to perplex and dash
Maturest counsels: for his thoughts were low;
To vice industrious, but to nobler deeds
Timorous and slothful: yet he pleased the ear,
And with persuasive accent thus began:
  "I should be much for open war, O Peers,
As not behind in hate, if what was urged   120
Main reason to persuade immediate war
Did not dissuade me most, and seem to cast
Ominous conjecture on the whole success;
When he who most excels in fact of arms,
In what he counsels and in what excels
Mistrustful, grounds his courage on despair
And utter dissolution, as the scope
Of all his aim, after some dire revenge.
First, what revenge? The towers of Heaven are filled
With armed watch, that render all access   130
Impregnable; oft on the bordering deep
Encamp their legions, or with obscure wing
Scout far and wide into the realm of Night,
Scorning surprise. Or could we break our way
By force, and at our heels all Hell should rise

With blackest insurrection, to confound
Heaven's purest light, yet our great enemy
All incorruptible would on his throne
Sit unpolluted, and the ethereal mould
Incapable of stain would soon expel   140
Her mischief, and purge off the baser fire,
Victorious. Thus repulsed, our final hope
Is flat despair: we must exasperate
The almighty victor to spend all his rage,
And that must end us, that must be our cure—
To be no more. Sad cure! for who would lose,
Though full of pain, this intellectual being,
Those thoughts that wander through eternity,
To perish rather, swallowed up and lost
In the wide womb of uncreated Night,   150
Devoid of sense and motion? And who knows,
Let this be good, whether our angry foe
Can give it, or will ever? How he can
Is doubtful: that he never will is sure.
Will he, so wise, let loose at once his ire,
Belike through impotence, or unaware,
To give his enemies their wish, and end
Them in his anger, whom his anger saves
To punish endless? 'Wherefore cease we, then?'
Say they who counsel war; 'we are decreed,   160
Reserved, and destined to eternal woe;
Whatever doing, what can we suffer more,
What can we suffer worse?' Is this then worst,
Thus sitting, thus consulting, thus in arms?
What when we fled amain, pursued and strook
With Heaven's afflicting thunder, and besought
The deep to shelter us? this Hell then seemed
A refuge from those wounds. Or when we lay
Chained on the burning lake? that sure was worse.
What if the breath that kindled those grim fires,   170

Awaked, should blow them into sevenfold rage,
And plunge us in the flames? or from above
Should intermitted vengeance arm again
His red right hand to plague us? What if all
Her stores were opened, and this firmament
Of Hell should spout her cataracts of fire,
Impendent horrors, threatening hideous fall
One day upon our heads; while we perhaps,
Designing or exhorting glorious war,
Caught in a fiery tempest shall be hurled,   180
Each on his rock transfixed, the sport and prey
Of racking whirlwinds, or for ever sunk
Under yon boiling ocean, wrapt in chains;
There to converse with everlasting groans,
Unrespited, unpitied, unreprieved,
Ages of hopeless end! This would be worse.
War therefore, open or concealed, alike
My voice dissuades; for what can force or guile
With him, or who deceive his mind, whose eye
Views all things at one view? He from Heaven's highth   190
All these our motions vain sees and derides,
Not more almighty to resist our might
Than wise to frustrate all our plots and wiles.
Shall we then live thus vile, the race of Heaven
Thus trampled, thus expelled to suffer here
Chains and these torments? Better these than worse,
By my advice; since fate inevitable
Subdues us, and omnipotent decree,
The victor's will. To suffer, as to do,
Our strength is equal, nor the law unjust   200
That so ordains: this was at first resolved,
If we were wise, against so great a foe
Contending, and so doubtful what might fall.
I laugh, when those who at the spear are bold
And vent'rous, if that fail them, shrink, and fear

What yet they know must follow—to endure
Exile, or ignominy, or bonds, or pain,
The sentence of their conqueror. This is now
Our doom; which if we can sustain and bear,
Our supreme foe in time may much remit   210
His anger, and perhaps, thus far removed,
Not mind us not offending, satisfied
With what is punished; whence these raging fires
Will slacken, if his breath stir not their flames.
Our purer essence then will overcome
Their noxious vapour, or inured not feel,
Or changed at length, and to the place conformed
In temper and in nature, will receive
Familiar the fierce heat, and void of pain;
This horror will grow mild, this darkness light;   220
Besides what hope the never-ending flight
Of future days may bring, what chance, what change
Worth waiting, since our present lot appears
For happy though but ill, for ill not worst,
If we procure not to ourselves more woe."
    Thus Belial, with words clothed in reason's garb,
Counselled ignoble ease, and peaceful sloth,
Not peace; and after him thus Mammon spake:
    "Either to disenthrone the King of Heaven
We war, if war be best, or to regain   230
Our own right lost: him to unthrone we then
May hope, when everlasting Fate shall yield
To fickle Chance, and Chaos judge the strife.
The former, vain to hope, argues as vain
The latter; for what place can be for us
Within Heaven's bound, unless Heaven's Lord supreme
We overpower? Suppose he should relent
And publish grace to all, on promise made
Of new subjection; with what eyes could we
Stand in his presence humble, and receive   240

Strict laws imposed, to celebrate his throne
With warbled hymns, and to his Godhead sing
Forced Halleluiahs; while he lordly sits
Our envied sovran, and his altar breathes
Ambrosial odours and ambrosial flowers,
Our servile offerings? This must be our task
In Heaven, this our delight; how wearisome
Eternity so spent in worship paid
To whom we hate! Let us not then pursue,
By force impossible, by leave obtained   250
Unacceptable, though in Heaven, our state
Of splendid vassalage; but rather seek
Our own good from ourselves, and from our own
Live to ourselves, though in this vast recess,
Free, and to none accountable, preferring
Hard liberty before the easy yoke
Of servile pomp. Our greatness will appear
Then most conspicuous, when great things of small,
Useful of hurtful, prosperous of adverse,
We can create, and in what place soe'er   260
Thrive under evil, and work ease out of pain
Through labour and endurance. This deep world
Of darkness do we dread? How oft amidst
Thick clouds and dark doth Heaven's all-ruling Sire
Choose to reside, his glory unobscured,
And with the majesty of darkness round
Covers his throne, from whence deep thunders roar,
Mustering their rage, and Heaven resembles Hell!
As he our darkness, cannot we his light
Imitate when we please? This desert soil   270
Wants not her hidden lustre; gems and gold;
Nor want we skill or art, from whence to raise
Magnificence; and what can Heaven show more?
Our torments also may in length of time
Become our elements, these piercing fires

As soft as now severe, our temper changed
Into their temper; which must needs remove
The sensible of pain. All things invite
To peaceful counsels, and the settled state
Of order, how in safety best we may   280
Compose our present evils, with regard
Of what we are and where, dismissing quite
All thoughts of war. Ye have what I advise."
   He scarce had finished, when such murmur filled
The assembly, as when hollow rocks retain
The sound of blustering winds, which all night long
Had roused the sea, now with hoarse cadence lull
Seafaring men o'erwatched, whose bark by chance,
Or pinnace, anchors in a craggy bay
After the tempest: such applause was heard   290
As Mammon ended, and his sentence pleased,
Advising peace; for such another field
They dreaded worse than Hell; so much the fear
Of thunder and the sword of Michaël
Wrought still within them; and no less desire
To found this nether empire, which might rise,
By policy, and long process of time,
In emulation opposite to Heaven.
Which when Beëlzebub perceived, than whom,
Satan except, none higher sat, with grave   300
Aspect he rose, and in his rising seemed
A pillar of state; deep on his front engraven
Deliberation sat and public care;
And princely counsel in his face yet shone,
Majestic though in ruin. Sage he stood,
With Atlantean shoulders fit to bear
The weight of mightiest monarchies; his look
Drew audience and attention still as night
Or summer's noontide air, while thus he spake:
   "Thrones and imperial Powers, Offspring of Heaven, 310

Ethereal Virtues! or these titles now
Must we renounce, and, changing style, be called
Princes of Hell? for so the popular vote
Inclines, here to continue, and build up here
A growing empire—doubtless! while we dream,
And know not that the King of Heaven hath doomed
This place our dungeon, not our safe retreat
Beyond his potent arm, to live exempt
From Heaven's high jurisdiction, in new league
Banded against his throne, but to remain   320
In strictest bondage, though thus far removed,
Under the inevitable curb, reserved
His captive multitude. For he, be sure,
In highth or depth, still first and last will reign
Sole king, and of his kingdom lose no part
By our revolt, but over Hell extend
His empire, and with iron sceptre rule
Us here, as with his golden those in Heaven.
What sit we then projecting peace and war?
War hath determined us, and foiled with loss   330
Irreparable; terms of peace yet none
Vouchsafed or sought; for what peace will be given
To us enslaved, but custody severe,
And stripes, and arbitrary punishment
Inflicted? and what peace can we return,
But, to our power, hostility and hate,
Untamed reluctance, and revenge, though slow,
Yet ever plotting how the conqueror least
May reap his conquest, and may least rejoice
In doing what we most in suffering feel?   340
Nor will occasion want, nor shall we need
With dangerous expedition to invade
Heaven, whose high walls fear no assault or siege,
Or ambush from the deep. What if we find
Some easier enterprise? There is a place

(If ancient and prophetic fame in Heaven
Err not), another world, the happy seat
Of some new race called Man, about this time
To be created like to us, though less
In power and excellence, but favoured more   350
Of him who rules above; so was his will
Pronounced among the gods, and by an oath,
That shook Heaven's whole circumference, confirmed.
Thither let us bend all our thoughts, to learn
What creatures there inhabit, of what mould,
Or substance, how endued, and what their power,
And where their weakness, how attempted best,
By force or subtlety. Though Heaven be shut,
And Heaven's high Arbitrator sit secure
In his own strength, this place may lie exposed,   360
The utmost border of his kingdom, left
To their defence who hold it; here, perhaps,
Some advantageous act may be achieved
By sudden onset: either with Hell-fire
To waste his whole creation, or possess
All as our own, and drive, as we are driven,
The puny habitants; or if not drive,
Seduce them to our party, that their God
May prove their foe, and with repenting hand
Abolish his own works. This would surpass   370
Common revenge, and interrupt his joy
In our confusion, and our joy upraise
In his disturbance; when his darling sons,
Hurled headlong to partake with us, shall curse
Their frail original, and faded bliss,
Faded so soon! Advise if this be worth
Attempting, or to sit in darkness here
Hatching vain empires." Thus Beëlzebub
Pleaded his devilish counsel, first devised
By Satan, and in part proposed; for whence,   380

But from the author of all ill, could spring
So deep a malice, to confound the race
Of Mankind in one root, and Earth with Hell,
To mingle and involve, done all to spite
The great Creator? But their spite still serves
His glory to augment. The bold design
Pleased highly those infernal States, and joy
Sparkled in all their eyes; with full assent
They vote: whereat his speech he thus renews:
    "Well have ye judged, well ended long debate,   390
Synod of gods, and, like to what ye are,
Great things resolved; which from the lowest deep
Will once more lift us up, in spite of fate,
Nearer our ancient seat; perhaps in view
Of those bright confines, whence, with neighbouring arms
And opportune excursion, we may chance
Re-enter Heaven; or else in some mild zone
Dwell not unvisited of Heaven's fair light,
Secure, and at the brightening orient beam
Purge off this gloom; the soft delicious air,   400
To heal the scar of these corrosive fires,
Shall breathe her balm. But first, whom shall we send
In search of this new world? whom shall we find
Sufficient? who shall tempt with wandering feet
The dark, unbottomed, infinite Abyss,
And through the palpable obscure find out
His uncouth way, or spread his aery flight,
Upborne with indefatigable wings
Over the vast abrupt, ere he arrive
The happy isle? What strength, what art, can then   410
Suffice, or what evasion bear him safe
Through the strict senteries and stations thick
Of Angels watching round? Here he had need
All circumspection, and we now no less
Choice in our suffrage; for on whom we send

The weight of all, and our last hope, relies."
　This said, he sat; and expectation held
His look suspense, awaiting who appeared
To second, or oppose, or undertake
The perilous attempt; but all sat mute,   420
Pondering the danger with deep thoughts; and each
In other's countenance read his own dismay,
Astonished. None among the choice and prime
Of those Heaven-warring champions could be found
So hardy as to proffer or accept,
Alone, the dreadful voyage; till at last
Satan, whom now transcendent glory raised
Above his fellows, with monarchal pride
Conscious of highest worth, unmoved thus spake:
　"O Progeny of Heaven, empyreal Thrones!   430
With reason hath deep silence and demur
Seized us, though undismayed. Long is the way
And hard, that out of Hell leads up to light;
Our prison strong, this huge convex of fire,
Outrageous to devour, immures us round
Ninefold, and gates of burning adamant,
Barred over us, prohibit all egress.
These passed, if any pass, the void profound
Of unessential Night receives him next,
Wide-gaping, and with utter loss of being   440
Threatens him, plunged in that abortive gulf.
If thence he scape into whatever world,
Or unknown region, what remains him less
Than unknown dangers and as hard escape?
But I should ill become this throne, O Peers,
And this imperial sovranty, adorned
With splendour, armed with power, if aught proposed
And judged of public moment, in the shape
Of difficulty or danger, could deter
Me from attempting. Wherefore do I assume   450

These royalties, and not refuse to reign,
Refusing to accept as great a share
Of hazard as of honour, due alike
To him who reigns, and so much to him due
Of hazard more, as he above the rest
High honoured sits? Go therefore, mighty Powers,
Terror of Heaven, though fallen; intend at home,
While here shall be our home, what best may ease
The present misery, and render Hell
More tolerable; if there be cure or charm   460
To respite, or deceive, or slack the pain
Of this ill mansion; intermit no watch
Against a wakeful foe, while I abroad
Through all the coasts of dark destruction seek
Deliverance for us all: this enterprise
None shall partake with me." Thus saying, rose
The Monarch, and prevented all reply;
Prudent, lest, from his resolution raised,
Others among the chief might offer now
(Certain to be refused) what erst they feared,   470
And, so refused, might in opinion stand
His rivals, winning cheap the high repute
Which he through hazard huge must earn. But they
Dreaded not more the adventure than his voice
Forbidding; and at once with him they rose;
Their rising all at once was as the sound
Of thunder heard remote. Towards him they bend
With awful reverence prone; and as a god
Extol him equal to the Highest in Heaven.
Nor failed they to express how much they praised   480
That for the general safety he despised
His own; for neither do the Spirits damned
Lose all their virtue; lest bad men should boast
Their specious deeds on Earth, which glory excites,
Or close ambition varnished o'er with zeal.

Thus they their doubtful consultations dark
Ended, rejoicing in their matchless Chief:
As when from mountain-tops the dusky clouds
Ascending, while the North-wind sleeps, o'erspread
Heaven's cheerful face, the louring element   490
Scowls o'er the darkened landskip snow or shower;
If chance the radiant sun with farewell sweet
Extend his evening beam, the fields revive,
The birds their notes renew, and bleating herds
Attest their joy, that hill and valley rings.
O shame to men! Devil with devil damned
Firm concord holds, men only disagree
Of creatures rational, though under hope
Of heavenly grace; and, God proclaiming peace,
Yet live in hatred, enmity, and strife   500
Among themselves, and levy cruel wars,
Wasting the Earth, each other to destroy:
As if (which might induce us to accord)
Man had not hellish foes enow besides,
That day and night for his destruction wait!
    The Stygian council thus dissolved; and forth
In order came the grand infernal Peers;
Midst came their mighty Paramount, and seemed
Alone the antagonist of Heaven, nor less
Than Hell's dread Emperor, with pomp supreme,   510
And god-like imitated state; him round
A globe of fiery Seraphim enclosed
With bright emblazonry, and horrent arms.
Then of their session ended they bid cry
With trumpet's regal sound the great result:
Toward the four winds four speedy Cherubim
Put to their mouths the sounding alchymy,
By harald's voice explained; the hollow Abyss
Heard far and wide, and all the host of Hell
With deafening shout returned them loud acclaim.   520

Thence more at ease their minds and somewhat raised
By false presumptuous hope, the ranged powers
Disband; and, wandering, each his several way
Pursues, as inclination or sad choice
Leads him perplexed, where he may likeliest find
Truce to his restless thoughts, and entertain
The irksome hours, till his great Chief return.
Part on the plain, or in the air sublime,
Upon the wing or in swift race contend,
As at the Olympian games or Pythian fields;   530
Part curb their fiery steeds, or shun the goal
With rapid wheels, or fronted brigads form:
As when, to warn proud cities, war appears
Waged in the troubled sky, and armies rush
To battle in the clouds; before each van
Prick forth the aery knights, and couch their spears,
Till thickest legions close; with feats of arms
From either end of Heaven the welkin burns.
Others, with vast Typhœan rage more fell,
Rend up both rocks and hills, and ride the air   540
In whirlwind; Hell scarce holds the wild uproar:
As when Alcides, from Œchalia crowned
With conquest, felt the envenomed robe, and tore
Through pain up by the roots Thessalian pines,
And Lichas from the top of Œta threw
Into the Euboic sea. Others more mild,
Retreated in a silent valley, sing
With notes angelical to many a harp
Their own heroic deeds and hapless fall
By doom of battle; and complain that Fate   550
Free Virtue should enthrall to Force or Chance.
Their song was partial, but the harmony
(What could it less when Spirits immortal sing?)
Suspended Hell, and took with ravishment
The thronging audience. In discourse more sweet

(For eloquence the soul, song charms the sense)
Others apart sat on a hill retired,
In thoughts more elevate, and reasoned high
Of providence, foreknowledge, will, and fate,
Fixed fate, free will, foreknowledge absolute,   560
And found no end, in wandering mazes lost.
Of good and evil much they argued then,
Of happiness and final misery,
Passion and apathy, and glory and shame,
Vain wisdom all, and false philosophy!
Yet with a pleasing sorcery could charm
Pain for a while or anguish, and excite
Fallacious hope, or arm the obdured breast
With stubborn patience as with triple steel.
Another part, in squadrons and gross bands,   570
On bold adventure to discover wide
That dismal world, if any clime perhaps
Might yield them easier habitation, bend
Four ways their flying march, along the banks
Of four infernal rivers that disgorge
Into the burning lake their baleful streams:
Abhorred Styx, the flood of deadly hate;
Sad Acheron of sorrow, black and deep;
Cocytus, named of lamentation loud
Heard on the rueful stream; fierce Phlegethon,   580
Whose waves of torrent fire inflame with rage.
Far off from these a slow and silent stream,
Lethe, the river of oblivion, rolls
Her watery labyrinth, whereof who drinks
Forthwith his former state and being forgets,
Forgets both joy and grief, pleasure and pain.
Beyond this flood a frozen continent
Lies dark and wild, beat with perpetual storms
Of whirlwind and dire hail, which on firm land
Thaws not, but gathers heap, and ruin seems   590

Of ancient pile; all else deep snow and ice,
A gulf profound as that Serbonian bog
Betwixt Damiata and Mount Casius old,
Where armies whole have sunk: the parching air
Burns frore, and cold performs the effect of fire.
Thither, by harpy-footed Furies haled,
At certain revolutions all the damned
Are brought; and feel by turns the bitter change
Of fierce extremes, extremes by change more fierce,
From beds of raging fire to starve in ice   600
Their soft ethereal warmth, and there to pine
Immovable, infixed, and frozen round
Periods of time; thence hurried back to fire.
They ferry over this Lethean sound
Both to and fro, their sorrow to augment,
And wish and struggle, as they pass, to reach
The tempting stream, with one small drop to lose
In sweet forgetfulness all pain and woe,
All in one moment, and so near the brink;
But Fate withstands, and, to oppose the attempt,   610
Medusa with Gorgonian terror guards
The ford, and of itself the water flies
All taste of living wight, as once it fled
The lip of Tantalus. Thus roving on
In confused march forlorn, the adventurous bands,
With shuddering horror pale, and eyes aghast,
Viewed first their lamentable lot, and found
No rest. Through many a dark and dreary vale
They passed, and many a region dolorous,
O'er many a frozen, many a fiery Alp,   620
Rocks, caves, lakes, fens, bogs, dens, and shades of death,
A universe of death, which God by curse
Created evil, for evil only good,
Where all life dies, death lives, and Nature breeds,
Perverse, all monstrous, all prodigious things,

Abominable, inutterable, and worse
Than fables yet have feigned, or fear conceived,
Gorgons, and Hydras, and Chimæras dire.
    Meanwhile the Adversary of God and Man,
Satan, with thoughts inflamed of highest design,   630
Puts on swift wings, and toward the gates of Hell
Explores his solitary flight; sometimes
He scours the right hand coast, sometimes the left;
Now shaves with level wing the deep, then soars
Up to the fiery concave towering high.
As when far off at sea a fleet descried
Hangs in the clouds, by equinoctial winds
Close sailing from Bengala, or the isles
Of Ternate and Tidore, whence merchants bring
Their spicy drugs; they on the trading flood,   640
Through the wide Ethiopian to the Cape,
Ply stemming nightly toward the pole: so seemed
Far off the flying Fiend. At last appear
Hell-bounds, high reaching to the horrid roof,
And thrice threefold the gates; three folds were brass,
Three iron, three of adamantine rock,
Impenetrable, impaled with circling fire,
Yet unconsumed. Before the gates there sat
On either side a formidable Shape.
The one seemed woman to the waist, and fair,   650
But ended foul in many a scaly fold
Voluminous and vast, a serpent armed
With mortal sting. About her middle round
A cry of Hell-hounds never-ceasing barked
With wide Cerberean mouths full loud, and rung
A hideous peal; yet, when they list, would creep,
If aught disturbed their noise, into her womb,
And kennel there, yet there still barked and howled
Within unseen. Far less abhorred than these
Vexed Scylla, bathing in the sea that parts   660

Calabria from the hoarse Trinacrian shore;
Nor uglier follow the night-hag, when, called
In secret, riding through the air she comes,
Lured with the smell of infant blood, to dance
With Lapland witches, while the labouring moon
Eclipses at their charms. The other Shape—
If shape it might be called that shape had none
Distinguishable in member, joint, or limb;
Or substance might be called that shadow seemed,
For each seemed either—black it stood as Night,   670
Fierce as ten Furies, terrible as Hell,
And shook a dreadful dart; what seemed his head
The likeness of a kingly crown had on.
Satan was now at hand, and from his seat
The monster moving onward came as fast,
With horrid strides; Hell trembled as he strode.
The undaunted Fiend what this might be admired,
Admired, not feared—God and his Son except,
Created thing naught valued he nor shunned—
And with disdainful look thus first began: 680
    "Whence and what art thou, execrable Shape,
That dar'st, though grim and terrible, advance
Thy miscreated front athwart my way
To yonder gates? Through them I mean to pass,
That be assured, without leave asked of thee.
Retire, or taste thy folly, and learn by proof,
Hell-born, not to contend with Spirits of Heaven."
    To whom the Goblin, full of wrath, replied:
"Art thou that Traitor-Angel, art thou he,
Who first broke peace in Heaven and faith, till then   690
Unbroken, and in proud rebellious arms
Drew after him the third part of Heaven's sons,
Conjured against the Highest, for which both thou
And they, outcast from God, are here condemned
To waste eternal days in woe and pain?

And reckon'st thou thyself with Spirits of Heaven,
Hell-doomed, and breath'st defiance here and scorn,
Where I reign king, and, to enrage thee more,
Thy king and lord? Back to thy punishment,
False fugitive, and to thy speed add wings,   700
Lest with a whip of scorpions I pursue
Thy lingering, or with one stroke of this dart
Strange horror seize thee, and pangs unfelt before."
    So spake the grisly Terror, and in shape,
So speaking and so threatening, grew tenfold
More dreadful and deform. On the other side,
Incensed with indignation, Satan stood
Unterrified, and like a comet burned,
That fires the length of Ophiuchus huge
In the artic sky, and from his horrid hair   710
Shakes pestilence and war. Each at the head
Levelled his deadly aim; their fatal hands
No second stroke intend; and such a frown
Each cast at the other, as when two black clouds,
With Heaven's artillery fraught, come rattling on
Over the Caspian, then stand front to front
Hovering a space, till winds the signal blow
To join their dark encounter in mid-air:
So frowned the mighty combatants, that Hell
Grew darker at their frown; so matched they stood;   720
For never but once more was either like
To meet so great a foe. And now great deeds
Had been achieved, whereof all Hell had rung,
Had not the snaky Sorceress, that sat
Fast by Hell-gate and kept the fatal key,
Risen, and with hideous outcry rushed between.
    "O father, what intends thy hand", she cried,
"Against thy only son? What fury, O son,
Possesses thee to bend that mortal dart
Against thy father's head? and know'st for whom;   730

For him who sits above, and laughs the while
At thee ordained his drudge, to execute
Whate'er his wrath, which he calls justice, bids—
His wrath, which one day will destroy ye both!"
   She spake, and at her words the hellish Pest
Forbore; then these to her Satan returned:
   "So strange thy outcry, and thy words so strange
Thou interposest, that my sudden hand,
Prevented, spares to tell thee yet by deeds
What it intends, till first I know of thee   740
What thing thou art, thus double-formed, and why,
In this infernal vale first met, thou call'st
Me father, and that phantasm call'st my son.
I know thee not, nor ever saw till now
Sight more detestable than him and thee."
   To whom thus the Portress of Hell-gate replied:
"Hast thou forgot me then, and do I seem
Now in thine eye so foul? once deemed so fair
In Heaven, when at the assembly, and in sight
Of all the Seraphim with thee combined   750
In bold conspiracy against Heaven's King,
All on a sudden miserable pain
Surprised thee; dim thine eyes, and dizzy swum
In darkness, while thy head flames thick and fast
Threw forth, till on the left side opening wide,
Likest to thee in shape and countenance bright,
Then shining Heavenly-fair, a goddess armed,
Out of thy head I sprung. Amazement seized
All the host of Heaven; back they recoiled afraid
At first, and called me *Sin*, and for a sign   760
Portentous held me; but, familiar grown,
I pleased, and with attractive graces won
The most averse, thee chiefly, who full oft
Thyself in me thy perfect image viewing
Becam'st enamoured; and such joy thou took'st

With me in secret, that my womb conceived
A growing burden. Meanwhile war arose,
And fields were fought in Heaven; wherein remained
(For what could else?) to our almighty foe
Clear victory, to our part loss and rout   770
Through all the Empyrean. Down they fell,
Driven headlong from the pitch of Heaven, down
Into this deep, and in the general fall
I also; at which time this powerful key
Into my hands was given, with charge to keep
These gates for ever shut, which none can pass
Without my opening. Pensive here I sat
Alone; but long I sat not, till my womb,
Pregnant by thee, and now excessive grown,
Prodigious motion felt and rueful throes.   780
At last this odious offspring whom thou seest,
Thine own begotten, breaking violent way,
Tore through my entrails, that, with fear and pain
Distorted, all my nether shape thus grew
Transformed; but he, my inbred enemy,
Forth issued, brandishing his fatal dart,
Made to destroy. I fled, and cried out *Death!*
Hell trembled at the hideous name, and sighed
From all her caves, and back resounded *Death!*
I fled; but he pursued (though more, it seems,   790
Inflamed with lust than rage) and, swifter far,
Me overtook, his mother, all dismayed,
And, in embraces forcible and foul
Engendering with me, of that rape begot
These yelling monsters, that with ceaseless cry
Surround me, as thou saw'st, hourly conceived
And hourly born, with sorrow infinite
To me; for, when they list, into the womb
That bred them they return, and howl, and gnaw
My bowels, their repast; then, bursting forth   800

PL   5

Afresh, with conscious terrors vex me round,
That rest or intermission none I find.
Before mine eyes in opposition sits
Grim Death, my son and foe, who sets them on,
And me, his parent, would full soon devour
For want of other prey, but that he knows
His end with mine involved, and knows that I
Should prove a bitter morsel, and his bane,
Whenever that shall be; so Fate pronounced.
But thou, O father, I forewarn thee, shun   810
His deadly arrow; neither vainly hope
To be invulnerable in those bright arms,
Though tempered heavenly; for that mortal dint,
Save he who reigns above, none can resist."
    She finished; and the subtle Fiend his lore
Soon learned, now milder, and thus answered smooth:
    "Dear daughter—since thou claim'st me for thy sire,
And my fair son here show'st me, the dear pledge
Of dalliance had with thee in Heaven, and joys
Then sweet, now sad to mention, through dire change   820
Befallen us unforeseen, unthought of—know,
I come no enemy, but to set free
From out this dark and dismal house of pain
Both him and thee, and all the Heavenly host
Of Spirits that, in our just pretences armed,
Fell with us from on high. From them I go
This uncouth errand sole, and one for all
Myself expose, with lonely steps to tread
The unfounded deep, and through the void immense
To search with wandering quest a place foretold   830
Should be, and, by concurring signs, ere now
Created vast and round, a place of bliss
In the purlieus of Heaven, and therein placed
A race of upstart creatures, to supply
Perhaps our vacant room, though more removed,

Lest Heaven, surcharged with potent multitude,
Might hap to move new broils. Be this, or aught
Than this more secret, now designed, I haste
To know; and, this once known, shall soon return,
And bring ye to the place where thou and Death   840
Shall dwell at ease, and up and down unseen
Wing silently the buxom air, embalmed
With odours: there ye shall be fed and filled
Immeasurably; all things shall be your prey."
   He ceased, for both seemed highly pleased, and Death
Grinned horrible a ghastly smile, to hear
His famine should be filled, and blessed his maw
Destined to that good hour. No less rejoiced
His mother bad, and thus bespake her sire:
   "The key of this infernal pit, by due   850
And by command of Heaven's all-powerful King,
I keep, by him forbidden to unlock
These adamantine gates; against all force
Death ready stands to interpose his dart,
Fearless to be o'ermatched by living might.
But what owe I to his commands above,
Who hates me, and hath hither thrust me down
Into this gloom of Tartarus profound,
To sit in hateful office here confined,
Inhabitant of Heaven and Heavenly-born,   860
Here in perpetual agony and pain,
With terrors and with clamours compassed round
Of mine own brood, that on my bowels feed?
Thou art my father, thou my author, thou
My being gav'st me; whom should I obey
But thee? whom follow? Thou wilt bring me soon
To that new world of light and bliss, among
The gods who live at ease, where I shall reign
At thy right hand voluptuous, as beseems
Thy daughter and thy darling, without end."   870

Thus saying, from her side the fatal key,
Sad instrument of all our woe, she took;
And, towards the gate rolling her bestial train,
Forthwith the huge portcullis high up-drew,
Which but herself not all the Stygian powers
Could once have moved; then in the key-hole turns
The intricate wards, and every bolt and bar
Of massy iron or solid rock with ease
Unfastens: on a sudden open fly,
With impetuous recoil and jarring sound,   880
The infernal doors, and on their hinges grate
Harsh thunder, that the lowest bottom shook
Of Erebus. She opened, but to shut
Excelled her power; the gates wide open stood,
That with extended wings a bannered host,
Under spread ensigns marching, might pass through
With horse and chariots ranked in loose array;
So wide they stood, and like a furnace-mouth
Cast forth redounding smoke and ruddy flame.
Before their eyes in sudden view appear   890
The secrets of the hoary deep, a dark
Illimitable ocean, without bound,
Without dimension; where length, breadth, and highth,
And time, and place, are lost; where eldest Night
And Chaos, ancestors of Nature, hold
Eternal anarchy, amidst the noise
Of endless wars, and by confusion stand.
For Hot, Cold, Moist, and Dry, four champions fierce,
Strive here for mastery, and to battle bring
Their embryon atoms; they around the flag   900
Of each his faction, in their several clans,
Light-armed or heavy, sharp, smooth, swift, or slow,
Swarm populous, unnumbered as the sands
Of Barca or Cyrene's torrid soil,
Levied to side with warring winds, and poise

Their lighter wings. To whom these most adhere
He rules a moment; Chaos umpire sits,
And by decision more embroils the fray
By which he reigns; next him, high arbiter,
Chance governs all. Into this wild Abyss, 910
The womb of Nature, and perhaps her grave,
Of neither sea, nor shore, nor air, nor fire,
But all these in their pregnant causes mixed
Confusedly, and which thus must ever fight,
Unless the Almighty Maker them ordain
His dark materials to create more worlds—
Into this wild Abyss the wary Fiend
Stood on the brink of Hell and looked a while,
Pondering his voyage; for no narrow frith
He had to cross. Nor was his ear less pealed 920
With noises loud and ruinous (to compare
Great things with small) than when Bellona storms,
With all her battering engines bent to rase
Some capital city; or less than if this frame
Of Heaven were falling, and these elements
In mutiny had from her axle torn
The steadfast Earth. At last his sail-broad vans
He spreads for flight, and in the surging smoke
Uplifted spurns the ground; thence many a league,
As in a cloudy chair, ascending rides 930
Audacious; but, that seat soon failing, meets
A vast vacuity: all unawares,
Fluttering his pennons vain, plumb-down he drops
Ten thousand fathom deep, and to this hour
Down had been falling, had not by ill chance
The strong rebuff of some tumultuous cloud,
Instinct with fire and nitre, hurried him
As many miles aloft; that fury stayed—
Quenched in a boggy Syrtis, neither sea,
Nor good dry land—nigh foundered, on he fares, 940

Treading the crude consistence, half on foot,
Half flying; behoves him now both oar and sail.
As when a gryphon through the wilderness
With winged course, o'er hill or moory dale,
Pursues the Arimaspian, who by stealth
Had from his wakeful custody purloined
The guarded gold: so eagerly the Fiend
O'er bog or steep, through strait, rough, dense, or rare,
With head, hands, wings, or feet, pursues his way,
And swims, or sinks, or wades, or creeps, or flies.   950
At length a universal hubbub wild
Of stunning sounds and voices all confused,
Borne through the hollow dark, assaults his ear
With loudest vehemence. Thither he plies
Undaunted, to meet there whatever Power
Or spirit of the nethermost Abyss
Might in that noise reside, of whom to ask
Which way the nearest coast of darkness lies
Bordering on light; when straight behold the throne
Of Chaos, and his dark pavilion spread   960
Wide on the wasteful Deep! With him enthroned
Sat sable-vested Night, eldest of things,
The consort of his reign; and by them stood
Orcus and Ades, and the dreaded name
Of Demogorgon; Rumour next and Chance,
And Tumult and Confusion all embroiled,
And Discord with a thousand various mouths.
    To whom Satan, turning boldly, thus: "Ye Powers
And Spirits of this nethermost Abyss,
Chaos and ancient Night, I come no spy,   970
With purpose to explore or to disturb
The secrets of your realm; but, by constraint
Wandering this darksome desert, as my way
Lies through your spacious empire up to light,
Alone and without guide, half lost, I seek,

What readiest path leads where your gloomy bounds
Confine with Heaven; or if some other place,
From your dominion won, the Ethereal King
Possesses lately, thither to arrive
I travel this profound. Direct my course: 980
Directed, no mean recompense it brings
To your behoof, if I that region lost,
All usurpation thence expelled, reduce
To her original darkness and your sway
(Which is my present journey), and once more
Erect the standard there of ancient Night.
Yours be the advantage all, mine the revenge!"
   Thus Satan; and him thus the Anarch old,
With faltering speech and visage incomposed,
Answered: "I know thee, stranger, who thou art,   990
That mighty leading Angel, who of late
Made head against Heaven's King, though overthrown.
I saw and heard; for such a numerous host
Fled not in silence through the frighted deep,
With ruin upon ruin, rout on rout,
Confusion worse confounded; and Heaven-gates
Poured out by millions her victorious bands,
Pursuing. I upon my frontiers here
Keep residence; if all I can will serve
That little which is left so to defend,   1000
Encroached on still through our intestine broils
Weakening the sceptre of old Night: first Hell,
Your dungeon, stretching far and wide beneath;
Now lately Heaven and Earth, another world
Hung o'er my realm, linked in a golden chain
To that side Heaven from whence your legions fell.
If that way be your walk, you have not far;
So much the nearer danger. Go, and speed!
Havoc, and spoil, and ruin, are my gain."
   He ceased; and Satan stayed not to reply,   1010

But, glad that now his sea should find a shore,
With fresh alacrity and force renewed
Springs upward, like a pyramid of fire,
Into the wild expanse, and through the shock
Of fighting elements, on all sides round
Environed, wins his way; harder beset
And more endangered, than when Argo passed
Through Bosporus betwixt the justling rocks;
Or when Ulysses on the larboard shunned
Charybdis, and by the other whirlpool steered: 1020
So he with difficulty and labour hard
Moved on: with difficulty and labour he;
But, he once passed, soon after, when Man fell,
Strange alteration! Sin and Death amain,
Following his track (such was the will of Heaven)
Paved after him a broad and beaten way
Over the dark Abyss, whose boiling gulf
Tamely endured a bridge of wondrous length,
From Hell continued, reaching the utmost orb
Of this frail world; by which the Spirits perverse   1030
With easy intercourse pass to and fro
To tempt or punish mortals, except whom
God and good Angels guard by special grace.
    But now at last the sacred influence
Of light appears, and from the walls of Heaven
Shoots far into the bosom of dim Night
A glimmering dawn. Here Nature first begins
Her farthest verge, and Chaos to retire,
As from her outmost works, a broken foe,
With tumult less and with less hostile din;   1040
That Satan with less toil, and now with ease,
Wafts on the calmer wave by dubious light,
And, like a weather-beaten vessel, holds
Gladly the port, though shrouds and tackle torn;
Or in the emptier waste, resembling air,

Weighs his spread wings, at leisure to behold
Far off the empyreal Heaven, extended wide
In circuit, undetermined square or round,
With opal towers and battlements adorned
Of living sapphire, once his native seat;   1050
And fast by, hanging in a golden chain,
This pendent world, in bigness as a star
Of smallest magnitude close by the moon.
Thither, full fraught with mischievous revenge,
Accurst, and in a cursed hour, he hies.

NOTES

Abbreviations:

M. = Milton, or Milton's poetry, as distinguished from his prose.

G. = Glossary.

P. W. = Milton's prose-works.

Other books of *Paradise Lost* are indicated by Roman numerals.

COMMENDATORY VERSES

First printed in 2nd ed. 1674. I number the lines of each poem for convenience of reference.

I. The Latin elegiacs: the author of these was Samuel Barrow, a Cambridge man of note. Born in 1625 he graduated from Trinity in 1643, and afterwards attained to some celebrity in medicine. He was appointed Physician in Ordinary to Charles II in August, 1660, and died in 1682. His Royalist sympathies evidently did not prevent him from being an admirer of Milton. Curiously enough, his poetic summary of the contents of the Epic includes no direct reference to the Temptation and Fall of Man. He is most struck with the war in Heaven and Satan's expulsion.

1. *Amissam*; the masculine were more correct; cf. the title of Hogg's once well-known translation—*Paraphrasis Poetica in tria Johannis Miltoni Poemata, viz. Paradisum Amissum, Paradisum Recuperatum, et Samsonem Agonisten* (1690).

9. *pontum*; no doubt, the right reading. It is strange, however, that Masson and others who print *pontum* do not note that both the 2nd and 3rd eds. of *P. L.* have *portum* (which Keightley retained, with what sense is not clear).

15. *futurum*, so 2nd and 3rd eds., but many later texts print *futura*. As the line stands it seems to mean (if we may reproduce the baldness of the original), 'who could believe that there would be any one who would conceive hopes of these things?' i.e. be so ambitious. But probably the author intended *futura* (or wrote *hoc*).

17–38. These lines, nearly half the poem, allude to bk. VI of *P. L.*; see VI. 246–327, 634–69, 669, 670, 749–879.

30. *Currus animes*, the Cherubic chariot (VI. 750–6).

39–42. Lauder placed these verses—ironically—on the title-page of his *Essay* (1750).

42. Alluding to the Homeric "Battle of the Frogs and Mice"; and the Virgilian (?) "Culex". Cf. Dryden's lines on Milton.

II. The English verses: the writer, 'A. M.', was Andrew Marvell (1620–1678), poet and politician. In 1657 he had been made assistant secretary to Milton while the latter still held office under the Council. At the Restoration he did Milton good service—"acted vigorously in his behalf and made a considerable party for him" (says Phillips, *Memoir*). I think that Marvell's poetry shows signs of Milton's influence (see *Lyc.* p. 128, Pitt Press ed.). There are many variations of reading in some reprints of these verses.

37–40. See *P. L.* I. 13, 14. A correspondent of *Notes and Queries* points out that "the bird" (39) meant is the bird of Paradise and that Marvell refers to the old notion, believed till the end of the last century, that it was footless: cf. "always keeps on wing".

9. *Samson Agonistes* had been published (1671).

11. *soon*. Todd (1809) *still*.

12. *success*, result, issue, see *P. L.* II. 9.

15. *he perplexed*. Todd *he'd perplex*.

21, 22. See 47, *infra*.

26. *pretend*, claim falsely.

31. *that majesty*. Keightley, Masson ('Globe' ed.) *the*.

42. *expense*. Pickering's ed., Keightley and others *expanse*.

43. See *P. L.* III. 33–6.

47–50. A sarcasm against Dryden, who, as the champion of rhymed plays, had under the name of 'Bayes' been satirised in Buckingham's *Rehearsal* (1671)—an attack which he repaid with interest in *Absalom and Achitopel*. Dryden (as we learn from Aubrey) on one of his visits to Milton asked permission to "put his *Paradise Lost* into a drama in rhyme. Mr Milton received him cordially, and told him he would give him leave to tag his verses": the outcome being his opera *The State of Innocence and Fall of Man* (see *Introduct.* p. xxiii), published in 1674, the very year in which, apparently, Marvell wrote these verses. Milton may have talked the matter over with Marvell (so Masson thinks); or, perhaps, it had become a piece of contemporary gossip among literary men. Either way, the reference here is not to be mistaken.

49. *fancies*. Keightley *faces*. *points*, the tagged laces used to tie parts of the dress, especially the breeches; mentioned often in Shak.

51, 52. *the mode*, the fashion of rhyming. He means that he would use the word 'praise' rather than the weaker term 'commend', had he not to find a rhyme with 'offend'. Many texts of the last century transposed the words 'offend' and 'commend'—a needless change.

THE VERSE

For some general remarks on Milton's attitude towards rhyme see *Introduction*, pp. lxii–lxv.

1. *rime*, see G.

10. Cf. the similar appeal to the example of Italian writers in the Preface to *S. A.* Italian works in blank verse (*versi sciolti*) which illustrate what Milton says in both places are:—Trissino's tragedy *Sofonisba*, written about 1514 and his heroic poem *Italia Liberata*, published 1548 (cf. Johnson's *Life* of M. *ad fin.*); Ruccelai's *Rosmunda* (1516), modelled on *Sofonisba*; Tasso's poem on the Creation; and Alamanni's didactic work *La Coltivazione* (1546). The influence of Italian poetry on Milton is seen also in the free ('Apolelymenos') measures of the choruses of *S. A.*, and in *Lyc.*; cf. Pitt Press *S. A.* p. 65, and *Lyc.* pp. xliii, xliv.

"Among the *Spanish* poets, Mr Bowle mentions Francisco de Aldana, who translated the *Epistles* of Ovid into Spanish blank verse; and Gonsalvo Perez, who, in like manner, translated the *Odyssey* of Homer" (Todd).

12. Scarcely pleasant reading for Dryden who had defended rhyme (see *Introduction*, p. lxiii), and whose rhymed dramas were appearing in quick succession. We have, I believe, a similar hit at him in the Preface to *S. A.* (see Pitt Press ed. pp. 60, 61). In the Preface to his Juvenal Dryden retorted that whatever might be Milton's "alleged" reasons for "the abolishing of rhyme", the real reason was "that rhyme was not his talent": which we may accept—or not.

14. See *Introduction*, p. lxix, lxx.

20. Practically it was quite true that *Paradise Lost* was 'the first great English poem, of a non-dramatic type, written in blank verse, though Surrey had used a rhymeless measure in his translation of the second (1557) and fourth (1548) books of the *Æneid*; cf. Ascham's *Schoolmaster* (1570), "The noble Lord Th' Earle of Surrey, first of all English men, in translating the fourth booke of Virgill...auoyded the fault of Ryming" (Bohn's ed. p. 217). There are also some blank verse pieces by Nicholas

Grimald in Tottel's *Miscellany* (1557)—e.g. "The Death of Zoroas", Arber's ed. pp. 120–3, and "Ciceroes death", pp. 123–5. And Gascoigne's *Steele Glas* (1576) is "written without rime", as he notes in the "Epistle Dedicatorie" (Arber, p. 45). But these works, though interesting to the student, have no great intrinsic merit, and Milton's claim is substantially unimpeachable. The next long epic after *P. L.* in blank verse was Phillips's *Cider* (1706), an imitation of the *Georgics*; and Thomson (*Autumn*) in addressing Phillips says:

> "the second thou
> Who nobly durst in rhyme-unfettered verse
> With British freedom sing the British song";

an obvious allusion to Milton (whom Thomson imitates constantly) and this Preface.

BOOK I

1–5. Like Homer and Virgil he indicates the theme of his poem at the outset. Cf. the beginning of *Par. Reg.* (with its allusions to these lines):

> "I who erewhile the happy Garden sung
> By one man's disobedience lost, now sing
> Recovered Paradise to all mankind,
> By one man's firm obedience fully tried
> Through all temptation, and the Tempter foiled
> In all his wiles, defeated and repulsed,
> And Eden raised in the waste wilderness."

4. *one greater Man*, the Messiah; see *Rom.* v. 19.

6–16. The invocation of the Muse is an epic convention; like Dante and Tasso, M. follows therein Homer and Virgil. The significance lies in his choice of a power to be addressed: not one of the Nine Muses to whom a Greek or Roman poet would have appealed, but the Muse of sacred song, the Heavenly power which inspired Moses on Sinai, and David on Zion, and the other prophets of Israel. Twice he speaks of great singers as "taught by the Heavenly Muse" (III. 19, *Com.* 515), and in VII. 1–4 he gives her the name "Urania", 'the Heavenly': following possibly Drummond of Hawthornden who called one section of his poems "Urania, or Spiritual Poems"; certainly followed by Shelley, *Adonais* II–IV (and by Tennyson, *In Memoriam*, XXXVII?). Book VII. 1–39, where, having completed half his task, the poet petitions the Muse afresh, should be compared with this passage.

6. See VII. 5–7. Perhaps *secret* = Lat. *secretus*, apart, retired.

7. *Oreb, or . . . Sinai.* M. may be referring to the *two* occasions on which Moses received a Divine communication—(i) when the Lord appeared to him in a burning bush, *Exod.* iii; (ii) when he was given the Law, *Exod.* xix–xxxi. Myself, I believe that only the latter is intended, and that M., contrasting *Exod.* xix. 20 with *Deut.* iv. 10, does not decide whether the mountain where Moses received the Law should be called 'Oreb or Sinai'. The accounts can be harmonised easily: Horeb was the whole range, Sinai its lower part. Why in *P. L.* (cf. XI. 74) M. prefers 'Oreb' to 'Horeb', I do not know: in the Trinity MSS. I find the entry, "the massacre in Horeb".

8. *that shepherd*, Moses, who "kept the flock of Jethro" on Horeb, *Exod.* iii. 1. *first taught*, in *Genesis* i.

9, 10. *the Heavens*, i.e. the sky and starry realms of this Universe, not the Empyrean. *Chaos* = 'vast Abyss', l. 21; see *Appen.* p. 133.

10–12. Cf. III. 30, 31.

Siloa's brook; more familiar to us in the description "pool", through *John* ix. 7, 11; but Isaiah's words, of which M. may be thinking—"the waters of Shiloah that go softly", viii. 6—imply that the waters of the 'pool' overflowed into the garden below and so formed a streamlet, which would find its way into the Kidron. Josephus notes the abundant water of Siloa (which he always calls a spring, πηγή), *Bellum Judaicum* v. 4. 1. The form *Siloa* illustrates Milton's dislike of *sh*; see note on 398. The Septuagint has Σιλωάμ, the Vulgate *Siloe*.

Why does M. specially refer to Siloa? The reason, I think, is this. The classical Muses (says Hesiod, *Theog.*) frequent "the dark-coloured spring (Aganippe)...and altar of Zeus"—κρήνην ἰοειδέα...καὶ βωμὸν ἐρισθενέος Κρονίωνος. Imitating that passage in *Lyc.* 15, 16, M. addresses the Muses as "Sisters of the sacred well, That from beneath the seat of Jove doth spring". (He connects the spring with the altar—cf. *Il Pen.* 48—to show the sanctity of poetic inspiration.) Here he takes Hesiod's thought, which he before presented in its classical dress, and gives it a Scriptural investiture: the result being a complete parallel between the classical Muses who haunt the spring that rises by the altar of Zeus, and the Heavenly Muse who haunts the spring that flows by the Temple ("the oracle") of the Almighty.

12, 13, *fast by*, close by. Siloa was outside Jerusalem, in the valley that skirted Mt Moriah on which stood the Temple. *oracle*, "thy holy oracle", *Psalm* xxviii. 2.

14. The metaphor in "flight", "soar", is a favourite with M. Cf. VII. 3, 4, "above the Olympian hill I soar, Above the flight of Pegasean wing"; also III. 13, IX. 45. *no middle flight*, i.e. he will ascend to the highest Empyrean.

14, 15. He hopes to be filled with a higher inspiration, so as to treat of higher things, than the classical poets whose inspiration came from the Muses of antiquity. *The Aonian mount*, Helicon, in Bœotia; sacred to the Muses—whence their title *Aonides*. Pope calls them "Aonian maids" (*Messiah*), and Campbell, "Aonian Muses" (*Pleasures of Hope*).

15. *pursues*, treats of; "in the sense of the Latin *sequor*. *E noto fictum carmen sequar*, Horace, *Ars Poetica* 240" (Keightley).

16. This claim to novelty of theme recalls *Comus*, 44, 45:
          " I will tell you now
    What never yet was heard *in tale or song*,"
i.e. "in prose or rhyme" (a phrase of Ariosto). Similar claims might be instanced in Virgil, Spenser, and other poets, e.g. Horace's *carmina non prius | audita...canto* (*Od*. III. 2–4). *rhyme*, verse; see G.

17–26. Cf. similar invocation of the Holy Spirit *P. R*. I. 8–17: a higher power than the Muse addressed above. "There can be little doubt that Milton believed himself to be, in some real sense, an inspired man" (Masson). In *Church Gov*. he says that a great poem can only be achieved through "devout prayer to that eternal Spirit, who can enrich with all utterance and knowledge" (*P. W*. II. 481); and in *Christian Doct*. VI he explains that he means by the Spirit "that impulse or voice of God by which the prophets were inspired".

19, 20. *for thou know'st*. Cf. Homer, *Il*. II. 484, ἔσπετε νῦν μοι, Μοῦσαι... | ὑμεῖς γὰρ θεαί ἐστε, πάρεστέ τε, ἴστε τε πάντα; and Theocritus, XXII. 116, εἰπὲ θεά, σὺ γὰρ οἶσθα.

20, 21. Cf. account of the Creation, VII. 234, 235, "on the watery calm His brooding wings the Spirit of God outspread". In *Gen*. i. 2 the Heb. verb rendered "moved" in A. V. (*ferebatur* in Vulgate) means either 'fluttered' (Luther has *schwebete*), as in *Deut*. xxxii. 11, where it is used of an eagle hovering; or 'brooded' (*incubabat* in Basil and others of the Latin Fathers) like a bird hatching eggs. Cf. Sir Thomas Browne, *Religio*, XXXII, "This is that gentle heat that brooded on the waters, and in six days hatched the world."

21. *dove-like*. The allusion, I believe, is to the descent of the Holy Ghost "in a bodily shape like a dove" at the baptism of our Lord (*Luke* iij. 22); cf. *P. R.* I. 30, 83. This I infer from a passage in Milton's theological treatise, *Christian Doctrine* VI.

Abyss, Chaos; see G.

24. *argument*, subject = Lat. *argumentum*; cf. IX. 28.

25. *assert*, vindicate; cf. Pope, "Sedition silence, and assert the throne".

26. Cf. *S. A.* 293, 294, "Just are the ways of God, And justifiable to men"—the Scriptural reference being to passages like *Ps.* cxlv. 17 and *Rev.* XV. 3, "just and true are thy ways". Pope professed the same design; cf. the *Essay on Man*, I. 15, 16:

"Laugh where we must, be candid where we can,
    But vindicate the ways of God to man."

to men, i.e. "justify" to men.

29. *grand*, i.e. first, original—cf. "grandfather".

31, 32. i.e. transgress his will because of ("for") one restraint. Keightley makes "for one restraint" qualify what follows— 'lords of the world (cf. IX. 658), but for a single restraint'.

33. *Iliad* I. 8.

35. See *Appen.* pp. 142, 143, on "Satan's motives etc".

36. *what time*, at the time when, Lat. *quo tempore*. "What time I am afraid, I will trust in thee", *Ps.* lvi. 3. So *Com.* 291, *Lyc.* 28.

39. *peers*, equals, Lat. *pares*, cf. *Lyc.* 9; so *peer-less*, unequalled.

40. See *Isaiah* xiv. 12–14.

45, 46. *flaming*; cf. *Luke* x. 18, "I beheld Satan as lightning fall from heaven". *the ethereal sky*, the Empyrean; see *Appen.* pp. 131, 132. *combustion*; see G.

48. *in chains*. Cf. 2 *Pet.* ii. 4, "if God spared not the angels . . . but . . . delivered them into chains of *darkness*" (see l. 72); also *Jude* 6, *Rev.* xx. 1, 2. Same allusion II. 169, 183, 196, III. 82.

50. *nine*, traditionally a significant number, being a multiple of three (see 619). Their fall from Heaven lasted nine days (VI. 871), as did that of the Titans in Hesiod (*Theogony* 722).

55. *pain*, physical suffering. Cf. 125, 147, 336: the point is emphasised by Milton (and entirely lost if we misinterpret "pain" = punishment). Later, M. shows how the fallen angels first became sensible of pain through their sin (see VI. 327, note).

56, 57. *baleful*, full of woe, see G. *witnessed*, showed, testified to.

58. Scan *obdúrate*, as always in M.; cf. VI, 790.

59. Second Ed. has "Angels kenn". Throughout the volume the apostrophe indicative of the genitive was omitted (as often happened then): hence 'Angels' may have stood for 'Angel's' or 'Angels'' (cf. 754 and the common misreading, caused by this ambiguity, XII. 229, note). Some modern texts print "Angel's ken", making "ken" a noun. But M. uses "ken" as a verb v. 265, XI. 396, and I prefer to take it so here—with the sense, 'as far as angels see'. Cf. 2 *Henry VI.* III. 2. 101, "As far as I could ken thy chalky cliffs".

63. *no light*, i.e. there *was*. It was a popular belief that the flames of Hell gave no light (Keightley). *darkness visible*, an obvious oxymoron (see 692). What M. means is—not absolute darkness ('pitch darkness', as we say), for then the "*sights* of woe" would have been invisible—but the gloom which half conceals and half reveals objects, and itself (to borrow Pope's words) "strikes the sense no less than light". Mr Beeching aptly reminds us of *Job* X. 22.

66, 67. Doubtless from Eurip. *Troades*, 676, οὐδ᾽ ὃ πᾶσι λείπεται βροτοῖς | ξύνεστιν ἐλπίς ('even hope, which remains to all mortals, is not here'). Probably too there is an echo of Dante's famous words—"All hope abandon, ye who enter here"—placed over the gates of hell, *Inferno* III. 9.

68. *urges*, afflicts, plies—Lat. *urgere*; cf. "exercise", II. 89.

70. Cf. VI. 738, and see *Appen.* p. 134.

72. *utter darkness*; again III. 16, v. 614. *utter* = outer, see G.

73. Cf. v. 613, "Cast out from God and blessed vision".

74, 75. He makes the distance of Hell from the Empyrean = three times the distance of the Earth ("the centre") from the "utmost pole" of the globe or Universe (i.e. that point in the surface of the globe which is nearest to the Empyrean). The calculation is suggested by *Iliad* VIII. 16, *Æn.* VI. 578.

79–81. Beëlzebub is called Satan's "next subordinate" v. 671; see II. 299, note.

81, 82. *Satan* = 'adversary': a name first given to him when he rebelled: his "former name" being thenceforth heard no more (v. 658, 659). It is not, I think, clear whether this "former name" was "Lucifer" (cf. VII. 131-3), or some other title which, like the titles of the other rebels, was utterly blotted out (cf. ll. 361-3, note, VI. 376-80). I believe, however, that M. means us to understand that both "Lucifer" and "Satan" were later names, given after the rebellion.

84, 85. *beest*, see G. There is a double allusion—to *Isai*. xiv. 12, "how art thou fallen", and *Æn*. II. 274, *quantum mutatus ab illo | Hectore qui redit*.

86. *didst*; grammar requires *did*: the sense implies 'thou'.

87–90. Cf. v. 676–8, where Satan says to Beëlzebub that they had ever been wont to share each other's thoughts and "were one". To Beëlzebub he first hinted his purpose to rebel (v. 673).

87. *if he*, i.e. if *thou beest* (from 84) he; the sentence is not completed (the figure of speech called *anacoluthon*). M. often uses this abrupt style to suggest the speaker's agitation; cf. v. 30 *et seq*.

91, 92. *into what...from what*; cf. v. 543, "O fall From what high state of bliss into what woe"; and *P. R.* II. 30, 31. An imitation perhaps of Gk. οἷος...οἷος—as in Soph. *Trach*. 994, οἵαν ἀνθ' οἵων θυμάτων χάριν, 'what a return (i.e. how poor) for what sacrifices' (i.e. how great); and *Elect*. 751, οἷ' ἔργα δράσας οἷα λαγχάνει κακά.

93. *his thunder*. Cf. account of the battle III. 393, VI. 836.

94. *for*, because of. Satan's defiant spirit recalls the stubborn attitude of Prometheus towards Zeus in Æschylus's play.

97. *fixed mind*; cf. *Il Pen*. 4, Spenser *F. Q.* IV. 7. 16, "Yet nothing could my fixed mind remove" (change). *fixed*, steadfast.

98. *high disdain*. A common phrase with 'our old poets'— Spenser (cf. *F. Q.* I. I. 19), Sylvester and others; taken from the *alto sdegno* of Italian writers (Todd).

from sense of, i.e. disdain springing from a feeling of.

104. *dubious*, because the battle lasted for three days (bk. VI.).

105. *shook his throne*. A boastful exaggeration; see VI. 833, 834. *field*, battle (II. 768); so Lat. *campus*. The Second Ed. has the note of interrogation at the end of the line.

107. *study*, pursuit of; 'study', like Lat. *studium*, often meant 'endeavour'; cf. *Lear* I. I. 279, "let your study be to content your lord", and XI. 577.

108–11. The Second Ed. has at the end of 108 a colon; of 109 a note of interrogation; and in 111 a full stop after *me*. This punctuation, variously altered in many texts, I retain. Some editors remove the interrogation in 109, treating the line as a relative clause, as though Satan said: 'I retain my will (106), my hate (107), my courage (108), and all other qualities in me that cannot be overcome.' This gives good sense—but not Milton's. The line is interrogative, and Satan asks: 'to retain one's hate, one's courage etc., is not that to be still unsubdued:

in what else but this lies the test of being not overcome?' In one of the last of Tonson's editions (1738), being the fifteenth (of a poem which some assure us was "not appreciated"), I find the line bracketed, i.e. treated as a parenthesis—as it really is.

109. *what...else*; to be taken together; cf. 683.

110. Regarding 109 as parenthetical, I take "that glory" to refer back to 108: 'never' (says Satan) 'shall the Victor extort from me the glory—to him—of my submission'. Some explain —'the glory (i.e. Satan's) of not being overcome'; but does this suit "extort"?

114. *doubted his empire*. Again an exaggeration.

115. Scan *ignomy*; see II. 207, note. *beneath*, worse than.

116. *by fate*; important because Satan denies (v. 860–3) that the angels were created by the Almighty: we were, he says, self-begotten "By our own quickening power, when *fatal course* Had circled his full orb" (i.e. at the time decreed by the course of fate). Fate, not the Almighty, he recognizes as superior. *gods*= divine beings.

117. Can the fiery substance (see II. 139–42, 274, 275, notes) of their forms perish ("fail")? Satan thinks not: Moloch and Belial are less certain (II. 99, 146–54). *empyreal*; see G.

120. *successful hope*, hope of success; so in Shak. often. Cf. "sterile curse"=curse of sterility, *Julius C.* I. 2. 9; "fruitful prognostication"=prognostication of fruitfulness, *Antony*, I. 2. 53.

122. *grand*, great (like F. *grand*); cf. II. 507.

123. *triumphs*; scan as a trochee, *tríumphs*.

124. *tyranny*. M. makes him use the most offensive word—not "monarchy", as in 42, where the poet was speaking in his own person. See II. 59, note.

128. *throned powers*; Satan's followers in general ("throned" —cf. 360—merely suggesting their dignity): not the particular Order of the Hierarchies called Thrones (737, note), since M. makes Satan belong to the Order of Archangels.

130. *conduct*, command, as of a general.

138. See 117, note. *essences*, see 425.

139. *remains*; singular, because "mind and spirit" form one idea—a common usage in Shak.; cf. *Troilus*, IV. 5. 170, "faith and troth bids them". See *Lycidas*, 7.

141. *though...glory extinct*. Cf. 394, "though...cries un-heard", and *S. A.* 738. I think that these are absolute construc-tions, modelled perhaps on the Lat. ablative absolute; but there

may be an ellipse of the auxiliary verb. *extinct*, quenched (like a flame).

144. *of force*, perforce; so IV. 813.

148. *suffice*, satisfy = Lat. *sufficere*.

149–52. "They (evil angels) are sometimes permitted to wander through the whole earth, the *air* (cf. 430), the heaven itself, to execute the judgments of God", *Christian Doct.* IX. *thralls*, slaves; see *enthrall* in G.

152. *gloomy deep*, Chaos.

155, 156. *to undergo*, i.e. so as to undergo (not dependent on 'avail', 153). *fiend*, 'one who hates', from A.S. *féon*, to hate.

157, 158. *Cherub*; see G. *Doing or suffering*, i.e. whether in an active or passive state; cf. the common antithesis δρᾶν... παθεῖν; see II. 199.

167. *if I fail not*, if I am not mistaken, Lat. *ni fallor*.

170. *his ministers*, the good angels; really they had no share in the expulsion of the rebels, which was due to the Messiah, "sole victor" (VI. 880); Satan, one of the outcast, did not know this.

171–7. See VI. 858–79. *laid*, i.e. to rest, stilled; cf. *P. R.* IV. 429, and Tennyson, *Margaret*, "Your spirit is the calmed sea, Laid by the tumult of the fight", and *Queen Mary*, I. 5, "God lay the waves and strow the storms at sea". So *sternere* (*Æn.* V. 763) and *ponere* in Lat.; cf. *ponere freta*, Horace, *Od.* I. 3. 15.

176. *his* = *its* (see G.); or he may be personifying "thunder".

178, 179. *slip*, let slip; cf. *Macbeth*, II. 3. 52, "I have almost slipped the hour". *satiate*; see G.

185. *harbour*, dwell; cf. V. 99.

186. *afflicted* = Lat. *afflictus*, struck down. *powers*, forces.

187. *offend* = Lat. *offendere*, to strike at, harm; cf. VI. 465.

191. Cf. VI. 787, "hope conceiving from despair". *if not*, i.e. if we may not gain reinforcement.

193. *uplift*, uplifted.

197. *as whom*, as those whom. *fables*, the mythological stories of the classics; M. generally speaks of them contemptuously as "fabulous".

198. *Earth-born*, the Giants; like the Titans (with whom writers confused them much) they were reputed the offspring of Uranus and Ge (Earth); see 509, note, and 778. *that warred* refers to the Giants only; the legend of their conflict with Zeus (or Jove) seems to be due to the earlier revolt of the Titans against Uranus.

199. *Briareos or Typhon*; the former (*centumgeminus Briareus*, *Æn.* VI. 287), being the son of Uranus, is meant to represent the Titans—the latter, the Giants. The legends about both were conflicting. Scan *Briáreos*, though classically the name is *Briáreus*.

or Typhon. For the comparison see Fairfax, II. 91, "He looked like huge Tiphoius loos'd from hell". Typhon, or Typhœus, is commonly described as a hundred-headed monster, who, trying to seize sovereignty over gods and men, was killed by Zeus with a thunderbolt.

200. *Tarsus*, the capital of Cilicia; M. alludes here to Pindar and Æschylus who describe Typhon as living in "a Cilician *den*"; cf. Æsch. *P. V.* 351, τὸν γηγενῆ τε Κιλικίων οἰκήτορα | ἄντρων...Τυφῶνα ('the *earth-born* inhabitant of Cilician dens'), where Æsch. seems to be quoting Pindar, *Pyth.* I. 17, [Typhon] τόν ποτε | Κιλίκιον θρέψεν πολυώνυμον ἄντρον. So *Pyth.* 8. 16, Τυφὼς Κίλιξ. See II. 539, *Nat. Ode*, 226 ("Typhon huge ending in snaky twine").

201. The Bibles of that time identified the Leviathan with the whale, and M. probably did so; but the Heb. *livyáthán* was used of any huge monster, e.g. the crocodile, *Psalm* lxxiv. 14.

202. *ocean-stream*; Homer's ῥόος (or ποταμὸς) ὠκεάνοιο.

203–208. Todd quotes a story to this effect from the Swedish writer Olaus Magnus, whose *History of the Northern Nations* had been Englished (1658). Evidently some remarkable 'traveller's tales' as to the size of whales were in circulation: Heylin, *Cosmography* (1682 ed.) tells us of 'Leviathans' four acres big (III. 191, 192). Cf. Milton's own description VII. 412–15:

> "there leviathan,
> *Hugest* of living creatures, on the deep
> Stretched *like a promontory*, *sleeps* or swims,
> And *seems a moving land.*"

204. *pilot*, steersman, cf. *S. A.* 198; or master of the vessel.

night-foundered, benighted—lit. 'plunged or sunk in night' (and so unable to continue his course). Cf. *Comus*, 483; see *founder* in G.

206. i.e. with *anchor fixed* in his rind. Such inversions of the order of words are common in Shakespeare; cf. *Richard II.* III. I. 9. As a matter of natural history, whales have not "scaly rinds"; but M. alludes to *Job* xli. 15 (where, however, the crocodile is meant).

207, 208. *the lee*, the sheltered side. *invests*, wraps, Lat. *investit*.

211. *heaved*, lifted; cf. Germ. *heben*. To "heave the head" occurs in *S. A.* 197, *Comus*, 885, *L'Allegro*, 145; Dryden borrowed it (*St Cecilia's Day*).

213. *at large*, free to carry out his designs.

221. *rears*, raises, as often in Spenser and Shakespeare.

223. *spires*, tongues or columns of flame.

226. *incumbent*; in the literal sense 'leaning, resting, on' (Lat. *incumbens*).

230-3. This notion of earthquakes being caused by escape of winds from underground recurs in VI. 195-8, *S. A.* 1647, 1648.

232. *Pelorus*, the north-east promontory of Sicily, now Cape Faro; near Ætna, by whose volcanic action M. implies that it was affected.

233-6. Editors compare *Æneid* III. 571-7.

233. *whose*. The antecedent is Pelorus as well as Ætna, the description that follows being applied as much to the one as to the other.

234. *fuelled*, serving as fuel, or 'rich in fuel'.

235. *sublimed*; see G.

236. *involved*, wrapped in (Lat. *involvere*).

239. *scaped*; see G. *Stygian flood*, the "fiery gulf" (52).

242. In M. and Shak. *clime* means (1) climate, temperature—so probably here and at 297; (2) region, realm—cf. II. 572 and *The Merchant of Venice*, II. 1. 10, "The best-regarded virgins of our clime".

244-6. *change for*, take in exchange for. *sovran*; see G.

248. i.e. they were his equals in reason, but not in power.

253. Cf. Horace's *cœlum non animum mutant qui trans mare currunt* (*Epist.* I. 2. 27).

254. *its*, see G.

255. A reminiscence, I suppose, of *Midsummer N. D.* II. 1. 243, "I'll follow thee and make a hell of heaven". Hartley Coleridge says, "One sinful wish would make a hell of heaven". For this conception of Hell as not a place, but a mental state, of punishment, see IV. 20-3. Sir Thomas Browne writes, *Religio Med.* LI, "every devil is an hell unto himself; he holds enough of torture in his own *ubi*". In Marlowe's *Faustus*, when the Doctor asks "Where is the place that men call hell?", Mephistophiles replies, "Hell hath no limits, nor is circumscribed In one self place; for where we (evil spirits) are is hell" (V. 119, 120—see Dr Ward's ed. p. 157).

257. *all but less than* = nearly equal to. The phrase is a combination of 'only less than' and 'all but equal to' (Beeching).

259. i.e. in building Hell the Almighty has created a place such that he could never grudge Satan its possession.

261–3. When William Lauder published in 1750 his infamous *Essay* on Milton, the object of which was to show that the poet had 'plagiarised' from a number of obscure writers (mostly foreign scholars of the 16th and 17th cents.), he took these three lines, translated them into what he conceived to be Iambic verse, said that he had found them in the *Adamus Exul* (1601) of Grotius, and printed them as a convincing proof of Milton's dishonesty. His version runs—or limps—thus: *nam, me judice, | regnare dignum est ambitu, etsi in Tartaro; | alto præesse Tartaro siquidem* (sic) *juvat, | cælis quam in ipsis servi obire munia.* In 1752 he reprinted the *Adamus* in his *Delectus*, but did not venture to interpolate his forgery. The mischief, however, had been done; for Bishop Newton, being completely deceived, printed the lines in his notes on this passage as genuine, and remarked that M. had evidently 'translated' them from Grotius. Of course the fraud was eventually exposed; none the less, the lines still find their way periodically from the Bishop's notes into modern editions. For him it may be said that he had no reason to suspect Lauder, and probably no opportunity of consulting the *Adamus*, a very scarce work, of which the British Museum has a single original copy.

263. Probably the germ of this famous line (varied VI. 183) is Homer, *Od.* XI. 488, where Achilles (in Hades) says that he would rather serve on earth as a poor man's slave, than reign over all the dead. Fletcher says of the fallen angels, " In Heaven they scorn'd to serve, so now in Hell they reign" (*Purple Island* VII. 10).

266. Cf. "forgetful lake", II. 74. *astonished, oblivious*, see G.

268. *mansion*, dwelling-place, abode (Lat. *manere*, to remain).

276, 277. "On the rough edge of battle ere it joined ", VI. 108. Cf. Lat. *acies*, the front line of a fight.

281. *amazed*, utterly confounded; a far stronger word then than now. *astound = astonish*.

282. *pernicious*, destructive, ruinous; some, however, explain it 'great', 'excessive'.

284. *his shield*, described again VI. 254–6.

285. *temper* = a thing tempered (cf. II. 813): abstract for concrete.

288. *optic glass*; apparently not an uncommon phrase for the telescope; I find it in Giles Fletcher, *Christ's Victory on Earth*, 60, "all her optique glasses shattered", and in Henry More, *Song of the Soul*, "The Opticke glasse has shown to sight The dissolution of these starrie crouds" (p. 212, Cambridge ed. 1647). Cf. "optic tube", III. 590 (borrowed by Thomson, *Autumn*). Galileo did not invent the telescope, but he developed it: hence it is generally associated with his name; cf. Bacon, "those glasses (*illa perspicilla*) discovered by the memorable efforts of Galileo", *Novum Organon*, XXXIX. A *Tuscan* by birth, Galileo (cf. v. 262, note) passed the latter part of his life in, or near, Florence. M. saw him (1638–9); cf. *Areopagitica*. "There (in Italy) it was that I found and visited the famous Galileo, grown old, a prisoner to the Inquisition, for thinking in astronomy otherwise than the Franciscan and Dominican licensers thought", *P. W.* II. 82. Near the Villa d' Arcetri where Galileo then lived, "an old tower is still pointed out as having once been his observatory" (Masson).

289, 290. There is true pathos in the mention, here and ll. 302–4, of Italian scenes. M. is revisiting in memory places associated with what was, perhaps, the happiest period of his whole life—his stay in Italy (see *Life*): "times when...I tasted bliss without alloy" (as he wrote in 1647, *Letter*). He always spoke of Italy with deepest affection: especially of Florence which he loved for its language (*Letter*, 1638), "its genius and taste" (*Second Defence*), and the friends whom he should ever remember with pleasure (*vestri nunquam meminisse pigebit*— *Epitaphium Damonis* 125).

Fesolè, classical *Fæsulæ*; a hill about three miles north-east of Florence. *Valdarno*, the valley of the river Arno, in which Florence lies. Here (290) M. has in mind Galileo's later residence at the Villa d'Arcetri, on the left bank of the Arno, i.e. west of the main part of the city. There is a passage in one of Milton's *Letters* from Florence, in which he speaks of his delight in "visiting the stream of the Arno, and the hills of Fæsolæ" (modern Italian form *Fiesole*).

291. Cf. v. 261–3. Apparently M. knew that the 'spots' in the moon are unevennesses on its surface caused by mountains and valleys, though in v. 420 (see note) he attributes them to 'vapours'.

292, 293. *his spear...the mast.* I find the comparison twice in Fairfax, *Tasso*; cf. III..17, "Mast-great the spear was which the gallant bore", and VI. 39, "These sons of Mars bore (instead of spears) Two knotty masts, which none but they could lift".

293. *Norwegian hills*. Norway, of course, was a great timber-emporium: thence, writes Hexham's *Mercator* (1636), "the high *masts* for shipping, the plankes and boords of Oak and *firre trees* [cf. 292, "tallest *pine*"] are sent yeerely in great abundance into Germanie, Holland, France, *England*, Spayne, and other places" (I. 93). And Jonson says that the appearance of the tall-masted vessels of the Armada was as if "half of Norway with her fir trees came", *Prince Henry's Barriers*.

294. *ammiral*, see G.

296. *marle*, soil; more correctly used of rich, moist earth. *those*, i.e. the well-known, famous (Lat. *illi*).

298. Cf. VI. 214, "And flying vaulted either host with fire" (said of fiery darts), with *P.R.* I. 116, "Hell's deep-vaulted den".

299. *nathless*=not the less: A.S. *ná*=not.

302. The comparison of a multitude to fallen autumnal leaves is found in Homer, Virgil, Dante, and other epic poets. Cf. Dryden (who has obviously recollected this passage), "Thick as the leaves in autumn strew the woods...the army stands", *Æn.* VI. 428. Note that M. was himself at Florence in the autumn (September, 1638).

303, 304. See 289, note. *Vallombrosa*, 'Shady Valley'; about 18 miles from Florence. The name is applied not only to the valley itself, but to the wood-covered hill rising therefrom. On this hill stands a monastery (now disused) where M. was said to have spent some days (a tradition of which Wordsworth makes effective use in his "At Vallombrosa"), and in the chapel an organ used to be shown as that on which M. played—*Notes and Queries*, V. v. 306. The reference to the fallen leaves is appropriate, since the approach to the convent was through forests of chestnut and beech trees, deciduous species. Dean Stanley wrote, "inasmuch as the whole mountain is furrowed with streams, which gave to the place its original name of *Bellacqua*, the leaves constantly falling on these streams, and almost choking their currents, give the exact picture" painted by M.: "an instance" (he added) "of the tenacity of Milton's memory in retaining, through all the vicissitudes of civil war, age, and blindness, the precise recollection of what he had seen in early youth"—*Notes and Queries*, V. XI. 488, 489.

embower, form as it were bowers.

304. *sedge*; "in allusion to the Hebrew name of the Red Sea, Yâm Sûf, i.e. Sea of Sedge, on account of the quantity of sea-

weed in it" (Keightley). As the angels are afloat on waves (of fire), the simile is in the highest degree appropriate.

305. The rising of the constellation Orion (at midsummer) and his setting (at the beginning of November) being attended with storms, the name became proverbial of rain and "fierce winds". Cf. Virg. *Æn.* I. 535, *nimbosus Orion*, IV. 52, *aquosus Orion*; and Grotius, *Adamus Exul—illic procellis tumidus Orion furit.* So Marlowe, *Faustus*, III. 2, "Orion's drizzling look"; Drummond, *Entertainment*, "That no Orion do with storms them blast"; and Heywood's *Hierarchie,* "Orion...riseth in the winter season, disturbing both earth and sea with showres and tempests" (ed. 1635, p. 177).

armed; from Virg. *Æn.* III. 517, *armatumque auro circumspicit Oriona.* "After his death, Orion [the great hunter] was placed among the Stars where he appears as a giant with a girdle, sword...and club" (*Class. Dict.*): hence armed.

306–11. *Exodus* xiv. 5–29. See again XII. 206–10.

vexed; in the sense ('to disturb violently, to buffet') of Lat. *vexare,* as applied to a storm, e.g. in Horace, *Odes* II. 9. 3.

307. Late Greek writers (cf. the XIth *Oration* of Isocrates) speak of an Egyptian king Busiris, unknown to Homer and Hesiod, and not mentioned in Egyptian records. Some describe him as builder of Thebes. Legend said that he was slain by Hercules—an event depicted often on vases. Why M. identifies him with the Pharaoh who perished in the Red Sea, no one has ever explained. Some editors say that M. 'follows' Raleigh's *History*—which is not so: for Raleigh expressly states that Busiris was "the first oppressor of the Israelites" (p. 204), and that after *two* intervening reigns came "Cenchres, drowned in the Red Sea" (p. 197, 1621 ed.). Cf. again p. 218, "through which (i.e. Red Sea) Moses past, and in which Pharaoh, otherwise called Cenchres, perished". Either M. follows some unknown authority, or he treats 'Busiris' as a general title for the rulers of Egypt, like 'Pharaoh'.

Memphian=Egyptian; so in 694; I note the same use in Sylvester; cf. "The *Memphian* Sages then, and subtill Priests", where the margin has, "The Magicians of Egypt" (Grosart's ed. I. 187). He calls the Egyptians variously "Memphites", "Memphists", and "Memphians". Memphis was the ancient capital (before Thebes) of Egypt; founded by Menes (1st monarch of 1st dynasty), and called—by the Egyptians *Men nefer*, 'the good station', from its position at the apex of the Delta—by the Arabs *Memf*, whence European form of the name.

chivalry, forces, as *P. R.* III. 344. In neither place need we limit it to 'cavalry' (with which 'chivalry' is etymologically identical).

308. *perfidious*; he had given the Israelites leave to go.

309. "Israel dwelt...in the country of Goshen", *Gen.* xlvii. 27.

312. *abject*, cast down; see G.

313. *Under amazement of*, utterly confounded by.

317. *if*; the clause qualifies "lost". *astonishment*, see G.

320. *virtue*, valour, Lat. *virtus*.

321. *vales of Heaven*, see *Appen.* p. 132. In v. 642–55 he describes the angels sleeping in Heaven, "among the trees of life".

329. *Transfix*, pierce through and fasten to; cf. II. 181.

335. *nor did they not*, i.e. and they did—Lat. *neque non*.

337. For "obey *to*" (Fr. *obéir à*), cf. Greene, *Friar Bacon*, IX. 142, "I charge thee to obey to Vandermast", Shak. *Troilus*, III. 1. 165, and *The Phœnix*, 4, "To whose sound chaste wings obey". There is a single instance in the Bible—*Romans* vi. 16.

338–43. *Exod.* X. 12–15. See the account of the ten Plagues in XII. 185, 186. *Amram's son*, Moses; see *Exod.* vi. 20.

340. *pitchy*, dark as pitch; cf. 1 *Henry VI*. II. 2. 1, 2:

> "The day begins to break, and night is fled,
> Whose pitchy mantle over-veil'd the earth."

341. *warping*, undulating forward; see G.

345. *cope*, roof, covering, cf. IV. 992; akin to *cap*, *cape*.

347, 348. *spear...waving*; absolute use. *Sultan*, see G.

351–55. Alluding to invasions of Italy and Roman empire by Goths (as early as 248 A.D.); Huns, notably under Attila, who was finally defeated at Châlons-sur-Marne, 451; and Vandals. Genseric, or Gaiseric, leader of the Vandals, crossed from Spain into Numidia, 428, captured Carthage, 439, and built up an empire in Africa.

Observe the effectiveness of the three similes whereby M. conveys an impression of the numbers of the angels. They are compared—resting on the water, to fallen leaves (or floating sea-weed): flying, to a cloud of locusts that "darkens" the land (*Exod.* X. 15): alighted, to a vast host that throngs a plain. Each aspect has its proper simile.

351. *a multitude*, see II. 692, note.

353. *Rhene*, from Lat. *Rhenus*=Rhine, and *Danaw* or *Donau*, Germ. form of Danube, were current forms in 17th cent.; I find them in Heylin's *Cosmography* (1682 ed.) and

Hexham's *Mercator* (1636), perhaps the two most popular geographical works of the time. So "Rhenish wine" = Rhine wine, *The Merchant of Venice*, I. 2. 104, *Hamlet*, I. 4. 10.

355. *beneath*, south of; alluding to the Vandals.

356. *every...each*. A favourite variation with Milton; cf. *Comus*, 19, "Of every salt flood and each ebbing stream", and 311, "I know each lane and every alley green". Etymologically *ever-y = ever-each*.

360. See 128.

361-75. Again in VI. 379, 380, he tells us that the original names of the apostate angels were "Cancelled from Heaven and sacred memory". How then to describe them? He must give them *some* titles. So he adopts (see *Appen.* pp. 144-6) the view that they became the gods of heathenism, oriental and classical, and here, by anticipation, uses those "new names" (365) which later ages assigned to them.

363. Bentley thought that M. dictated *Book* (which some modern texts print); cf. *Rev.* iii. 5. A passage in *Christian Doct.* IV seems to me to make this probable—"mention is frequently made of those who are written among the living and of the book of life, but never of the book of death".

370, 371. See *Romans* i. 23.

372. *religions*, religious rites. *full of pomp*; M. often expresses dislike of ceremony and ritual in worship (see XII. 534).

376. *who first, who last;* τίνα πρῶτον, τίνα δ' ὕστατον, *Iliad* v. 703. The long list of the deities is intended as a counterpart to Homer's catalogue of the ships and Virgil's list of warriors (Addison).

381. Those who led astray "the chosen people" come first.

382-91. Texts probably glanced at are: 1 *Pet.* v. 8; *Ezek.* vii. 20, xliii. 8; *Exod.* xxv. 22; 2 *Kings* xix. 15. For the setting up of altars to heathen gods *inside* the Temple, see Manasseh's reign, 2 *Kings* xxi.

386. *thundering*; "perhaps taken from *Exodus* xx, where Jehovah thunders the Ten Commandments from Sinai" (Beeching).

386, 387. *throned between*. The reference is to the golden images of Cherubim, with expanded wings, placed over the mercy-seat covering the ark in the Tabernacle. Cf. *Psalm* lxxx. 1.

389. *abominations*, the regular Bible word for idolatrous worship.

391. *affront*; commonly taken here in its primary sense 'to

confront', 'face' (Lat. *ad+frons*)—cf. *Hamlet*, III. 1. 31; but
IX. 328 and *P. R.* III. 161 make the ordinary sense—'to insult'—
more likely.

392. *Moloch.* God of the Sun as a destroying power; "the
abomination of the children of Ammon", 1 *Kings* xi. 7;
worshipped with human sacrifices, 2 *Kings* xxiii. 10, *Ps.* cvi. 37,
38. The name, better written 'Molech' (as by Sandys), means
'King' (cf. *Amos* v. 26, margin), and M. generally adds "King"
(cf. II. 43, VI. 357). With these lines, 392–6, cf. *Nat. Ode*, 205–10.

394, 395. *though...cries unheard.* See 141, note.

396. Sandys, whose *Relation* of his travels in Palestine was
certainly known to Milton, gives, no doubt, the picture of the
idol handed down by Jewish tradition, and describes it as "of
brasse, hauing the head of a Calfe, the rest of a kingly figure,
with armes extended to receive the miserable sacrifice, seared
to death with his burning embracements. For the Idol was
hollow within, filled with fire. And least their lamentable
shreeks should sad the hearts of their parents, the Priests of
Molech did deafe their eares with the continual clang of
trumpets and timbrels," *Relation*, p. 186. This sacrifice of
children by fire was due to the notion that the fierce summer
heat of the god would be allayed thereby (Sayce).

396–9. *Rabba*, capital of Ammonites—"the city of *waters*",
2 *Sam.* xii. 27: *Argob*, district of mountain range of *Bashan*:
Arnon, boundary river between Moab and Amorites: all E. of
Jordan. Part of this territory (as Keightley notes) belonged to—
not the Ammonites, spite of their claim (*Judg.* xi. 13)—but the
Amorites. As we look, however, at a map of Palestine we must
recollect that M. could not do so.

398. *Basan*; the form used in the Septuagint, Vulgate, and
Prayer-Book. M. always avoids *sh*; cf. 'Hesebon' 408, 'Chemos'
406, 'Sittim' 413, 'Beërsaba'=Beersheba, III. 536, 'Silo'=
Shilo, *S. A.* 1647. It will generally be found that he has the
authority of either the Septuagint or Vulgate (or both) for his
Scriptural proper names, where they differ in form from the
Authorised Version.

401–3. Solomon, persuaded by his wives (cf. 444–6), built
"high places" to Moloch, Chemos and Astarte on the Mount of
Olives (1 *Kings* xi. 5–7)—thence called the "Mount of Corruption" (2 *Kings* xxiii. 13), and later, the "Mount of Offence".
These titles M. glances at here (403), and in 416, 443.

401. *by fraud*, by deceit.

402. *His temple*, i.e. of Moloch.

404. The valley of Hinnom, lying S. and S.W. of Jerusalem, skirted the southern part of Olivet. Having been the scene of rites paid to Moloch, it was "defiled" (cf. l. 418) by Josiah (2 *Kings* xxiii. 10), and made the common refuse-place of Jerusalem. Previously it formed part of royal gardens; Sandys says, "We descended into the valley of Gehinnon, which divideth the Mount Sion from the Mountaine of Offence... This valley is but streight (i.e. narrow); heretofore most delightful, planted with *groves*, and watered with fountains," *Relation*, p. 186. The 'grove' of Hinnom is not directly mentioned in Scripture: did M. take the idea from Sandys?

405. *Gehenna*, hell, Gk. form of *Ge Hinnom*, 'Valley of Hinnom'.

406. "Moloch and Chemos ('the abomination of Moab') are joined, 1 *Kings* xi. 7. And it was a natural transition from the god of the Ammonites to the god of their neighbours the Moabites" (Newton). Chemos (really the same deity as Moloch) was often identified with Baal-Peor (412).

obscene, foul; referring to the character of the rites with which he was worshipped. *dread*, i.e. object of dread.

407-11. Roughly speaking, all the places here mentioned (of which the sites are known) lay in the territory assigned (*Numb.* xxxii) to the tribe of Reuben—a region fringing east shore of the Dead Sea, bounded S. by river Arnon, N. by Mt Nebo. It had belonged to the Moabites till it was won from them by the Amorites (*Numb.* xxi. 26).

407. *from Aroer to Nebo*, i.e. from S. to N. of the region— *Aroer* being a small town on the bank of the Arnon; cf. Tennyson, *Dream of Fair Women*, "from Aroer on Arnon unto Minneth". *Nebo*, the mountain (forming part of the range of *Abarim*) from whose summit, Pisgah, Moses saw the Promised Land (*Deut.* xxxii. 49, xxxiv. 1).

408. *Hesebon*, "the city of Sihon the king of the Amorites", *Numb.* xxi, 26. For 'Hesebon', not 'Hesbbon', see on 398.

410. The germ of the line lies in *Isai.* xvi. 8, "the *vine* of Sibmah" (and verse 9). "Several rock-cut wine-presses are to be seen here, and these are probably the remains of the vineyard industry for which Sibmah was once so famous" (Murray's *Palestine*, 1892 ed. p. 173); the "flowery dale" is now "quite barren and uncultivated" (*ibid.*).

411. *Elealè*, mod. El-'Al, 'the High'; about 1½ miles from Hesebon (*Murray*, p. 186). the *Asphaltic pool* = the Dead Sea; cf. Blount, *Glossographia*, "Asphaltick of or belonging to the

Dead Sea, or Lake called Asphaltites"; and Sandys' *Relation*, p. 141, "that cursed lake Asphaltites: so named of the Bitumen which it vomiteth". In *Eikonoklastes* M. speaks of "the apples of Asphaltis"=Dead Sea fruit (*P. W.* I. 461). The bitumen or 'asphaltus' (cf. 729) floating on its surface is called "slime" in *Gen.* xi. 3 (cf. *P. L.* x. 298), or 'Jews' Pitch'.

412–14. *Peor*, Baal-Peor. *Sittim*; see *Numb.* xxv; it was situated "in the plains of Moab". *to do rites* = Ιερά ρέзειν, *sacra facere* ('to *sacrifice*'); cf. *Comus*, 535, "Doing abhorred rites to Hecate". *cost them woe*, i.e. the plague wherein died "twenty and four thousand" (*Numb.* xxv. 9).

415–18. He means that in later times, under Solomon, the rites (='orgies') of Chemos were introduced at Jerusalem. *of scandal*, i.e. of 'offence' or 'stumbling', see 403. *grove*, see 404, note. *homicide*; he received human sacrifice (392–6). *Josiah*, see 404, note.

415. *orgies*, cf. Jonson, *Hymenæi* (footnote), "δργια with the Greeks value the same that *ceremoniæ* with the Latins; and imply all sorts of rites". *enlarged*, carried still further.

419–21. *bordering*, i.e. Palestine, on north. *the brook*, the Besor, "the river of Egypt". These limits comprise Canaan.

422. *Baälim*. The supreme male deity of Phoenician and Canaanitish nations was the Sun-god, Baal: worshipped in different places under different aspects and titles—e.g. Baal-Berith, Baal-Zebub, Baal-Peor. The collective name of all these manifestations of the gods was 'Baälim' (plural). So 'Ashtaroth' (plural) was collective name of different manifestations of the moon-goddess Ashtoreth (sing.), the supreme female deity of these nations, and counterpart of Baal.

423, 424. Imitated by Pope, *Rape of the Lock*, 69, 70:
"For Spirits, freed from mortal laws, with ease
    Assume what sexes and what shapes they please."
Pope imitates Milton much—often most wittily.

424–9. Repeated VI. 351–3, where he says that spirits "limb themselves", as they like, and assume "colour, shape, or size", according to their pleasure. *essence pure*=the "liquid texture" of spirits, VI. 348.

428. *what shape they choose*. See 789, 790. Satan takes several "shapes" in *P. L.*: e.g. in IV. 402, 403, he is first a lion (an allusion to I *Peter* v. 8), then a tiger. In works on demonology popular in 17th cent. evil spirits often appear in shape of wild animals—see "Digression of Spirits" in Burton's *Anatomy*, I. ii. I. 2. Thus in the *Faust-buch* (1587), chap. XXIII, numerous

spirits are introduced to Faustus, each in form of some animal; see Dr Ward's *Faustus*, p. 141.

429. *dilated*, expanded. *obscure*, dark. M. invests the angels with a radiance (see *Appen*. p. 143) which they can lay aside.

433. Cf. "living Dread", *S. A.* 1673, "living God" in Scripture.

434–6. *bowing...bowed.* Sarcastic play on words (see 642).

435–7. I keep the punctuation of the original eds., which makes 'bowed' the main verb, 'sunk' a participle. Some editors, by inserting a comma after 'heads', just reverse the relation of 'bowed' and 'sunk'.

438–41. See 422, note. *Astoreth*, or Astarte, identical with Assyrian Istar and Greek Aphrodite, was symbolised in the religion of Phœnicians by the planet Venus or the Moon: in the latter case she was represented as horned like the crescent moon. Cf. Selden, *de Dis Syris—Lunam autem se ostendit Astarte, cum fronte corniculata fuerit conspicua* (1629 ed., p. 246). So M. regards her here and *Nat. Ode*, 200, "moonèd Ashtaroth, *Heaven's queen*"—a title due to her as moon-goddess (*Jeremiah* vii. 18). Cf. "Assyrian queen" (i.e. Istar), *Com.* 1002. The name is cognate with Sanskrit *tara* or *stara*, L. *stella*, E. *star*.

Sidon was the oldest, and for a time the chief, city of Phœnicia.

443–6. See 401, note, and cf. *P. R.* II. 169–71. *large*; "God gave Solomon...largeness of heart", I *Kings* iv. 29.

446–52. "In vain the Tyrian maids their wounded Thammuz mourn", *Nat. Ode*, 204. According to the legend, Thammuz, son of Cyneras, King of Byblus in Phœnicia, was slain by a boar in Lebanon; but every year his blood flowed afresh, and he came to life again—there being annual festivals in his honour at Byblus and elsewhere, first to lament his death, then to celebrate his revival. Thammuz, 'Sun of Life', is the Greek Adonis (the god of the solar year), and the story symbolises alternation of summer and winter. The notion of his blood flowing again was due to the reddening of the waters of the river Adonis through the peculiar red mud brought down by spring torrents from the Lebanon heights. M. alludes to the story, IX. 440, *Mansus*, 11.

449. *ditty*; strictly the words alone of a song; Lat. *dictatum*.

450, 451, *smooth*, smooth-flowing. *native*, i.e. from the river's source. *ran purple*, i.e. with reddened waters; *purple*, see G.

454–7. *Ezek.* viii. 14. Probably the Jews owed this worship to their intercourse with Phœnicians.

457–61. "Behold, Dagon was fallen upon his face to the ground before the ark of the Lord; and the head of Dagon and both the palms of his hands were cut off upon the threshold", 1 *Sam.* v. 4. *Dagon*, the national god of the Philistines. His worship seems to have been introduced from Babylonia, since cuneiform Assyrian inscriptions mention a god *Dakan* or *Dagan*, probably identical with Dagon. The name has also been derived (i) from Heb. *Dag*, a fish, (ii) from Heb. word for 'corn', Dagon being the god also of agriculture.

458. *in earnest*, with better reason than the mourners just mentioned. *captive ark*, see 1 *Sam.* v. 2.

460. *grunsel*, threshold; see G.

463. *downward fish*; a symbol that he was a "sea-idol" (*S. A.* 13), the Philistines themselves being a race who had come into Canaan over the sea (from Crete), and dwelt along sea-coast. Cf. 1 *Sam.* v. 4, margin. Probably M. connected the name with *Dag*, a fish.

464–6. He mentions the five chief cities of the Philistines, Ashdod and Gaza (cf. *S. A., passim*) being principal seats of worship of Dagon. *Azotus*, Greek form of Ashdod, cf. *Acts* viii. 40; used in Vulgate; Selden, *de Dis Syriis* (p. 262), says, *In Azoto sive Asdodo...fanum celebre erat Dagonis. Ascalon=* Askelon; so Septuagint and Vulgate. *Accaron=*Ekron, as in Vulgate, which also has *Accaronitæ=*people of Ekron (see 398, note). These must have been current forms in 17th cent.: cf. Sandys' *Relation*, p. 153, "Ten miles North of Ascalon along the shore stands Azotus: and eight miles beyond that Acharon, now places of no reckoning". Cf. also Scot, *Discovery*, 1584, "Belzebub the god of Acharon" (VII. xiii), and Heywood's *Hierarchie*, "Baalzebub, of the Accarronites", p. 40. *Gaza*, modern Guzzeh; on borders of desert that separates Palestine from Egypt: hence "frontier bounds".

467–9. *Rimmon*, Syrian deity of *Damascus* (2 *Kings* v. 18), which lay between the rivers *Abana* and *Pharpar* (2 *Kings* v. 12).

471–6. *a leper*, Naaman (2 *Kings* v.). For the Syrian altar of Ahaz, see 2 *Kings* xvi. *sottish*, foolish.

476–82. Cf. *Nat. Ode*, 211, 212, "The brutish gods of Nile... Isis and Orus" (with Osiris, 213–15). *brutish*, because the religion of the Egyptians consisted in a pantheistic worship of nature that took animals for its symbols. Thus *Osiris*, their chief god, was worshipped under symbol of sacred bull, Apis: cf. Pope's line, "the dull ox...Is now a victim, and now Egypt's god" (*Essay on Man*, I. 64). Of *Isis*, 'goddess of the earth',

Herodotus says, "the statue of this goddess has the form of a woman but with horns like a cow" (Rawlinson, II. 73). *Anubis* again was represented with a jackal's head, which the Greeks and Romans changed to that of a dog (cf. Plato, *Gorg.* 482 B and Virg. *Æn.* VIII. 698, *latrator Anubis*). *Orus* (or *Horus*), 'path of the sun', was their Sun-god.

477. *crew*; a depreciatory word in Milton (except in *L'Allegro*, 38), being used often of Satan and his followers; cf. 51, 751.

479. *abused*, deceived, deluded—a common sense in Shak.; cf. *Cymbeline*, III. 4. 123, "my master is abused"; so *Lear*, IV. 1. 24.

482–4. The worship by Israelites of the golden calf in the wilderness (*Exod.* xxxii) is traced to Egyptian cult of Apis. *borrowed* i.e. from Egyptians, whom they "spoiled", *Exod.* xii. 35, 36.

484–6. *rebel king*, Jeroboam, a rebel against Rehoboam (who succeeded Solomon); he "doubled" the sin because he "made *two* calves of gold", setting one in Bethel, the other in Dan (1 *Kings* xii. 20, 28, 29). With l. 486 cf. *Psalm* cvi. 20.

487–9. The tenth plague, *Exod.* xii. See XII. 189, 190. *he passed*, i.e. Israel.

489. "The Lord smote all the first-born in the land of Egypt...and all the first-born of cattle", *Exod.* xii. 29. *bleating*; their deity Ammon was worshipped under the form of a ram.

490. Strictly, *Belial* was not the name of any god, but an abstract word meaning 'that which is without profit' = worthlessness, wickedness: hence generally found in phrases like 'son (or man) of Belial' (501, 502). It has been treated so in the Bible sometimes, but more often—incorrectly—as a proper name. M. makes Belial a type of effeminacy and lust (cf. *P. R.* II. 150, "Belial, the dissolutest spirit that fell, The sensualest"), and rightly does not limit his worship to any particular place— although, to gratify his own hostility to the Church (493–6) and the court (497), he cannot refrain from indicating his opinion as to where Belial is most prevalent. Cf. *P. R.* II, where Satan, speaking to Belial, says (182, 183):

"Have we not seen, or by relation heard,
    In courts and regal chambers how thou lurk'st?"
Compare 497.

495. See 1 *Samuel* ii. 12–17.

497. Charles II was then on the throne. The Licenser might have been expected to raise objections to the line.

502. *flown*, flushed; the combination of the abstract word, "insolence", with the literal "wine", suggests the classical figure called *zeugma*.

503–5. *Gen*. xix, *Judg*. xix. The First Ed. had:
> "when hospitable Dores
> Yielded thir Matrons to prevent worse rape."

503. *Witness*, i.e. let the streets bear witness, be a proof.

506. *prime*, first, foremost.

507. *were long to tell*. Cf. x. 469, XII. 261; an imitation of the Latin—cf. Lucretius IV. 1166, *cetera de genere hoc longum est si dicere coner*. Spenser has it, *F. Q.* II. 7. 14, also Drayton, *Polyolbion* xv (Keightley). *were*, would be; the subjunctive, rare now, but common in Elizabethan English (Abbott).

508. i.e. held (=considered) by Javan's descendants (the Greeks) to be gods.

confessed later, admitted to be of later origin.

Javan, the son of Japhet; see *Genesis* x. 2. He stands for the Greek race; the name being the same word as *Ion* (older form 'Ιάων), whence *Ionians*, the section of the Greeks with whom Orientals were best acquainted through Phœnician trade. Cf. "isles of *Javan*"=isles of Greece, *S. A.* 715, 716; see *Isai.* lxvi. 19.

509, 510. *Heaven and Earth*, i.e. Uranus and Ge (or Gaia), whose 12 sons, according to the ordinary mythology, were called Titans (see 198, note). One of them, Cronos (=Saturn in Roman mythology) deposed his eldest brother (cf. 511, 512), and afterwards was himself expelled by his own son Zeus=Jove, whose mother was Rhea (cf. 512-14). In 510 M. uses Titan as a name for the eldest (cf. "firstborn") of the 12 Titans.

enormous, monstrous.

513. *like measure*, similar treatment.

514, 515. *Ida* the mountain in Crete where Jove was born. In *Il Pen.* 29 M. associates "Ida's inmost grove" with Saturn.

515, 516. *Olympus*, mountain range between Thessaly and Macedonia; early Greek poets speak of it—literally—as being abode of Zeus and other deities. *snowy*; "its chief summit is covered with perpetual snow" (*Class. Dict.*): hence Homer's epithet νιφόεις.

middle air, "i.e. the air between earth and heaven" (Beeching); but a then current theory of mediæval physics divided the air into 3 regions (*äeris trina spatia*, as I find in the *Adamus Exul* of Grotius), and I conjecture that M. refers to this view here, and means the middle region of the three; so in *P. R.* II. 117

where, alluding to *Ephes.* ii. 2, he makes "the middle *region* of *thick* air" (i.e. not the pure "æther") the meeting-place of Satan and his followers. Cf. again a note in Jonson's *Masque of Hymen* (*ad fin.*), which says that part of the scenery representing clouds opened and "revealed the three regions of air" (then described). See *Appen.* pp. 147–9 for a fuller consideration of the point.

517, 518. *Delphian cliff*; seat of famous oracle of Apollo; on southern slope of Mt Parnassus. Keightley quotes from Soph. *Œdip. Rex* 463, Δελφὶς πέτρα; cf. "steep of Delphos" (with same reference to Apollo), *Nat. Ode*, 178, and Gray, *Progress of Poesy*, 66. *Dodona*, in Epirus; here was an oracle of Zeus.

519, 520. *Doric land*, Greece. According to the common tradition, Saturn came alone to Italy ("the Hesperian fields").

521. *the Celtic*, i.e. 'fields' (from l. 520)—cf. *Com.* 60, "Roving the Celtic and Iberian fields"; or he may be imitating Greek ἡ Κελτική (i.e. χώρα or γῆ, country): in either case he means France—perhaps too Spain. *utmost isles*, e.g. Britain (cf. Virg. *Ecl.* 1. 67 *toto divisos orbe Britannos*) and '*ultima* Thule'. *utmost*, furthest.

523. *damp*, depressed; cf. "damp" (n.), depression, XI. 293.

528. *recollecting*, re-collecting, getting back again.

532. "A *clarion* is a small shrill treble trumpet" (Hume).

534. *Azazel*, from *Levit.* xvi. 8, where the A. V. has "the scapegoat", while the margin has "Azazel", which the R. V. adopts. That the word was the title of some evil demon is now generally held; and I suspect that in making him one of the fallen angels M. simply followed some tradition of the mediæval demonologists.

536. *advanced*, uplifted; cf. v. 588, "ensigns high advanced". It was the term for raising a standard; cf. *Romeo*, v. 3. 96, "death's pale flag is not advanced there", and *King John*, II. 1. 207.

538. *emblazed*=emblazoned: a term from heraldry. Cf. v. 592 and 2 *Henry VI.* IV. 10. 76, "wear it as a herald's coat, To emblaze the honour". The banner had rich devices portrayed on it.

540. *metal...blowing*, an absolute construction.

542. *Hell's concave*, the vaulted roof of Hell; cf. II. 635.

543. *reign*, realm; so "regency", v. 748. See II. 960–2.

546. *orient*, lustrous, bright; see G.

547, 548. *helms*, helmets. *serried*, locked together, Fr. *serré*.

549–62. Cromwell's Ironsides. Cf. VI. 63–6, where the host
"moved on
In silence their bright legions, to the sound
Of instrumental harmony, that breathed
Heroic ardour to adventurous deeds."
Here M. is thinking of the description in Thucydides (V. 70)
of the Spartans advancing at the battle of Mantinea ὑπὸ αὐλητῶν
πολλῶν, "to the strains of many *flute*-players" (Keightley).

550. The "Dorian" is one of the 'authentic' modes in music;
Plato calls it "the true Hellenic mode" (*Laches* 188 D), and "the
strain of courage", ἀνδρεία (*Rep.* 399 A), in contrast to the
effeminate "Lydian" mode (see *L' Allegro*, 136, note). It
inspires "a moderate and settled temper in the listener", says
Aristotle (*Pol.* VIII. 5). In *Areopagitica* M. speaks of music
which is "grave and Doric", *P. W.* II. 73. Many old German
chorales are written in this mode (Grove).

mood=mode; see G.

551–9. *recorders*, see G. In *On Education* M. dwells on the
influence of music upon character. The lines seem an expression
of his own devotion to the same art and inspiration.

556. *swage*, assuage; lit. to make sweet, Lat *suavis*.

561. *to*, to the sound of, Gk. ὑπό; cf. 550.

562. *the burnt soil*, see 228, 229.

563. *horrid*; probably in the lit. sense 'bristling' (Lat. *hor-
ridus*), i.e. with spears etc.; cf. II. 513 and VI. 82.

567, 568. *files*, ranks: "the files of war", VI. 339. *traverse*,
across.

573. I.e. since the creation of man, *post hominem creatum*: a
Latinism often used by M. with 'after'; cf. *S. A.* 1433, "after
his message told", *Com.* 48, "After the Tuscan mariners
transformed".

574. *embodied*, assembled, brought together.

574, 575. i.e. any other army, compared with this host of
angels, would be as absurdly inferior as an army of pygmies.

575. *that small infantry*, i.e. the Pygmies (cf. 780), the fabulous
little folk, of the height of a πυγμή (13½ inches), whom Homer
mentions, *Il.* III. 5. Sir Thomas Browne, not quite certain
whether to believe in them, is sure of one thing—that "if any
such nation there were, yet it is ridiculous what men have
delivered of them; that they fight with cranes upon the backs of
rams or partridges" (*Vulgar Errors* IV. xi).

576–87. Expanding the idea in 573–5, he takes the great
cycles of heroic story—Greek (576–9), British (579–81),

mediæval, whether French or Italian (582-7)—and says that all the warriors and armies severally associated with these stories could bear no comparison with Satan's followers.

577. *Phlegra*, the old name of the peninsula of Pallene in Macedonia, where (according to ancient legend) the Giants were born, and where they were vanquished by the Gods. Cf. Drummond:

> "they durst in the Phlegræan plain
> The mighty rulers of the sky defy."

577-9. Greek legend, as embodied in epic or tragic verse, centres mainly round Thebes, Troy (Ilium), and Mycenæ (the city of the Pelopidæ). Thus in his first *Elegy* M. epitomises the chief themes of Greek tragedy—*seu mæret Pelopeia domus, seu nobilis Ili,* | *aut luit incestos aula Creontis avos* (Creon was king of Thebes). Here he mentions only two of the cycles. By the "heroic race" that fought at *Thebes* he means (1) Polynices and his six companions whose exploit is told in Æschylus' play, *Septem contra Thebas*; (2) their descendants, the Epigoni, who ten years later destroyed Thebes. The heroes of the story of *Ilium* are those whom the *Iliad* presents to us. There "auxiliar gods" take part, some helping the Trojans, some the Greeks.

579-81. Cf. Milton's own account of his youthful studies: "hear me out now, readers, that I may tell ye whither my younger feet wandered; I betook me among those lofty *fables and romances*, which recount in solemn cantos deeds of knighthood", *Apol. for Smect., P. W.* III. 118. The interest of this reference to the legend of King Arthur is explained in *Introduction*. M. discusses the story at some length in his *Hist. of Britain*, and evidently had studied it closely.

580. *in fable*; an allusion, suggests Keightley, in particular to the *Historia Britonum* by Geoffrey of Monmouth, who gives one of our earliest versions (1140) of the Arthurian legend. No doubt M. is thinking of Geoffrey whom he used extensively in his *History*; but there he often refers to the Breton monk Nennius and to Gildas—yet earlier authorities than Geoffrey—likewise to William of Malmsbury: so that here we can scarcely limit the reference to any particular writer. 'Fable' is his favourite term in the *History* for these old Chronicles. *romance*; e.g. Mallory's *Morte Darthur*, published by Caxton, 1485 (the basis of Tennyson's *Idylls of the King*).

Uther's son, King Arthur, son of Uther Pendragon; cf. Tennyson, *Palace of Art*, "mythic Uther's deeply-wounded son". In *Epitaph. Damon.* 166-8 M. glances at the story of Arthur's birth.

581. The division of Arthur's "fabulous paladins" (as Drummond calls them, *Forth Feasting*, 1617) into "British and Armoric" coincides with *P. R.* II. 360, 361, "Knights of Logres or of Lyones, Lancelot or Pelleas or Pellenore": where Logres = Britain, more strictly England east of river Severn; and Lyones = Brittany (according to one theory), whence came Sir Tristram. *Armoric*, of Armorica = Brittany: "it was first called *Armorica* from its situation on the Sea, as the word importeth in the old language of that people" (Heylin, I. 167). Brittany is closely connected with the Arthurian legend.

Begirt with, surrounded by. Cf. Gray, *The Bard*, III.

583–7. The names are associated with romances (mainly Italian) in prose or verse; see *Appen.* pp. 150–3. *jousted*, tilted.

586. *his peerage*, the 'douze pairs' (i.e. *peers*) or 12 'paladins' of France (*P. R.* III. 343): the most famous being Roland, the Achilles or brave man, and Oliver, the Ulysses or wise man, of the Old French epic poems and prose-romances which narrate the exploits of Charlemagne and his knights.

587. *Fontarabbia*, modern Fuenterrabia, a frontier fortress on Bay of Biscay—S. of Biarritz. Its position made it the scene of many encounters between Spanish and French.

588. *observed*, obeyed.

591–4. *Appen.* p. 143. *her*; he personifies "form"; see *its* in G.

like a tower; cf. Tennyson's *Ode* (38) on the Duke of Wellington.

596–9. The lines to which the Licenser for the Press took exception when the MS. of the poem was submitted to him. Censure of such innocuous verses becomes doubly ridiculous when we remember certain later passages. Doubtless the Licenser did not get far in his reading; it must have been a shock to him if he ever discovered that he had tacitly approved the attack on the Church in XII. 507–35.

597. *eclipse*; proverbially of evil omen, the precursor of trouble. *disastrous*, boding disaster; see G.

601. *intrenched*, cut into; cf. O.F. *trencher*, to cut.

603. *considerate*, considering, full of thought. Cf. *Areopagitica*, "let us be more considerate builders, more wise", *P. W.* II. 93.

605–12. See *Appen.* p. 142.

605. *remorse*, pity. *passion*, deep feeling (but not anger).

606. *fellows of*, partners in.

609. *amerced of*, deprived of, lit. 'fined with loss of'; see G.

613–15. *scathed*, damaged; see G. Whether lightning can be said to 'singe' the top of a tree seems doubtful. *blasted heath*; see *Macbeth*, I. 3. 77. *blasted*, withered by the lightning (612).

619. *thrice*, a conventional number; cf. Ovid, *Met.* XI. 419, *ter conata loqui, ter fletibus ora rigavit. assayed*, tried; see G.

624. *event*, issue, result, Lat. *eventus*; so often in M. and Shak.

632. Scan *exîle*; cf. X. 484, *Richard II.* I. 3. 151.

633. *emptied Heaven*; a mere boast, see II. 692, note.

634. *self-raised*, see II. 75, 76.

642. *tempted...attempt.* There are not a few of these jingling phrases in M. Cf. "beseeching or besieging", v. 869, "feats of war defeats", *S. A.* 1278. Generally he expresses sarcasm or contempt by them. The use of this figure of speech (*paronomasia*) is specially common in late Latin writers; see Mayor's note on Cicero's 2nd *Philippic* XI. 13. M. uses it in his Latin writings; cf. the *Christian Doctrine*, I. 11, "*Natura natam* se fatetur...et *fatum* quid nisi *effatum* divinum omnipotentis cujuspiam numinis potest esse?" Something similar is found in Hebrew.

646. *to work*, to achieve.

650, 651. *rife*, prevalent. *fame*, report; see II. 346.

650–4. See II. 345–53, 830–5, and X. 481. The first hint of the design against mankind comes from Satan (cf. II. 379 *et seq.*), though Beëlzebub afterwards develops it (II. 345–78).

656. *eruption*, breaking forth from hell—sortie.

660. I.e. *pax desperatur*; cf. VI. 495, "nothing...to be despaired", *nil desperandum*.

662. *understood*, i.e. among themselves, and so secret.

668. Like Roman soldiers applauding an oration of their general.

670. *grisly*, horrible; cf. Germ. *grässlich, grausig*.

674. "It was the common opinion of chemists that metals were composed of sulphur and quicksilver" (Keightley).

675. *brigad*, so original eds., here and II. 532.

676. *pioners*, see G.

678. *cast*, form by throwing up the earth. *Mammon*, like "Belial", not really a proper name, but an abstract word = wealth.

679. *erected*, lofty, elevated; so Lat. *erectus* in same sense.

682. "And the street of the city was pure gold", *Rev.* xxi. 21.

683. *else*; separated from *aught*, with which it goes; cf. 109.

684. *vision beatific = Visio Beatifica*, the phrase used by Schoolmen to express "seeing" God (*Matthew* v. 8). Cf. "blessed vision", v. 613, "happy-making sight", *Ode on Time*, 18.

685. *Men also*, i.e. as well the fallen angels.

686. *ransacked*, pillaged, rifled. *the centre*; probably the centre of the earth; or the earth itself (see *Appen.* p. 136).

688. Horace's *aurum irrepertum et sic melius situm—Od.* III. 3. 49.

690. *ribs*, bars, large pieces. *admire*, wonder; see G.

692. Either "precious" is ironical, implying contempt, or "precious bane" is an oxymoron (see II. 252–7). *bane*, curse, evil.

694. Most editors take Babel = Babylon, but why not the Tower of Babel (cf. XII. 43–62)? There is a reference to Babylon in 717, and we do not want two references. *the works*, i.e. the Pyramids; cf. Jonson, *Prince Henry's Barriers*, "And did the barbarous Memphian heaps outclimb". *Memphian*, Egyptian; see 307, note.

697–9. Cf. Pliny, speaking of the Great Pyramid, "it is said (see Herodotus, II. 124), that in the building of it there were 366,000 men kept at worke twentie yeares" (Holland's *Pliny*, 1601, II. 577).

697. *and in an hour*, i.e. is performed (from 699).

702. *sluiced*, led by sluices; cf. Tennyson, *Arabian Nights*, "a broad canal From the main-river sluiced".

703. *founded*, melted; it seems impossible to follow the Second Ed. which reads *found out*.

704. *severing*, separating. The noun "bullion" (here used as adj.) meant a mass of unpurified gold or silver, "dross" being the scum that rises to the surface when such metal is melted: hence "bullion-dross" = scum rising from the bullion. *bullion*, see G.

708. M. might be expected to understand the mechanism of the organ, his favourite instrument (see *Life*).

710–17. Cf. Pope (who imitates the whole passage), *Temple of Fame*, 91, "The growing towers, like exhalations, rise"; and Tennyson, *Œnone*, "as yonder walls (i.e. of Troy) Rose slowly to a music slowly breathed". Peck noted that these lines read like an account of some Jacobean Masque, describing one of those elaborate structures of stage-architecture designed by Inigo Jones and brought on the scene by means of machinery, to the accompaniment of music. Thus I find that in Jonson's *Entertainment at Theobalds* the main scene represented "a

glorious place, figuring the seat of the household gods...erected
with *columns* (='pillars') and *architrave, frieze* and *cornice*".
(See Essay on Masque and Milton's connection therewith,
Comus, pp. 127–33). *symphonies*, i.e. the strains of the instru-
ments accompanying the voices.

713–716. *pilasters*, square columns usually set within a wall
and slightly projecting. *architrave*, the main or 'master' beam
(ἀρχή + *trabs*) that rests immediately upon a row of pillars, the
frieze coming just above, and the *cornice* projecting above the
frieze.

716. *bossy*, i.e. sculptures in relief.

717. *fretted gold*=gold wrought with designs, patterns;
see G.

717, 718. Not necessarily (as Bentley thought) a repetition of
694: since there 'Babel' may mean the Tower, while 'Memphian' may have the general sense 'Egyptian'.

718. *Alcairo*; he means Memphis, giving it the name of the
later capital built (10th cent. A.D.) some few miles from site of
its predecessor. The form "Alcairo" (Arab. *Al Kahirah*, the
City of Victory) seems to have been current then; compare
Hexham's *Mercator*, "Memphis...is called at this day (1636)
Cairo or *Alcairo*" (11. 427).

720. *Belus*. Cf. Sandys' *Relation*, "*Belus Priscus*, reputed a
God, and honored with Temples; called *Bel* by the Assyrians,
and *Baal* by the Hebrews" (p. 207). The famous temple of Bel
at Babylon (Herodotus, 1. 181–3), attributed to Semiramis, is
described by Raleigh, *History*, p. 183 (1621 ed.). *Serapis*;
there was a temple to him at Memphis, but more celebrated was
that at Alexandria, the *Serapeum* to which the great library was
attached. Serapis was identical with Greek Hades, whose
worship was introduced into Egypt by Ptolemy I, some of the
attributes of Osiris being transferred to him. 'Serăpis' and
'Serāpis' are found—the latter more correct.

723, 724. *Stood fixed*, i.e. was now complete (Lat. *stabat*),
having reached its appointed height. *discover*, reveal; F.
découvrir.

728, 729. *cresset*, a kind of hanging lamp, see G. *naphtha
and asphaltus*: the former the liquid (for the lamps), the latter the
solid substance (for the cressets). *asphaltus*, see 411, note. The
forms 'aspháltus' and 'aspháltum' were current till this cent.:
modern 'ásphalt' is from Fr. *asphalte*.

732. *the architect*. Masson says that Mammon is intended,
M. identifying him with Mulciber (or Vulcan). But (with

Mr Beeching) I cannot see that M. does this: he only says that Mammon discovered the gold out of which the fabric was made, and leaves us to infer from what follows that the architect was Vulcan or Mulciber. The attributes of the two deities Mammon and Vulcan are quite dissimilar.

733. *towered structure high.* The order of the words—a noun placed between two qualifying words—is a favourite with M. The idiom is Greek; in his note on *Lycidas*, 6 Mr Jerram quotes Hesiod, *Theogony*, 811, χάλκεος οὐδὸς ἀστεμφής, and Euripides, *Phœnissæ*, 234, νιφόβολον ὄρος ἱρόν. Gray probably borrowed the device from Milton; cf. his *Elegy* 53, "Full many a gem of purest ray serene". See II. 615, 616.

736. *gave to rule.* A Lat. idiom; cf. *Æneid* I. 66, *tibi divum pater...mulcere dedit flectus.* So in III. 243, XI. 339.

737. M. alludes to a mediaeval belief that the Heavenly beings were divided into Hierarchies and Orders; see *Appendix*, p. 153.

738, 739. *his name...in Greece,* Hephæstus, "the god of fire as used in art, and master of all the arts which need the aid of fire, especially of working in metal". All the palaces in Olympus (the heaven of the classical gods) were built by Hephæstus.

Ausonian land, Italy so called poetically from the *Ausones*, an ancient Latin race who dwelt on the west coast of Italy before its conquest by the Romans.

740. *Mulciber,* 'the softener, welder' (i.e. of metal), from Lat. *mulcere,* 'to soften'.

740–46. Partly a translation of *Iliad* I. 591 *et seq.*, where Hephæstus describes his fall. Cf. two allusions in Milton's Lat. poems: *sic dolet amissum proles Junonia cælum | inter Lemniacos præcipitata focos* (*Elegy* VII. 81, 82); and—*qualis in Ægeam proles Junonia Lemnon | deturbata sacro cecidit de limine cæli* (*Naturam Non Pati Senium,* 23).

741, 742. *angry*; because in a dispute between Jove and Juno, Vulcan took the part of Juno, his mother. *sheer,* 'clean' over; cf. IV. 182.

742–4. "We fall not from Virtue, like Vulcan from heaven, in a day", says Sir Thomas Browne, *Christian Morals,* I. 30.

746. *Lemnos,* sacred to Hephæstus, "the Lemnian God" (Spenser *Muiopotmos*); probably because it was volcanic. Scan the line

"On Lem|nos, th' Æg|'an isle|. Thus they |relate".

747. *erring,* i.e. incorrectly, erroneously. *rout,* company, band.

750. *engines*, contrivances; see G.

752. *harald*, herald; see G.

753. *awful*, inspiring awe, most solemn.

754. *trumpet's*. For the reason explained at 59, note, either *trumpet's* or *trumpets'* is possible here and in II. 515.

756. *Pandemonium*, 'the home of all the demons'; cf. x. 424. The word seems to have been coined by Milton (from Gk. πᾶν, 'all' + δαίμων, 'a demon'). Some prefer the form 'Pandæmonium'.

758. *squared regiment* = "perfect phalanx", 550.

763-6. "He alludes to those accounts of the single combats between the Saracens ('Panim chivalry') and Christians (cf. 582) in Spain and Palestine, of which the old romances are full" (Callander): using, as in *S. A.* in the dispute between Samson and Harapha, the technical terms of the mediæval duello. For a good description of such scenes, cf. *The Faerie Queene*, IV. 3. 4 *et seq.*

763. Possibly "covered field" = Fr. *champ clos*, the space for combat, enclosed with barriers or 'lists'; cf. *S. A.* 1087, "listed field". *champions*; the technical word for combatants— *campiones qui in campum descendunt et duello seu monomachia decertant* (Ducange).

764. *wont*, were wont; see G. *Soldan*; see G.

765, 766. *Panim*; see G. He mentions the two kinds of combat—(1) that fought out "to the utterance" (*Macbeth*, III. I. 72), i.e. till one of the fighters was killed: cf. "mortal duel", *S. A.* 1102; (2) that which was merely an exhibition of skill, spears and swords with blunted points being used. *career*, Fr. *carière*, a short gallop at high speed; another term peculiar to tournaments. Cf. *Animadversions*, "all this careering with spear in rest", *P. W.* III. 90.

767. Cf. II. 528.

768. The prevalence of *s* is meant to suggest the scene— 'sound echoing sense'; so that one is tempted to print with the original editions 'russling'.

768–75. *as bees*. The simile had been used by Homer, *Iliad* II. 87 *et seq.*, and Virgil, *Æneid* I. 430–6, VI. 707–9.

769. *Taurus*, one of the signs of the zodiac; strictly, the time of year defined is April 19–May 20. Cf. x. 671–3.

with; not 'in company with', since Taurus (as Bentley objected) is a fixed constellation, but 'in the neighbourhood of' (Beeching).

744. *expatiate* = Lat. *spatior*, 'walk abroad'; cf. Blount,

"Expatiate, to wander, to stray, to spread abroad". *confer*, confer *of*, discuss.

777–80. Spirits, we have seen (428), can contract themselves.

780, 781. Pliny (*Nat. History* VII. II. 26) placed the dwelling of the Pygmies (see 575, note) "beyond the source of the Ganges—even in the edge and skirts of the mountains". So *Batman vppon Bartholome* (1582 ed., p. 377), "Pigmei be little men of a cubite long...and they dwell in mountaines of Inde".

that, the well-known, whose name needs no mention.

781. *beyond the Indian mount*; probably he means Imaus (cf. III. 431), in classical writers (e.g. Pliny) the *western* chain of the Himalayas, i.e. between the Ganges and the Caspian. It should be noticed that 'extra Imaum' (i.e. East of or 'beyond') and 'intra Imaum' (i.e. West of) were phrases employed by map-makers of 17th cent. to describe (with convenient vagueness) regions of Central Asia. Thus in Mercator's map of 'Tartary' we have "Scythia extra"—and "Scythia intra—Imaum montem". Milton's readers might be reminded of this common distinction.

781–5. A reminiscence of *A Midsummer-Night's Dream*, II. 1. 28, 29, 141 (a play constantly imitated by Milton). Cf. too, Pope, *Rape of the Lock*, 31, "airy Elves by moonlight shadows seen". Commonly "fairies" and "elves" (more rustic in character) are distinguished. *sees, or dreams he sees*; from Virgil's *aut videt, aut vidisse putat*—*Æneid* VI. 454.

785, 786. *arbitress*, witness; cf. Horace's *non infideles arbitræ* | *Nox et Diana*—*Epod.* V. 48, 49. She comes "nearer to the earth" because influenced (II. 665) by the fairies. *pale*, with alarm.

790, 791. I.e. they had so contracted their forms that, though numberless, they had plenty of room to move about (Richardson).

795. *recess*, retirement. His sarcastic purpose in applying the ecclesiastical word "conclave" to the assembly of evil angels is unmistakable: that being the term specially applied to "the Meeting or Assembly of the Cardinals for the Election [of the Pope], or for any important affair of the Church" (Blount). Cf. his contemptuous reference in *Of Reformation* to the "councils (i.e. of the Church) and conclaves that demolish one another" (*P. W.* II. 389), and the similar use of "consistory" *P. R.* I. 42. Strictly 'conclave', like Lat. *conclave*, meant the room in which a meeting took place: then the meeting itself.

797. *frequent*=Lat. *frequens*, crowded, numerous; see G.

797, 798. *after...summons read.* Cf. 573 and Tennyson,

Pelleas and Ettarre, "after trumpet blown". *consult*, consultation; commonly the result of a consultation, i.e. a decision, decree—like Lat. *consultum*; e.g. in Dryden, *Fables*, "their grave consults dissolv'd in smoke".

BOOK II

1. Cf. the picture of Satan throned on "his royal seat", v. 756.

2. *Ormus*, ancient *Armuza*, a town situate on an island near the mouth of the Persian Gulf. Cf. Fairfax, XVII. 25, "Orms, plac'd in the wide Huge Persian bay, a town rich, fair, and large". Much celebrated as a mart for pearls and jewels; cf. Howell's *Familiar Letters*, "Ormus...the greatest Mart in all the Orient for all sorts of jewels" (Jacobs' ed. 1892, I. 157), and Marvell, *Song of the Emigrants*, "Jewels more rich than Ormus shows". Hexham (1636) calls it *Ormus Emporium*, and Heylin says, "in regard of the situation, it was one of the richest Empories in all the world; the wealth of Persia and East-India being brought hither" (*Cosmography*, 1682 ed., III. 143).

2, 3. Cf. *Love's Labour's Lost*, IV. 3. 222, 223:
> "like a rude and savage man of *Inde*,
> At the first opening of *the gorgeous east*."

The form *Ind* (or *Inde*) is common in poets—cf. *Comus*, 606. The first settlements of the East India Company dated from early in the 17th cent., and English people heard much concerning the wealth of India (cf. 638). See *Shakespeare's England*, I. 189.

3, 4. *or where*, i.e. of the places where. "It was the eastern ceremony, at the coronation of their kings, to powder them with gold-dust and seed-pearl" (Warburton); also to strew pearls and jewels at the monarch's feet. Shakespeare knew of the custom cf. *Antony and Cleopatra*, II. 5. 45, 46), which some traveller must have related. At the end of his *History of Moscovia* M. gives a list of authorities, mainly 'Voyages' and 'Travels' (e.g. Hakluyt and Purchas); and passages like this and III. 437–9 show how he used such sources of information.

4. Cf. Pope, *Temple of Fame*, 94, "With diamond flaming and barbaric gold". *Barbaricus* is an epithet of *aurum*, *Æn.* II. 504.

9. *success*, ill-fortune; see G.

10. *imaginations*, vain thoughts, schemes.

11. *Powers...Dominions*. For these titles, see *Appendix*, p. 153.

12–17. A parenthesis.

12. *for*. He calls them "Deities of *Heaven*" because he still regards Heaven as theirs. Exactly similar passages are X. 460, 461, and V. 361, 362 (note). In each case the clause introduced by *for* explains some particular word or phrase in the previous sentence.

14, 15. I.e. I do not consider Heaven lost. 'Give for lost', a common phrase; cf. *S. A.* 1697, "So Virtue, given for lost", and George Herbert, *Church Porch*, "Who say, 'I care not', those I give for lost". See too *The Winter's Tale*, III. 2. 96, "your favour I do give lost", i.e. consider it as lost. *Virtues*, see *Appendix*, p. 153.

16. I.e. than they would have been had they not fallen.

17. I.e. have such trust in themselves as not to fear.

20. Cf. I. 635-7. *counsel*, some needlessly change to *council*.

23. *unenvied*, not to be envied, unenvi*able*; see G.

27. *whom*, him whom.

29. *your bulwark*, as your defence; in apposition to *whom* (27).

26-30. Satan calls himself "only supreme in misery", IV. 91.

28. *the Thunderer*, the Almighty; an obviously fitting title here, see I. 93, 174-6, 258. Cf. *Tonans* applied to Jupiter.

39, 40. See I. 642, note.

43. See I. 392. Moloch ("furious king", VI. 357) is conspicuous in the great battle in Heaven (VI. 354-62). Newton reminds us of Homer's phrase σκηπτοῦχος βασιλεύς (*Il.* I. 279).

50. *recked*, cared, cf. 'reckless', careless, 'reckoning', care (*Lyc.* 116); *reck* = A.S. *récan*, to care, is common in Elizabethan writers. *thereafter*; 'accordingly' (i.e. as not fearing God), or 'thereupon'.

51. *sentence* = opinion, vote, Lat. *sententia*; cf. 291.

52. *more unexpert*, less experienced in them than in war.

59. I.e. the prison assigned by his tyranny. For Milton no word has worse associations than 'tyranny'; cf. *First Defence*, "the two greatest mischiefs of this life, and most pernicious to virtue, [are] tyranny and superstition"; and *The Ready Way*, "the most prevailing usurpers over mankind, superstition and tyranny" (*P. W.* I..212, II. 113). See I. 124, note.

60-70. Contrast Belial's reply, 129-42.

63. *tortures*, the things that torture us. *horrid*, see 513.

67. *fire and horror*, cf. I. 502, note. *equal*, i.e. to his.

69. *mixed*, filled. *Tartarean*; he applies to this nether world terms drawn from the classics—e.g. 'Tartarus' = Hell 858, VI. 54; 'Tartarean' and 'Stygian' 506 and I. 239 = belonging to Hell, infernal; 'Erebus' 883. Strictly, the practice involves

some incongruity of effect; cf. the mixture of classical and Scriptural allusions in *Lyc*. No doubt, M. was influenced by the Renaissance fashion of identifying the Hell of Christian theology with that of classical writers.

73, 74. *such*, i.e. those who think the way difficult. Used as a noun *drench* ('that which drenches' i.e. wets thoroughly) was, and is, commonly applied to a draught of physic for animals. Here therefore it is a contemptuous word—as in the *Animadversions*, "to diet their ignorance, and want of care, with the limited draught of a matin and even-song drench", *P. W.* III. 57. Moloch's object is to rouse them to action by taunts. *forgetful lake* = "oblivious pool", I. 266.

75–81. See I. 633, 634, and cf. the account of the expulsion of the angels from Heaven VI. 856–79. Not being subject to the law of gravitation they did not 'fall', but were driven down by force.

75. *proper*, natural = Lat. *proprius*, belonging to oneself.

77. *but* = 'that not'; usually in a negative clause; cf. *The Tempest*, I. 2. 209, "*not* a soul *but* felt a fever", i.e. *that* did *not*. So *Richard III*. I. 3. 186. (See Abbott, *Shakesp. Gram.* p. 84.)

79. *the deep*, Chaos; see *Appen.* p. 133.

82–4. *event*, issue (I. 624). The lines give a supposed objection from one of the audience.

83. *Our stronger*, our superior, our vanquisher.

89. *exercise*, torment; see G.

90–92. Thyer illustrates from Spenser, *Teares of the Muses*, 125, 126, "Ah, wretched world! and all that is therein, *The vassals of Gods wrath*, and slaves of sin"; and *A Midsummer-Night's Dream*, V. 1. 37, "To ease the anguish of a *torturing hour*". *inexorably*; so the original editions; he may have dictated *inexorable*.

92. *Calls*; singular because the two subjects really form a single idea ('punishment'); cf. I. 139.

97. *essential*, essence (see 439), substance, viz. of their angelic forms. In M. as in Shak. an adj. = a noun is very common (cf. 'obscure' 406, 'abrupt' 409): an illustration of Dr Abbott's remark that in Elizabethan E. "almost any part of speech can be used as any other part of speech" (*Shakesp. Gram.* p. 5).

99, 100. Cf. 146–54, and I. 117 (note).

100, 101. *at worst*, i.e. we have already reached the worst point (cf. 162, 163), short of absolute annihilation. To place 'at worst' between commas changes the sense. *by proof*, by experience.

104. *fatal*, upheld by fate (I. 133), hence secure.

106. *denounced*, threatened.

109. *Belial*; see I. 490, note. In the systems of the demonologists Belial holds high rank; Heywood (*Hierarchie*, 1635,
p. 436) makes him head of the fourth of the nine Orders into
which the fallen angels were divided (corresponding with the
nine Heavenly Orders—see p. 157). In assigning to Belial the
two qualities of personal beauty and persuasive speech M. has
followed (*more suo*) mediæval tradition. Cf. Scot's *Discovery
of Witchcraft* (1584), "This Beliall...taketh the form of a
beautifull Angell, he speaketh faire" (xv. 2). *humane*, polished,
refined.

113. *manna*, words sweet as manna, "the taste of [which]
was like wafers made with *honey*," *Exod.* xvi. 31.

113, 114. Alluding, as Bentley noted, to the profession of the
Sophists—τὸν ἥττω λόγον κρείττω ποιεῖν. The reproach was
made against Socrates; cf. Plato, *Apology* 18 B, which probably
alludes to the satirical lines about Socrates in Aristophanes'
Clouds, 111–15. So M. in *Tetrachordon*, "as was objected to
Socrates by them who could not resist his efficacy, that he ever
made the worse cause [i.e. λόγος] seem the better", *P. W.* III.
320. Blount (1672) defines a 'Sophister' as "a cunning or
cavilling disputer, who will make a false matter seem true".
dash, confound, cast down.

119. The first part of his speech answers Moloch point by
point.

123. *ominous*; a dissyllable, *i* being elided before pure *n*.

124. *in fact of arms* = Fr. *en fait d'armes*, i.e. in deeds, exploits;
fact = feat in sense as in etymology (Lat. *factum*). See 537.

127. *scope*, aim, mark; Gk σκοπός.

130. *render*; plural, because 'watch' = watchmen.

132. Scan *óbscure* (cf. *Hamlet*, IV. 5. 213), and see 210, note.

133. *scout*, reconnoitre; Fr. *écouter*, Lat. *auscultare*.

139–42. *mould*, substance, i.e. of the angels, whom Moloch
would assail with Hell-fire (67, 68). Spiritual frames, M. has
said (I. 117), are formed of an "empyreal substance", i.e. of
pure fire; cf. *Psalm* civ. 4, "Who maketh his angels spirits; his
ministers a flaming fire". And this fire, argues Belial here and
215, 216, will, through its greater purity, prevail over (i.e. be
insensible to) the "baser" fire of Hell.

143. *flat*, absolute, complete, Shakespeare has "flat perjury",
Much Ado About Nothing, IV. 2. 44; "flat rebellion", *King John*
III. 1. 298, etc.

155–9. This thought that the evil angels must live, so that they may suffer the more, is not peculiar to M. Thus Grotius (*Adamus Exul*), makes Satan say, *mors una... | mihi summa voti est; nec, quod extremum est malis, | licet perire;* and Sir Thomas Browne, *Religio Medici* LI, has, "the devil, were it in his power, would do the like [viz. destroy himself]; which being impossible, his miseries are endless, and he suffers most in that attribute... his immortality".

156. Ironical. *belike*, perhaps, no doubt; only here in M., but many times in Shakespeare; cf. *Hamlet*, III. 2. 305, "belike, he likes it not". *impotence*, lack of self-restraint (= Lat. *impotentia*).

159. *cease*, i.e. from war: 'why give up the struggle?'

160. *they who*, Moloch: a courteously indirect reference, consonant with Belial's "humane" character.

165. *what when*, i.e. how was it when—what was our state? Many texts print a note of exclamation (not in the original editions) after *what*, making the sentence an *anacoluthon*.

amain, with all speed. *strook*; Milton's preference for this form to *struck* is marked (Masson).

166. *afflicting*, perhaps in the lit. sense of *affligere*; see I. 186.

168, 169. See I. 51–3, 311–13. *chained*; see I. 48.

170. *Isaiah* xxx. 33.

174. *red right hand* = *rubens dextera* of Jupiter (Horace, *Od.* I. 2. 2).

175, 176. *her*, of Hell (176). *this firmament*, i.e. of "the horrid roof" (644) of Hell, to which he points. *cataracts*, floods, torrents; Gk. καταρράκτης, waterfall. See XI. 824, note.

180–2. Editors compare *Æn.* VI. 75, *rapidis ludibria ventis* ("the *sport* of every wind", Dryden), and 740, 741. Probably M. had in his thoughts *Measure for Measure*, III. I. 124–6:

"To be imprison'd in the viewless winds,
And blown with restless violence round about
The *pendent world*" [cf. 1052].

182. *racking*; Keightley says, "sweeping, driving along. Clouds thus driven are called the *rack*" (cf. "racking clouds", 3 *Henry VI.* II. I. 27). But perhaps = torturing. Cf. I. 126.

184. *converse*, dwell with; Lat. *cum*, with + *versari*, to dwell.

185. With M. (even in his prose, as Todd noted) and other poets a favourite arrangement of words, expressing emphasis; cf. v. 899, "Unshaken, unseduced, unterrified"; also *P. R.* III. 429, *Hamlet*, I. 5. 77. We may compare the repetition in the Greek dramatists of adjectives compounded with the negative prefix ά- (= Eng. *un*-); e.g. in Euripides, *Hecuba* 669, ἄπαις,

ἄνανδρος, ἄπολις, ἐξεφθαρμένη; and Sophocles, *Antigone* 1071, ἄμοιρον ἀκτέριστον, ἀνόσιον νέκυν.

187. See I. 661, 662.

190, 191. "He that sitteth in the heavens shall laugh", *Psalm* ii. 4. *motions*, proposals, schemes; cf. the use of 'motion' in politics, and the verb in IX. 229, "Well hast thou motioned".

194–6. A supposed objection; cf. 82–4, note.

199. *to suffer...to do. Et facere et pati fortia Romanum est*, Livy II. 12: *quidvis et facere et pati*, Horace, *Od.* III. 24. 43. "A man may confide in persons constituted for noble ends, who dare do and suffer"—Sir Thomas Browne, *Christian Morals*, I. 25.

207. *ignominy*; a trisyllable, as in I. 115, the unaccented vowel (*i*) being elided before pure *n*. The 1st Folio prints *ignomy* in I *Henry IV.* v. 4. 100, "Thy *ignomy* sleep with thee in the grave".

210. Scan *súpreme*. This throwing back of the accent in words like 'supreme', 'extreme', 'complete', 'obscure' (cf. 132), is usual in M. (and Shak.) when they precede a monosyllable or a noun accented on first syllable. Cf. I. 735, *Com.* 273, "Not any boast of skill, but éxtreme shift", 421, "She that has that, is clad in cómplete steel".

211. *far removed*; cf. 321, and see I. 74, 75, note.

215, 216. Cf. 139–42, note. *essence*, see 439. *vapour*, used of hot exhalations, as in XII. 635, "torrid heat and vapour".

inured, accustomed to the flames. To *inure* is literally 'to bring into practice' (=*ure*). For the obsolete noun *ure* (F. *œuvre*, 'work', Lat. *opera*) cf. Bacon's Essay *Of Stimulation*, "lest his hand should be out of ure", i.e. out of practice. Cf. '*manure*', to work with the hand, to cultivate.

217–19. Cf. 274–8. *temper*, nature, temperament.

219. *void of pain*; a consideration appropriate to Belial, who represents slothful ease and luxury.

220. *light*, a noun, surely; to take it as an adj., 'easy', is to lose the fine hyperbole that for them 'darkness' may become—'light'.

224. *for*, regarded as happy—looked at from that standpoint.

226–8. His counsel accords with his effeminate character (I. 490). *reason's garb.* Cf. *Com.* 759, "false rules...in reason's garb". *ignoble ease*=*ignobile otium*, Virg. *G.* IV. 564.

228. *thus Mammon.* See I. 678. His speech partly replies to Moloch (since he dismisses the notion of war altogether), partly carries Belial's counsel a step farther. The gist of what Belial

said was—'let us temporize, stay here and trust to chance—something may happen'. Mammon answers—'let us indeed stay here, but not idly look to the future: rather straightway set about founding a realm here to compensate for what we have lost there'. Belial, type of ease and sloth, stands, as it were, halfway between Moloch and Mammon.

231, 232. *then...when*, i.e. then only = 'never'. A favourite phrase; cf. IV. 970, "Then, when I am thy captive, talk of chains".

233. *the strife*, between Fate and Chance (cf. 907–10); or between the rebellious angels and the Almighty (less probable).

234, 235. *the former*, to unthrone the King of Heaven; *the latter*, to regain our lost rights. *to hope*, to hope *for*, cf. *S. A.* 838, note. *argues*, shows, proves (Lat. *arguere*); so often in M. and Shak.; cf. *S. A.* 1193, "which argued me no foe"; *Romeo*, II. 3. 33.

241–3. See V. 161–3, and contrast VI. 744.

244. *sovran*, see G. *breathes*, is fragant with.

245. *ambrosial*, often used by M., as by Tennyson, of that which delights the sense of taste or of smell. Cf. 'ambrosia' = fragrance v. 57. Strictly ἀμβροσία was the food of the gods.

249. *pursue*, seek after, try to regain, i.e. "our state" (251).

254. Horace, *Epist.* I. 18. 107, *et mihi vivam | quod superest ævi.* Note the oxymorons in these lines (252–7.

255–7. It was a favourite thought with Milton that many men would rather have "Bondage with ease than strenuous liberty" (*S. A.* 271): i.e. would sacrifice their freedom to save the trouble of maintaining it. See XII. 220, note. Sallust, his favourite historian (*Letter* to Lord Henry de Bras), makes Æmilius Lepidus say—*accipite otium cum servitio...mihi potior visa est periculosa libertas quieto servitio.*

263–7. Cf. *Psalms* xviii. 11, 13, xcvii. 2, "Clouds and darkness are round about him".

270–3. See I. 670 *et seq.*

271. *Wants not*, does not lack.

273. *magnificence*, such as the palace described, I. 710 *et seq.*

274, 275. All existing things were supposed to consist of four 'elements' or constituent parts—*fire, air* water, earth; and in each 'element' dwelt certain Spirits or 'dæmons' peculiar to it, ruling it, and partaking of its nature. Cf. *Il Pen.* 93, 94, "those dæmons that are found In *fire, air*, flood, or underground". That these 'dæmons' were the fallen angels was a

common view; see *Appen.* pp. 144–47, and cf. Satan's address
to his followers, *P. R.* II. 121–4:

"Princes, Heaven's ancient Sons, ethereal Thrones;
Demonian spirits now, from the *element*
Each of his reign allotted, rightlier called
Powers of *fire, air,* water and earth beneath!"

When M. makes Mammon say that their 'torments' (i.e.
Hell's fires) may become their 'element', he clearly alludes to
these mediæval beliefs; cf. 217–19, 397–402.

277. *needs,* of necessity—genitive case of *need.* A survival of
the O.E. adverbial use of the genitive; cf. *willes,* willingly,
sothes, truly, *dæies and nightes,* day and night.

278. *sensible,* sense: adj. for noun, cf. 97.

281. *compose,* adjust, i.e. adapt ourselves to.

282. *where,* so First Ed.; Second Ed. *were.*

284. Cf. V. 872, 873, "as the sound of waters deep. Hoarse
murmur echoed to his words applause."

287. *now…lull,* and which (viz. the winds) now lull.

288. *o'erwatched,* tired with watching; cf. *S. A.* 405.

292. *field,* battle; see 768, I. 105, note.

294. I.e. the "two-handed" sword, "from the armoury of
God" (VI. 251, 321), with which in the great battle in Heaven
Michael laid low the rebellious angels and disabled Satan
himself (VI. 320–7). Not mentioned in either *Daniel* or
Revelation.

299, 300. In Scripture Beël-zebub=Baal-zebub, 'Lord of
Flies', is the Sun-god of the Philistines, i.e. a local manifesta-
tion of the great deity Baal (see I. 422), his chief oracle being at
Ekron, "where answers seem to have been obtained from the
hum and motions of flies" (Sayce, *Bible and the Monuments*). In
P. L. he ranks next to Satan (see I. 79–81, V. 671, note), and in
Marlowe's *Faustus,* VI. 92, Lucifer (i.e. Satan) speaks of him as
"my companion-prince in hell". Perhaps this notion that he
was one of the chief of the infernal powers was due to the
rendering of *Mat.* xii. 24, where the title "prince of the devils"
is really applied to Beel-zebu*l,* 'Lord of the Heavenly Height'.

301, 302. Scan *aspéct,* as often in M. and Shak.; cf. V. 733,
VI. 450. Newton quotes 2 *Hen. VI.* I. I. 75, "Brave peers of
England, pillars of the state ". *front,* brow, Lat. *frons*; cf. *Hamlet,*
III. 4. 56.

304. *counsel*; he is great as statesman, not as warrior.

305. *majestic,* qualifying 'face'.

306. *Atlantean,* worthy of Atlas, one of the Titans, who as a

punishment for making war on Zeus was condemned to bear
heaven on his shoulders. Cf. Spenser, sonnet to Lord Burleigh:
> "As the wide compasse of the firmament
> On Atlas mighty shoulders is upstayd."

"The myth seems to have arisen from the idea that lofty
mountains supported the heaven" (*Class. Dict.*).

309. *thus he spake*; and what he says sweeps on one side the
main arguments of the previous speakers. 'War', he urges,
recognising their true position, 'with the Almighty (such as
Moloch counsels), *that* is ridiculous: peace (such as Belial and
Mammon dream of), *that* is not to be hoped for: suffer we must
and shall, but suffering may be lightened by revenge—and that
of a subtler kind than Moloch proposes (105)'. The speech of
each deity is carefully differentiated, and consistent with his
character.

311, 312. *these titles*, see I. 737. *style*, title, appellation; cf.
2 *Hen. VI.* I. 3. 51, "a queen in title and in style".

313. *for so*; alluding to the applause which Mammon had
(284).

315. In the original eds. 'doubtless' has a semicolon before
and after, i.e. it is a parenthetic sarcasm: 'build up here an
empire—as is so *very* likely!' Some remove the second semicolon and read "doubtless while we dream" = 'while we dream
undisturbed by any doubt'.

324. "I am Alpha and Omega, the first and the last", *Rev.* i.
11; also chaps. xxi. 6, xxii. 13. Same reference v. 165. Cf.
Jonson, *Masque of Augurs*, "Jove is that one, whom first, midst,
last you call". *highth or depth*, Heaven or Hell.

327, 328. "That golden sceptre which thou didst reject
> Is now an iron rod to bruise and break
> Thy disobedience";

so Abdiel warns Satan, v. 886-8. In each case there is an
allusion to *Ps.* ii. 9, "Thou shalt break them with a rod of iron"
(repeated *Rev.* ii. 27). The distinction between iron typifying
hostility and gold typifying benevolence is part of the symbolism in which M. delights. Cf. *Lyc.* 110, 111, where St Peter
bears "two massy keys"—the golden admitting to Heaven, the
iron excluding. A rod of gold, 'the Rod of Equity', is among
the regalia of the English Crown.

those, his loyal subjects, the angels who had not rebelled with
Satan.

330. *determined*, made an end of us, i.e. crushed us. Cf. VI.
318, XI. 227. Shak. used 'determine' as an intrans. verb = 'to

end', cf. *Coriol.* III. 3. 43, "must all determine here?" and v. 3. 120.

332. *vouchsafed*; First Ed. *voutsafed*, as always; rightly retained by those who think that M. wished to avoid *ch* before *s* in 'vou*ch*safe'.

336. *to*, to the best of; cf. *Winter's Tale*, v. 2 182, "I will prove so [i.e. valiant] to my power", and *Coriolanus*, II. 1. 262.

337. *untamed*, not to be tamed. *reluctance*, resistance, see G.

341. *want*, be wanting.

345-51. See 830, l. 650-4, note. *fame* = Lat. *fama* in lit. sense 'report'; cf. I. 651, Bacon, *Essay* xv, "as if fames were the relics of seditions past", and again, "these fames are a sign of trouble".

351-3. This seems to me inconsistent with Raphael's account in bk. VII. The 'Argument' there tells us "that God, *after* the expelling of Satan and his Angels out of Heaven, declared his pleasure to create another world, and other creatures to dwell therein". And Raphael's words (180-91) appear to imply that this declaration came as news to the angelic host, i.e. had not been preceded by any similar intimation. How then could it have been known to Beëlzebub, one of the outcast?

352, 353. *by an oath*. Cf. v. 607, *Gen.* xxii. 16, "By myself have I sworn, saith the LORD", *Isai.* xlv. 23. *that shook*; cf. *Æn.* IX. 106, *et totum nutu tremefecit Olympum*—itself from Homer, *Il.* I. 530, μέγαν δ' ἐλέλιξεν Ὄλυμπον, and echoed by Dryden, *Alexander's Feast*, 35-7, "Assumes the god,...And seems to shake the spheres". Epic poetry has its conventions and formulas, handed down from Homer to Virgil, from Virgil to the Italian poets, and so forth.

367. *puny*, see G.

375. First Ed. has 'originals', which shews that 'original' = originator, parent (i.e. Adam). Cf. *Church Gov.*, "run questing up as high as Adam to fetch their original", *P. W.* II. 449, and *Midsummer N.D.* II. 1. 117 "We are their parents and original". Some explain it = 'earliest condition, primitive state'.

376-8. *advise*, consider; see G. *or to*, i.e. whether it is better to. *vain empires*, such as Mammon foreshadowed.

379, 380. *devised by Satan*, see I. 650-4.

382, 383. *confound*, utterly ruin. *one root*, Adam (I *Cor.* xv. 22).

384, 385. See *Appen.* p. 143 on "Satan's motives etc.", and cf. Raphael's warning that Satan would plot Adam's fall, "As a despite done against the Most High" (VI. 905, 906).

387. *States*, often used by Shak. of a body of representatives or parliament; cf. *Troilus*, IV. 5. 65, "hail, all you states of Greece", and 2 *Hen. IV.* v. 2. 142, "we will accite [summon] all our states". So here; cf. phrase 'estates of the realm', and *états* in French.

391. *synod*, meeting, assembly; cf. VI. 156, XI. 67; Gk. σύν + ὁδός.

397-402. In later times, according to tradition, some of the outcast angels do become 'Spirits of air', and dwell in "*mild seats*" of the middle region of air. See *Appen.* pp. 144-49.

404. *tempt*, try, essay, Lat. *temptare*.

406, 407. *obscure*, obscurity: "palpable obscure" = "palpable darkness", XII. 188, i.e. "darkness which may be *felt*", *Exod.* x. 21. Drayton had used the phrase "darkness palpable", and the *Preface* to the A. V. speaks of "thick and palpable clouds of darkness". Without doubt, the original of all these passages was *Exod.* x. 21 in the Vulgate—*tenebræ tam densæ ut palpari queant*. (From Newton.) Lat. *palpare* = to stroke, feel. *uncouth*, strange, see G.

409. *vast abrupt*, the gulf between Hell and the World.

arrive, arrive *at*, reach: "if our things here below arrive him where he is", *Martin Bucer*, P. W. III. 282; so *Julius Caesar*, I. 2. 110, "But ere we could arrive the point proposed". In Elizabethan E. this omission of the preposition with verbs of 'motion' is common (Abbott, *Shakespearian* Grammar, pp. 132, 133).

410. *The...isle*, i.e. the Universe of this World, hung (1051) in Chaos, which is a kind of "sea" (1011): hence the peculiar fitness of comparing Satan, as he journeys through Chaos, to a vessel making for its port (1041-4). See again III. 76.

412, 413. *senteries*, so original eds., and metre requires the form (no more irregular than *sentry*, a corruption of *sentinel*). Perhaps 'sentery' was due to the notion that it = Fr. *sentier*, a path, Lat. *semita*. *stations* = Lat. *stationes*, guards, pickets.

413. *had*, would have.

415. *Choice*, care in selecting by vote some one to send.

418. *suspense*, in suspense.

423. *astonished*, see G. *prime*, chief, Lat. *primi*.

425. *hardy*, bold. *proffer*, offer himself, volunteer.

427-9. *Appen.* p. 143. *unmoved*, calm, not 'astonished'.

430. With this speech cf. *P. R.* I. 44-105. The scenes are similar. In each case Satan undertakes a design from which his followers shrink—here against Mankind, there against Christ.

And there he reminds them how he alone faced the former danger, and argues that, having succeeded once, he will succeed again.

431. *demur*, hesitation.

432, 433. An echo of *Æn.* VI. 126–9, where the Sibyl tells Æneas that the descent into Avernus is easy: " But to return, and view the cheerful skies, In this the task and mighty labour lies " (Dryden). The slow monosyllabic rhythm and the alliteration seem intended by Milton to suggest the laborious effort of ascent.

434–7. See 643–8. *convex*; if we interpret it of the vaulted roof alone, then it should be 'concave' (cf. 635), Satan being *inside*; but perhaps *convex*=circle. Hell is a dungeon ringed round with "bounds" of flame (I. 61, 62); and when Satan says "*this* convex" he points not merely to the roof, but to the fires on all sides.

438. *the void profound*=Lucretius' *inane profundum*. For the adjective *profound* used as a noun ('depth, abyss') cf. 97, note.

439. *unessential Night*, i.e. having no substance or being. *essence*=Lat. *essentia* (from *esse*)=Gk. οὐσία (or τὸ ὄν, that which really exists). Night, he means, is a mere vacuity (932).

441. *abortive*, monstrous, because unnatural, i.e. born prematurely. He speaks of the gulf as though it were some monstrosity horrible through premature birth. Others say 'rendering abortive'.

443. *remains*, awaits; for the singular verb see I. 139, note.

448. *moment*, importance. Cf. "of great moment", *Hamlet*, III. I. 86; "of no moment", 3 *Henry VI.* I. 2. 22.

450. *Me*; purposely emphatic by position.

452. *refusing*, if I refuse: honours and dangers go together.

457. *intend*, consider; see G.

461. *deceive*, beguile; cf. Cowper, "to deceive the time, not waste it". So. Lat. *decipere*—e.g. in Horace's *dulci laborum decipitur sono*=is beguiled into forgetting his troubles (*Od.* II. 13. 38).

462. *mansion*, see I. 268.

467. *prevented*, anticipated, forestalled; see G.

468. *raised*, encouraged; agreeing with 'others'; cf. 521.

470. *erst*, before, cf. I. 360; A.S. *ǽrest*, superl. of *ǽr*, soon.

471. *opinion*, public opinion, reputation.

474. Cf. I. 274–8, and v. 705, 706.

478. *awful*, full of awe, respect; cf. *Nat. Ode*, 59, note.

483–5. i.e. "Let not bad men set much store by those casual acts of seeming nobleness to which glory or ambition may doubtless spur even the worst of them; for neither have that other class of evil beings...lost such virtue as this" (Masson).

485. *close*, secret—often in Shak. Cf. Cotgrave, "Secret: Secret inward, privie, close". *varnished with*, speciously hidden by.

488–95. This simile is typical of many in Milton: similes classical in manner, more like Virgil's than Shakespeare's. The peculiarity is that he works the simile out, in all its bearings, into a picture complete in itself but rather detached from the context. Cf. I. 768–75.

489. *while the North-wind sleeps* = Homer's ὄφρ' εὕδῃσι μένος Βορέαο (*Il.* v. 522), "that wind generally...dispersing clouds" (Newton).

490, 491. *element*, sky; see G. *landskip*, see G.

492. *If chance*, if it chances that; cf. "how chance?" *Comus*, 508.

495. *rings*, for the singular verb cf. 443.

501. Dr Bradshaw notes that the phrase 'to levy war' (see XI. 219), which Johnson censured, was a technical term found in legal documents and statutes. He cites from one of Barrow's *Sermons* (May 29, 1676), "those in the late times who, instead of praying for their sovereign,...did raise tumults, and levy war against him". Add Tennyson, *Queen Mary*, II. 1, "must we levy war against the Queen's Grace?" Commonly 'levy' is used—and was (cf. Shak. often)—of raising troops.

503. *to accord*, to agree among ourselves.

508. *Paramount*, lord, chief; see G.

512. *globe*, compact band—cf. *P. R.* IV. 581; Lat. *globus* is used similarly of a close mass of men. *Seraphim*; see G.

513. *emblazonry*, i.e. shields 'emblazoned' (see I. 538) or figured with designs. *horrent*, bristling (see 63 and I. 563, note).

514. Only the great angels had taken part in the council (I. 792–7); the others were awaiting its result. *session*, sitting, council.

515. *trumpet's*, see I. 754, note.

516. i.e. towards the four quarters of the compass; cf. III. 326, and see *Ezekiel* xxxvii. 9, "Come from the four winds, O breath, and breathe upon these slain".

517, 518. *alchymy*, the trumpets made of alchymy. Misunderstanding the use of 'alchymy' (see G.), Bentley proposed

'Orichalc'; Gk. ὀρείχαλκος, Lat. *orichalcum* (cf. *Æn.* XII. 87), yellow copper ore, and the brass made therefrom. *harald*, see I. 752.

522. *ranged*, assembled in ranks.

526. *entertain*, pass, while away; cf. *Argument*, "to entertain the time", a phrase used by Shak.; cf. *Lucrece*, 1361, "The weary time she cannot entertain", and *Sonnet* XXXIX. The picture of the angels variously employed recalls (? was inspired by) Virgil's description of the souls of the blessed in Elysium with their diversions, *Æn.* VI. 640 *et seq.*

528–32. These "heroic games" (IV. 551, a similar scene) are Milton's counterpart to the Trojan sports, *Æn.* V. 577 *et seq.*, and those of the Myrmidons, withheld from war, *Iliad* II. 773 *et seq.*: whence too Pope's mock-heroic contests in the *Dunciad* ii.

528. *sublime* = Lat. *sublimis* in the literal sense 'aloft', 'uplifted'; cf. *P. R.* IV. 542, "through the air sublime".

530. Two of the great festivals of Greece were the *Olympic* games held every fifth year at Olympia, a small plain of *Elis* (cf. next note); and the *Pythian* at Delphi in honour of Apollo (the Pythian god).

531, 532. "Part curb the foaming steed", XI. 643, i.e. in horse-races. *or shun*; alluding (cf. *Areopagitica*, *P. W.* II. 68) to Horace, *Od.* I. I. 4, *metaque fervidis evitata rotis*, i.e. in chariot-races. To the chariot-races at Olympia M. refers in his sixth *Elegy* 26 (*volat Eleo pulvere fuscus eques*) in the lines on Pindar. *brigads*, see I. 675.

533. Keightley and Masson think that the *Aurora Borealis* is meant. *to warn*; because considered omens.

534. Newton quotes I *Henry IV*. I. I. 10, "like the meteors of a *troubled* heaven".

535. *van*, vanguard; Fr. *avant-garde*.

536. *prick*, ride; see G. *couch*; see G.

537, 538. *feats*, see 124. *welkin*, sky; see G.

539. *Typhœan*, see I. 199.

540. *ride the air*; *Macbeth*, IV. I. 138; see 662, note.

542. *Alcides*, Hercules, grandson of Alcæus. The story, as commonly told, was: Hercules, returning to Trachis from Œchalia where he had killed Eurytus (cf. Ovid, *victor ab Œchalia*, *Met.* IX. 135), landed at Cenæum, the N.W. promontory of Eubœa, and sent Lichas, his companion, to Trachis to fetch a white robe wherein to sacrifice to Zeus; Deianira, his wife, sent instead a robe dipped in what she thought to be a love-potion that would make Hercules true to her: the potion

was a poison, and when Hercules put the robe on it ate into his flesh, and could not be removed: in his agony he hurled (i.e. from Cenæum) Lichas into the sea, and himself *afterwards* ascended Mt Œta in Thessaly, raised a pile of wood, and was burnt thereon. The story forms the subject of Sophocles' *Trachiniæ*; told also by Ovid, *Met.* IX, whom M. follows closely. There is a fine application of it in *S. A.* 1038, 1039 (see Pitt Press ed.), where an ill-matched wife is likened to "a cleaving curse" to her husband.

Œchalia, a town in Thessaly. First Ed. *Oealia*.

543. *envenomed*, because steeped by Deianira in the blood of the Centaur Nessus, whom Hercules had slain with a poisoned arrow. Cf. M. in *In Obitum Procancel.* 9, 10 (alluding to same story), *ferus Hercules | Nessi venenatus cruore.*

545. *Lichas*; see *The Merchant of Venice*, II. 1. 32–5.

546. *Euboic sea*, between Eubœa and the mainland.

546–55. Heywood says of the infernal angels, "in Musicke they are skill'd" (*Hierarchie*, p. 441). *enthrall*, enslave; see G.

552. *partial*, prejudiced—in favour of themselves.

554. *suspended*, held rapt, thrilled. *took*, enchanted; see G.

557. Cf. Scott's happy allusion—"others apart sat on a bench retired, and reasoned highly on the doctrines of crime" (describing the lawyers at the trial of Effie Dean, *Heart of Midlothian*).

558–69. Contrast *Com.* 476–80 ("How charming is divine Philosophy" etc.), and cf. *S. A.* 300 *et seq.*, *P. R.* IV. 286 *et seq.*, where Greek philosophies are sneered at.

559, 560. M. is inclined to ridicule the angels for discussing such subjects: yet himself could not resist the pleasure of discoursing on free-will and predestination, not only in *Christian Doct.* (*P. W.* IV. 43–77), but even in *P. L.*—cf. III. 96–128, v. 524–34.

564, 565. Referring, I doubt not, primarily to the Stoics, whose philosophy he condemns in *P. R.* IV. 300 *et seq.*: 'apathy' (Gk. ά-, not + παθεῖν, to suffer) signifying in their system insensibility to suffering, hence freedom from 'passion' (see I. 605) or feeling—i.e. a passionless existence, "contemning all", *P. R.* IV. 304.

568, 569. Horace, *Od.* I. 3. 9, *illi robur et æs triplex | circa pectus erat*, where *æs*, like 'steel' here, is figurative.

obdured, hardened; cf. VI. 785.

570. *gross*, dense, compact.

571, 572. *wide*, far and wide. *clime*, region; see I. 242.

575, 576. In the main this picture of the infernal rivers is modelled on the classics—cf. *Æneid* VI. But M. has added some details e.g. the making of four rivers unite in the burning lakes. Note that he refers to the meaning of each river's name. *baleful*, see G.

577. *Styx*; from στυγεῖν, to hate, abhor; chief river of nether world, round which it flowed "with *nine* (see 645) circling streams" (Dryden) = *noviens Styx interfusa* (*Æn.* VI. 439).

578. *Acheron* = ὁ ἄχεα ῥέων, 'the stream of woe'.

579, 580. *Cocytus*; Gk. κωκυτός, wailing, from κωκύειν, to wail. Cf. Fairfax IV. 8, "Swift Cocytus stay'd his murmur shrill".

580, 581. *Phlegethon*; φλεγέθων, flaming; also called 'Pyriphlegethon'; waves of fire (Gk. πῦρ), not water, flowing in its 'torrent'.

583. *Lethe*; Gk. λήθη, a forgetting. "A river in the lower world was called Lethe. The souls of the departed drank of this river, and thus forgot all they had said or done in the upper world" (*Class Dict.*). Cf. Fairfax xv. 17, "the *silent streams* of Lethe flood", and Dryden, *Æn.* VI. 957, "The gliding Lethe leads her *silent* flood", and 968, "In Lethe's lake they long *oblivion* taste". There is extant a copy of Browne's *Britannia's Pastorals* with MS. notes pronounced by some to be by Milton, and over against a description of this river are written the words, "They who drinke of Lethe never think of love or ye world".

589. *dire hail*; Horace's *jam satis...diræ grandinis*, *Od.* I. 2. I, 2.

591. I.e. ruin of some ancient building; cf. "pile high-built", *S. A.* 1069. *all else*, so original eds.

592, 593. Lake Serbonis (now dried up) lay on the coast of Lower Egypt, separated from the sea by a narrow strip of sand (Herod. III. 5); close to Mt Casius (παρ᾽ ἣν τὸ Κάσιον ὄρος τείνει, Herod. II. 6), but rather E. than W. of it as Milton implies. *Damiata*, now Damietta, on easternmost mouth of Nile (it has been identified with Pelusium). Cf. *Orlando Fur.* xv. 48, "Then went Alfonso to the banks of Nile, To Damyat a citie thereabout" (Harington); and Fairfax, *Tasso*, xv. 16, "[Passed] Damiata next, where they behold How to the sea his tribute Nilus pays". M. may have introduced the name because of its occurrence in these Italian poems.

594. Primarily from Diodorus Siculus (I. 30. 4), who says of the Σιρβωνὶς λίμνη—πολλοὶ τῶν ἀγνοούντων τὴν ἰδιότητα τοῦ τόπου μετὰ στρατευμάτων ὅλων ἠφανίσθησαν. How this happened,

Sandys' *Relation* shows: the Lake, he says (and he had been there), was "bordred on each side with hills of sand, which being borne into the water by the winds so thickened the same, as not by the eye to be distinguished from a part of the Continent: by means whereof whole armies have bin devoured. For the sands neere-hand seeming firme, a good way entred slid farther off, and left no way of returning, but with a lingring cruelty swallowed the ingaged: whereupon it was called *Barathrum*....Close to this standeth the mountaine Cassius (no other than a huge mole of sand)", p. 137. Seemingly, the only historical basis of this story is the fact that when Darius Ochus, the Persian, invaded Egypt he lost part of his troops in the lake.

594, 595. *parching*, used of drying, withering effect of cold (cf. *Lyc.* 13, "parching wind") or heat (cf. XII. 636). *frore*, frosty, see G. *cold...fire*; Newton aptly quotes *Ecclus.* xliii. 21, "The *cold* north wind...*burneth* the wilderness, and consumeth the grass *as fire*"; and Virgil, *Georgic* I. 93, *ne...frigus adurat*. The *r...r* sound may be meant to suggest shuddering.

596–603. "The idea of making the pains of Hell consist in cold as well as heat [i.e. by alternations] was current in the Middle Ages...it seems to have come from the Rabbin [Jewish commentators], for they make the torments of Gehenna to consist of fire and of frost and snow" (Keightley). Cf. Dante, *Inferno* III. 86, 87, where Charon says, "Woe to you, depraved spirits! I come to lead you...into the eternal darkness, into fire and ice" (Carlyle), and *Purg.* III. 31, 32, "To suffer torments both of heat and cold that Power ordains" (A. J. Butler). I find the idea worked out in Giles Fletcher's *Christ's Victory on Earth*, 22, and in the *Faust-book* (1587), where Mephistophiles describes Hell to Faustus in a passage closely resembling these lines: also, when Faustus is suffered to visit Hell, out of curiosity, he finds there "a most pleasant, clear and cold water; into the which many tormented souls sprang out of the fire to cool themselves, but being so freezing cold, they were constrained to return again into the fire, and thus wearied themselves and spent their endless torments out of one labyrinth into another, one while in heat, another while in cold", Thoms' *English Prose Romances*, III. 194, 212 (see *Appen.* p. 135). The notion was known to Shakespeare; see *Measure for Measure*, III. I. 121 *et seq.*

596, 597. *harpy-footed*, with feet like the talons of Harpies (hideous winged creatures, with hooked claws, *uncæ manus*—see *Æn.* III. 211–18, *P. R.* II. 403). *haled=hauled*, dragged; in

First Ed. *hail'd*, i.e. summoned—a possible reading. *revolutions*, i.e. of time.

600. *starve*, afflict, perish with cold. O.E. *steruen*=to perish, die.

604. *sound*, strait; akin to *swim*, since A.S. *sund*='a strait of the sea that could be *swum* across'; cf. *Com.* 115, "sounds and seas".

611. *Medusa*, one of the three Gorgons (see 628); her hair being changed into serpents by Athene (cf. "snaky-headed Gorgon", *Com.* 447), her appearance became so terrible that all who looked at her were changed into stone.

612–14. According to legend, Tantalus, for divulging the secrets of Zeus, was "punished in the lower world by being afflicted with a raging thirst, and at the same time placed in the midst of a lake, the waters of which always receded from him as soon as he attempted to drink them" (*Class. Dict.*). See allusion *S. A.* 500, 501.

613. *wight*, person, being; a word (belonging more to popular ballad poetry) that Shak. seems to ridicule; cf. Pistol's use of it, *Merry Wives*, I. 3. 23, 40, *Hen. V.* II. I. 64. Really same as *whit* (where *h* is misplaced). A.S. *wiht*=creature.

615, 616. See I. 733, note.

617. *first*, for the first time.

620. *Alp*, see G.

621. The number of monosyllables suggests variety i.e. of scenery.

625. *prodigious*, unnatural, monstrous.

628. Cf. x. 524 (for rhythm), *Com.* 517 ("dire Chimeras and enchanted isles"). Hesiod mentions three *Gorgons*, daughters of Phorcys, monsters with wings and brazen claws, and hissing serpents, instead of hair, on their heads (see 611). The Lernean *Hydra* was a serpent with nine heads that ravaged the country near Argos; slain by Hercules (his 2nd 'labour'). In *Of Reformation* M. has the phrase "a continual hydra of mischief and molestation", *P. W.* II. 411. The *Chimera* was a fire-breathing monster, πρόσθε λέων, ὄπιθεν δὲ δράκων, μέσση δὲ χίμαιρα (*Il.* VI. 181), i.e. part lion, part dragon, part goat. Perhaps M. mentions these three monsters together because Virgil (*Æn.* VI. 287–9) and Tasso (Fairfax IV. 5) had done the same.

634. *shaves*, skims; cf. *radit iter liquidum*, Virg. *Æn.* V. 217.

635. *concave*, roof, see 434. Bentley omitted everything from "towering" to "fiend" 643 (inclusive), as "silly and pedantical".

Note how fully the simile is worked out, beyond the precise point of comparison (see 488, note): how also the proper names convey an impression of mysterious remoteness (see I. 582).

637–40. *hangs*, i.e. seems to the distant spectator to be in the clouds. *equinoctial winds*, "the trade-winds, which blow from east to west at the time of the equinoxes" (Bradshaw); afterwards (640) M. transfers 'trading' from the wind to the sea. *close*, i.e. together, so as to form, seen from far, a single object—like the single figure of Satan. M. had in his mind's eye a fleet of East Indiamen (Newton).

638. *Bengala*, a relic of the old form *Bangálá* = Bengal. In Hexham's ed. of *Mercator's Atlas* the bay of Bengal is marked 'Golfo di *Bengala*' in the map of Asia. Some of our earliest trading-settlements were along the Bengal coast (cf. 2, note).

639. *Ternate and Tidore*, two of the Moluccas or '*Spice* Islands' in the Malay Archipelago, close together. Hexham describes the 'Molluccoes' as "famous throughout the world, in regard of the abundance of all sorts of sweete *spices*, but especially for the Cloues which come from them... *Tidor* and *Ternate* are the principallest" (II. 423, 424).

640. *they*, the ships. *flood*; used similarly of the sea by Shakespeare, e.g. in *A Midsummer-Night's Dream*, II. I. 127, "Marking the embarked traders on the flood".

641. There seems to be an error here on Milton's part. A glance at the map (but let us remember that *he* could not see one) will show that he uses "the wide Ethiopian" (i.e. sea) = the Indian Ocean—that is, the ocean *east* of Africa. But was the term so applied? In Hexham's *Mercator*, in the map of Africa, I find the name *Oceanus Æthiopicus* given to the sea *west* of Africa—what we call the 'South Atlantic'; and in the letterpress the terms 'Æthiopicke Ocean', 'Æthiopicke Sea', are always used so. The same is the case in Heylin's map of Africa; while, speaking of the Atlantic, he says, "some parts hereof, which wash the *Westerne* Shores of *Œthiopia Inferior*, be called the Œthiopick Ocean" (*Cosmog*. Lib. IV. 71). Both authorities therefore are against Milton, and one can scarce do else than conclude that the title 'Ethiopian' really belonged to the South Atlantic (or *western* sea), not to the Indian Ocean (or *eastern* = *Oceanus Orientalis* in *Mercator*). In maps of the 17th century Ethiopia is the name of a region of Southern Africa: hence 'Ethiopian' as a title of the sea that washed its—western?—coasts.

641, 642. *Cape*, of Good Hope. *stemming*, pressing forward, i.e. breasting the waves; cf. *Julius C.* I. 2. 109. *the pole*, the South Pole.

643–8. Cf. 434–7. Nine is a sacred number; see 577, note, and I. 50. *impaled*, encircled; cf. *paling, pale*. The double alliteration (*i*...*i* and *p*...*p*) has a fine effect of emphasis.

648. The basis of the allegory of Sin and Death lies—appropriately—in Scripture: "Then when lust hath conceived, it bringeth forth sin: and sin, when it is finished, bringeth forth death", *James* i. 15. In IX. 12 Death is called the 'shadow' of Sin, and in the poem we never meet with them apart. How far M. means us to read an allegorical meaning into his description is hard to say. I cannot, e.g., think with Keightley that the "yelling monsters" (795) should be regarded as typifying "the mental torments that are the consequence of sin". To me they seem to be introduced—without any allegorical intent whatever —partly because they intensify the element of mere horror, partly for the sake of the literary parallel. On the other hand, the "mortal sting" is plainly symbolical; cf. I *Cor.* xv. 56. A strain therefore of allegory *is* present: individual judgment must say where.

650. *the one*. Milton's figure of Sin is own sister to Spenser's Error (*F. Q.* I. I. 14, 15) and Phineas Fletcher's Hamartia or Sin (*Purple I.* XII. 27—cf. also his *Apollyonists*, 1627, I. 10 *et seq.*): their common origin being the classical accounts of Scylla, notably Ovid's (*Met.* XIV) and Virgil's (*Æn.* III. 424 *et seq.*). It is therefore as a 'study' in a familiar style, not as a fresh creation, that the picture should be viewed: comparison it challenges—and bears, originality it does not claim. So with his figure of Death (see 666, note).

651, 652. So Hesiod describes Echidna, *Theogony* 298.

voluminous; perhaps with the literal sense 'in rolls or folds' (Lat. *volumen*, from *volvere*, to roll); cf. Pope, *Windsor Forest*, "The silver eel in shining volumes roll'd".

654–6. *cry*, pack; see G. *Cerberean*, as of Cerberus, the many-headed dog that guarded the entrance to Hades. *list*, wished, chose.

659–61. According to the legend, Circe threw magic herbs into the waters where Scylla bathed, so that she was changed in the way M. implies. *abhorred*, to be abhorred. *Calabria*, in South Italy. *Trinacria*, Sicily, so called from its triangular shape.

662. *the night-hag*; probably Hecate, goddess of sorcery, is meant; cf. *Macbeth*, III. 5 (from which M. quotes in *Comus*, 1017),

especially l. 20, where Hecate says, "I am for the air", meaning that she will "ride through the air". See *Comus*, 135.

called, i.e. invoked to take part in rites; cf. *Macbeth*, III. 5. 8 and 34 ("Hark! I am call'd").

664. *infant blood*; alluding to an ancient superstition. When the witches in Jonson's *Masque of Queens* assemble and relate what they have been doing, one says: "Under a cradle I did creep, By day; and when the child was asleep, At night I sucked the breath"; whereto the next: "I had a dagger: what did I with that? Killed an infant." In the footnote Jonson adds, "Their killing of infants is common...Sprenger reports that a witch confessed to have killed above forty infants...which she had offered to the devil"; and then he cites authorities, e.g. Horace, *Epod.* v and Lucan, *Phars.* VI. Cf., perhaps, *Macbeth*, IV. I. 30. *to dance*, like the witches in *Macbeth*; cf. IV. I. 132, stage-direction, "The Witches dance, and then vanish, with Hecate". So Jonson makes his witches, in the midst of their rites, fall "into a sudden magical dance"—commenting that this is in accordance with tradition (*Masque of Queens*). Upon the significance of the custom, see Tylor's *Primitive Culture*, II. 133.

665. *Lapland* was traditionally a home of witchcraft; cf. Burton's *Anatomy*, I. II. 1, 2 ("Digression of Spirits"), and Shak., *Comedy of E.* IV. 3. 11, "Lapland sorcerers". Heylin calls the Laplanders "great sorcerers" (*Cosmog.* II. 122). Their chief instrument of divination was an oval cylinder or drum figured with various designs, notably of the moon and heavenly bodies. See "Regnard's Journey to Lapland" (1681), which contains a full account of the 'sorcerers' and their incantations; also the narrative of Leems (1767)—on the "Magic Arts of the Laplanders" (both in Pinkerton's *Voyages*, 1808, vol. I).

665, 666. The belief that the moon (see l. 785, 786, note) and heavenly bodies are affected by magic is very old and widespread. Cf. Pliny. *N. H.* II. xii. 1, "As for the Moone, mortall men imagine that by Magicke sorcerie, and charms, she is inchaunted" (Holland I. 9). The superstition has two main aspects: (i) the moon may be 'drawn down'; cf. *deducere lunam*, Virg. *Ecl.* VIII. 69, *trahere lunam*, Ovid, *Met.* VII. 197—with Horace, *Epod.* v. 45, 46, XVII. 57, 58, Martial, *Ep.* IX. 30. So in Marlowe's *Faustus*, III. 38, the Doctor claims that Mephistophiles must do "whatever Faustus shall command, Be it to make the moon drop from her sphere". See also next note. (ii) The moon may be 'eclipsed'—as here—i.e. made to hide her light;

of. Greene's *Friar Bacon*, II. 48, where Bacon says that he can "dim fair Luna to a dark eclipse" (with XI. 14–16). So Fairfax IX. 15, "The moon and stars for fear of sprites were fled", and XIII. 9, "At those strange speeches [incantations]...The feeble moon her silver beams retires".

labouring; cf. Cowper (translating Milton's Italian sonnet to Diodati), "And *from her sphere draw down* the *labouring* moon". So Lat. *labores* = eclipse, *laborare*, to suffer eclipse. Cf. Virg. G. II. 478, *defectus solis varios, lunæque labores*.

666. *the other*, see 650, note. Joseph Warton thought that M. owed the "person of Death" to the θάνατος of Eurip. *Alcestis*. But Death as a personified figure had been described by Spenser (*F. Q.* VII. 7. 46), and introduced (as Todd noted) in 'Morality' and early Elizabethan plays. I daresay too that a similar allegorical presentment might be found in some popular *Book of Emblems*, or in the famous wood-cuts, *The Dance of Death* (1538). In any case we must remember that the tendency to personify (fostered by the very important influence of the Masque) was a characteristic of early 17th century poetry.

670. Cf. Homer's ἐρεμνῇ νυκτὶ ἐοικώς, *Od.* XI. 605 (Newton).

672. The 'dart' of Death, a symbol of the force by which humanity is laid low, is mentioned, XI. 491. *what seemed*; purposely vague—the more effective (cf. IV. 990). In his fine criticism of this passage Coleridge notes how the abstract vagueness of such description appeals to the imagination with a subtle force which concrete, more clearly defined, imagery would lack altogether.

673. *kingly crown*; *Job* xviii. 14, *Rev.* vi. 2.

677. *admired*, wondered; see G.

678, 679. Strictly, the construction includes "God and his Son" among "created things"—but the sense is clear.

686, 687. *taste*, i.e. its effects.

688. *Goblin*, demon, evil spirit; see G.

692, 693. See *Rev.* xii. 4, and cf. v. 710 ("Drew after him the third part of Heaven's host"), VI. 156. In IX. 141, 142 Satan boasts that his followers were "well-nigh half" the angels. Their number was a point of dispute among the School-men. *conjured*, see G.

695. *waste*, spend, pass; cf. *The Tempest*, v. 302.

701. Cf. I *Kings* xii. 11, "I will chastise you with scorpions".

whip of scorpions, a metaphor for a severe scourge.

706. *deform* = Lat. *deformis*, hideous, unsightly.

706–11. Cf. IV. 985 *et seq*. (Satan's meeting with Gabriel).

708. The comparison of a warrior clad in armour to a comet is at least as old as the *Æneid* (X. 272, 273), and is finely employed by Tasso. The vast scale of the simile here conveys a profound impression of Satan's majesty.

709. *Ophiuchus*, a constellation of the northern (cf. "arctic") hemisphere, consisting of some 80 stars and extending about forty degrees in length: lit. 'the Serpent-holder', from Gk. ὄφις a snake and ἔχειν; Lat. *Anguitenens* or *Serpentarius*; cf. Heywood's *Hierarchie*, "The Serpentarius (Ophiuchus who Is also call'd) the Astrologians show To be a young man rounded with a snake, Stucke full of starry lights" (p. 124). I find an apt illustration of the whole passage in Henry More's *Song of the Soul* (Cambridge ed. 1647, p. 210):

"Ye flaming comets wandering on high,
And new-fixt starres found in that Circle blue,
The one espide in glittering Cassiopie,
The other near to Ophiuchus high."

710, 711. The appearance of a comet was traditionally held an omen—generally of disaster. Cf. a passage in *Batman vppon Bartholome* (1582), VIII. 32, curiously like this: "*Cometa* is a starre beclipped with burning gleames...and is sodeinly bred and betokeneth changing of kings, and is a token of *pestilence or of war*...and they spread their beames toward the *North*" (= "arctic sky"). *horrid hair*, i.e. the tail of the *comet* (= κομήτης, long-haired, from κόμη, hair). Cf. I *Hen. VI*. I. I. 2, 3, "Comets, importing change of times and states, Brandish your crystal tresses in the sky"; and Drummond, "Comets' locks, portending harm and wrath", *Poems*, 1856 ed., p. 239.

711. Cf. the encounter of Michael and Satan in the battle in Heaven, compared to the clash of two planets, VI. 310–19.

715, 716. Cf. Dryden, "Lightning and thunder (*heaven's artillery*) As harbingers before th' Almighty fly". But the phrase was common, due perhaps to Juvenal XIII. 33. *Caspian*; chosen as typical in poets of a tempestuous region; cf. Fairfax, *Tasso* VI. 38.

717. *a space*, a short while. *the signal*; a metaphor from trumpets sounding a charge.

719. *so*, thus; completing the simile; cf. 947, I. 209, 311, 775 *that*, so that; a constant use in M. Cf. *The Tempest*, I. 2. 370, 371:

"I'll make thee roar,
That beasts shall tremble at thy din."

721, 722. *foe*, i.e. Christ. See 1 *Cor.* xv. 26, *Heb.* ii. 14.

730. *and know'st*, though knowing; in original eds. not a question.

739. *spares to*, refrains from; cf. Lat. *parcere* followed by infinitive. So M. in prose; cf. *Of Reformation*, "neither doth the author spare to record", *P. W.* II. 411.

746. Phineas Fletcher in his *Apollyonists* has the line, "The *Porter* to th' infernall gate is *Sin*".

755–8. As Athene sprang from the head of Zeus.

772. *pitch*, height; also used of depth.

787–9. Cf. Virgil, *Georgic* IV. 525–7 (with Pope's imitation, *St Cecilia's Day*, VI), where the river-banks re-echo the name 'Eurydice'; also Tennyson's *Merlin and Vivien* (end).

795. See 648, note (on the use of allegory here).

803. I.e. on the opposite side of the gate—see 649.

809. So Satan recognises Fate as the highest power (I. 116, note).

813. To *temper* metal is to harden it by cooling after it has been heated; cf. I. 285, VI. 322. *mortal dint*, deadly blow.

815. *lore*, lesson, what he had to learn (*lore* and *learn* cognate). Note the change in his tone; contrast 817, 818 with 744, 755. When in bk. IX. Eve tells (659–63) Satan that she may not touch the forbidden fruit under pain of death, Satan affects (695) not to know what death is. He is 'the father of lies'.

818. *pledge*; cf. the use of Lat. *pignus*.

823. Cf. VI. 877, "Hell...the house of woe and pain".

825. *pretences*, claims—or designs, ambitions; cf. VI. 421.

827. *uncouth*; see G.

829, 830. *unfounded*, bottomless, lit. 'having no base' (Lat. *fundus*). *quest*, search (Lat. *quærere*). *foretold*; see 345–53.

832, 833. Contrast 1048. *purlieus*; see G.

836, 837. *surcharged*, overfull. *broils*, turmoils; Fr. *brouiller*.

839–44. Cf. X. 397–409, where after the Temptation Satan bids Sin and Death make Mankind their prey and the Earth their possession—"There dwell, and reign in bliss", 399.

842. *buxom*, yielding; see G. Cf. V. 270, "winnows the buxom air", and *The Faerie Queene*, I. 11. 37, "scourge the buxome aire". The phrase is a reminiscence, as Keightley noted, of Horace's *pete cedentem* ['yielding'] *aera disco* (*Sat.* II. 2. 13). *embalmed*, made fragrant; cf. *balmy*=fragrant, from *balm*= aromatic resin or oil.

847. *maw*, stomach, Germ. *magen*; rather of animals than men.

855. *might*; 3rd ed. *wight* (from 613?).

868. Homer's θεοὶ ῥεῖα ζώοντες, *Il.* VI. 138; cf. *Com.* 2–6, and Tennyson, *Œnone*:

> "the Gods who have attain'd
> Rest in a happy place and quiet seats
> Above the thunder, with undying bliss."

869. As the Son sits at the right hand of the Father (v. 606, VI. 892); profane sarcasm, I suppose, is intended.

874. *portcullis*, see G.

883, 884. That Sin cannot close the gates is symbolical.

886. *that*, so that; cf. 719.

889. *redounding*, in clouds, volleys; Lat. *redundare*, to overflow.

890. In this picture of Chaos, to be compared with Ovid's, *Met.* I. 5–20, Milton labours (as Masson notes) to convey to the reader an impression of the utter confusion of the scene described: heaping image on image, idea on idea, by which the imagination may be baffled, and the mind bewildered with an insistent sense of the inconceivable. Take e.g. lines 892–4: each successive notion eludes the fancy. And the rhythm heightens the effect. It is to this part of *P. L.* that M. alludes in III. 16, 18, "Through utter and through *middle* darkness borne,... I sung of Chaos and eternal night": where I interpret "utter"=the darkness of Hell, as in I. 72, V. 614, and "middle"=that of Chaos, between Hell and Heaven.

891. "One would think the deep to be hoary", *Job* xli. 32.

895, 896. *Nature*, the created Universe. *anarchy*, see 993, note.

898. The four 'elements' are meant; see 274, note, III. 714, 715 (closely parallel); and cf. Dryden, *St Cecilia's Day*, 1–10:

> "From harmony, from heav'nly harmony
> This universal *frame* [cf. 924] began.
> When Nature underneath a heap
> Of *jarring atoms* lay,
> And could not heave her head,
> The tuneful voice was heard from high:
> Arise, ye more than dead.
> Then *cold and hot and moist and dry*
> In order to their stations leap,
> And Musick's pow'r obey."

900. *embryon*, embryo; the common form in Elizabethan E.

903, 904. *unnumbered*, innumerable; see 23, note. *Barca*... *Cyrene*, the chief cities of Cyrenaica in northern Africa, a region often treated as typical of sand. Cf. Fairfax XVII. 5, "From Syria's coasts as far as Cirene sands", and the *Taming of a Shrew* (not Shakespeare's), "hew'd thee smaller than the Libian sandes".

905, 906. *levied*, raised (Fr. *lever*), but also with the notion 'to levy troops'—cf. "*warring* winds"; it qualifies "sands". *poise*, give weight to (Fr. *peser*); dependent, like "to side", on "levied". *their wings*, i.e. of the winds. *lighter*, which would be too light but for the sand.

906, 907. I.e. the element, or 'champion', to whom for the moment most atoms cling, is victor. *umpire*, as judge; see G.

911. As Nature, i.e. the Universe, was born out of Chaos (= "this Abyss"), so may she at last fall back again into Chaos. He is varying an old thought, that all things proceed from Nature and, perishing, pass back into Nature. Cf. *Romeo*, II. 3. 9, 10, "The earth that's nature's mother is her tomb; What is her burying *grave* that is her *womb*"; and Tennyson, *Lucretius*, "the womb and tomb of all, Great Nature" (from Lucret. V. 260, *omniparens, eadem rerum commune sepulcrum*).

912. Again the 'elements' are meant: "sea" = water, of. V. 416.

918, 919. i.e. standing looked. *frith*, channel, estuary; same as *firth* (metathesis of *r* is common); akin to *ford, fiord, ferry*.

920. *pealed*, deafened, dinned; cf. *S. A.* 235.

921, 922. Cf. Virgil's *parvis componere magna solebam, Ecl.* I. 24; so VI. 310, 311, X. 306, *P. R.* IV. 563. *Bellona*, goddess of war.

923. *engines*; probably cannon are meant; see G.

924. *frame*, fabric, structure; see G.

927. *vans*, wings, Ital. *vanni*; see G.

933. *pennons*, i.e. pinions, Lat. *pennæ*. *plumb*, see G.

937. *Instinct*, filled, charged with. *nitre*, saltpetre.

938, 939. *stayed*, having been stopped. *Syrtis*, see G.

940. *foundered*, sunk; see G. *fares*, journeys; see G.

941. *consistence*, substance or mixture, of sea and land.

943–7. Cf. Herod. III. 116, "The northern parts of Europe are very much richer in gold than any other region: but how it is procured I have no certain knowledge. The story runs, that the one-eyed Arimaspi purloin it from the griffins" (Rawlinson); and IV. 13, 27, where he speaks of "the gold-guarding (χρυσοφύλακες) griffins". Pliny (*N. H.* VII. 1) says that these Arimaspi live near the Scythians, "toward the pole Arkticke", and that they "maintaine warre ordinarily about the mettall mines of gold, especially with griffons, a kind of wild beasts that flie, and use to fetch gold out of the veines of those mines: which savage beasts strive as eagerly to keepe and hold those golden mines, as the Arimaspians to disseize them thereof, and to get away the gold from them" (Holland, I. 154). See Lucan, *Pharsal.* III. 280, VII. 756. The legend, which Sir Thomas Browne places among his *Vulgar Errors*, III. xi, may have had some connection with the fact that gold is found in the Ural mountains near which the Arimaspi were thought to dwell.

943. *gryphon*, a mythic monster; "sum men seyn that thei han the body upward as an eagle, and benethe as a lyoune.... But a griffoun hathe the body more gret, and is more strong thanne viij. lyouns, and more gret and stongere than an c (i.e. 100) egles, suche as we han amonges us"—Sir John Mandeville, who knew a country where the 'griffoun' was quite common. Jonson makes it a type of "swiftness and strength", *Masque of Queens*. See G.

945. *Arimaspian*; Herod. (IV. 27) interprets Greek Ἀριμασπός = μουνόφθαλμος, as coming from two Scythian words—ἄριμα = ἕν, 'one', and σποῦ = ὀφθαλμός, 'eye'. Rawlinson (III. 192) says that ἄριμα = ϝάριμα, and may be cognate with πρῶτος, *primus, first*: σποῦ being cognate with Lat. *speculor, specto* etc.—from root *spic* or *spec*, 'to see'.

948. *dense, or rare*, i.e. matter now thick, packed close—now thin; 'dense', or 'condense' (VI. 353), and 'rare' are exact opposites.

951. *hubbub*, see G.

958, 959. I.e. the nearest way to the point where darkness borders on light. There should be no comma after "lies".

959–67. This picture of the palace of Chaos is as conventional and classical as that of Sin (650, note). Cf. the 'cave of Death', thronged with personified 'Shapes' of evil and disease (XI. 469–93); or the abode of Murder, on whom attend such abstractions as *Timor, Dolus, Furor* (*In Quintum Nov.* 138–54). So Spenser describes the palace of Pluto: Payne and Strife at his side: Revenge, Treason, Hate hard by: Care guarding the door (*F. Q.* II. 7. 21–5). Such passages owe their similarity to their common origin, viz. Virgil's account of the realm of Pluto, *Æn.* VI. 273–81. Of ll. 959–63 Pope has a most felicitous parody in the *Dunciad* IV. (*ad fin.*); see also canto I, where he makes Dulness the "Daughter of Chaos and eternal Night".

960, 961. *pavilion*, see G. *wasteful deep*, again VI. 862. *wide...* *wasteful* (= vast, desolate), Milton's favourite form of alliteration. Cf. *Nat. Ode* 51, 64, *Arc.* 47, *Lyc.* 13, and compounds like 'wide-wasting' VI. 253, XI. 487, 'wide-waving' XI. 121, 'wide-watered' *Il Pen.* 75.

962. In Eurip. *Ion*, 1150 μελάμπεπλος is said of night.

964. *Orcus, Ades*; Lat. and Greek names of Pluto, god of Hell.

964, 965. *Name of Demogorgon* = Demogorgon himself; a Latinism. *Demogorgon*, a deity supposed to be alluded to by Lucan, *Pharsal.* VI. 744, and said to be first mentioned by name by Lactantius (fourth cent. A.D.): also to be mentioned by Italian writers, Boccaccio, Boiardo, Tasso, and Ariosto. Be all this as it may, Demogorgon was certainly a demon very much 'dreaded'. Spenser makes him the lord of Chaos—"Downe in the bottome of the deepe Abysse", *Faerie Q.* IV. 2. 47; Marlowe recognizes him as co-ruler with Beelzebub of the nether world, *Faustus*, III. 18; Greene speaks of "Demogorgon, master of the fates", *Friar Bacon* XI. 110, and "Demogorgon, ruler of the fates", *Orlando Fur.*; and he is an important character in Shelley's *Prometheus Unbound*. Apparently too he is identical with the "Gorgon prince of darkness and dead night" at the sound of whose *name* "Cocytus quakes and Styx is put to flight" (*F. Q.* I. I. 37). The name has been considered a corruption of δημιουργός; it is at least noticeable that Demogorgon became the patron of alchemists.

966. *all embroiled*, mixed in turmoil together; cf. 837.

967. "A thousand busy tongues the goddess bears"—Pope describing Fame (*Temple of Fame*).

972. *secrets*; perhaps 'secret places', Lat. *secreta*, as in 891 (Newton).

977. *confine with*, border on; Lat. *cum*+*finis*, a boundary.

983–6. Cf. 665–7, where Adam tells Eve that the stars shine, "Lest total darkness should by night regain Her *old possession*".

989. *incomposed*, disturbed, *dis*composed (Lat. *incompositus*).

993–8. "Nine days they fell; confounded Chaos roared,
    And felt tenfold confusion in their fall
    Through his wild *anarchy* [cf. 896]; so huge a rout
    Encumbered him with ruin" (VI. 871–4).

1001–5. *Appendix*, p. 134.

1001. *our*, so original eds.; changed by some to *your*. The point of *our* seems to me to be that Chaos thereby proclaims himself an ally with Satan against their common foe—their cause is the same.

1004, 1005. *Heaven*, the sky of this world. *chain*, see 1051.

1006. *Heaven*; here the Empyrean is meant.

1007–9. Chaos, we see, directs Satan's course, as he had been asked (980), and wishes him good speed. Yet when Satan, after the Temptation, descends to Hell and announces to his followers the result of his mission (X. 460 *et seq.*), he pretends that Chaos had "fiercely opposed" (478) his journey: his object being to exalt himself in their eyes by exaggerating the dangers overcome. Herein are revealed the two great aspects of his character— proud self-esteem (see *Appen.* p. 142), and duplicity.

1011. In XI. 750 M. likens the waters left by the Flood to a "sea without shore"—imitating Ovid, *Met.* I. 292, *deerant quoque litora ponto*. So Thomson, describing the Deluge, "A shoreless ocean tumbled round the globe", *Spring*.

1017, 1018. *Argo*, the vessel in which Jason and the 50 Argonauts sailed to Aea (afterwards called Colchis) to fetch the golden fleece. *Bosporus*, the Thracian Bosporus, now Straits of Constantinople; connecting the Propontis (Sea of Marmara) with the Pontus Euxinus (Black Sea). At its eastern entrance, i.e. where it opens into the Black Sea, stood two rocks, one on either side, the *Symplegades*, so called (from Gk συν + πλήσσειν, to strike), because when a ship was passing through they clashed together and crushed it. By the advice of the seer Phineus and the help of Hera, the Argonauts managed to pass, and thenceforth the rocks were fixed motionless. Juvenal calls them *concurrentia saxa* (*Sat.* XV. 19), i.e. 'justling' (see G.).

1019, 1020. *Scylla* and *Charybdis* (660) were two rocks, close together, in the Straits of Messina between Italy and Sicily. The currents or 'whirlpools' were so strong that sailors seeking to avoid the one rock were generally driven on the other: whence the proverbial line, from the *Alexandreis* of Philip Gualtier, *incidis in Scyllam cupiens vitare Charybdim. larboard*, the left side of a ship; Ulysses, by steering to the left, nearer to Scylla, thus avoided Charybdis on his right.

1028. *a bridge*, described X. 293 *et seq.* See *Appen.* p. 135.

1032, 1033. For the thought that Guardian Angels watch over men, see *Com.* 219, 220, 455–69, *S. A.* 1431 (Pitt Press note), and *Christian Doct.* IX, where he deals with the ministry on earth of Angels.

1034. Cf. again IX. 107, "precious beams of sacred influence" (said of the stars), and 192, "when as sacred light began to dawn". *sacred*, "since God is light", III. 3. *influence*, see G.

1042–4. *wafts*, see G. *holds*, makes for; he is thinking of Lat. *tenere*, which implies, however, reaching a destination (*portum, terram etc.*). Cf. Ovid, *Heroides* XVIII. 198, *et teneant portus naufraga membra tuos*.

1046. *weighs*, balances.

1048. *undetermined*, qualifying 'heaven'. "Its extent was such that from the portion that was seen the eye could not determine whether its margin was straight or curved" (Keightley). See X. 381.

1051. See *Appen.* p. 134. *golden chain*; alluding to Homer's story of the golden chain of Zeus, suspended from Heaven, whereby he can draw up the gods, and the earth and sea, and the whole universe, though they cannot draw him down (*Il.* VIII. 18–27). Cf. Bacon, *Advancement of Learn.* III. 2, "that excellent and divine fable of the Golden Chain", *illustris illa et divina de aurea catena fabula*; and Chapman, *Shadow of Night,* "The golden chain of Homer's high device". Plato (*Theaetetus* 153 C) interprets it of the Sun. It is curious to note how poets apply the story. Dryden, in his character of "The Good Parson", says, "For, letting down the golden chain from high, He drew his audience upward to the sky". Pope, speaking of the order and design in nature, says, "Is the great chain that draws all to agree, And drawn supports, upheld by God or thee?" (*Essay on Man* I. 33, 34). Jonson writes of marriage, "Such was the golden chain let down from heaven" (*Masque of Hymen*— see his note); and Tennyson of prayer, "For so the whole round earth is every way Bound by gold chains about the feet of God" (*Morte D'Arthur*).

1052, 1053. I.e. the Universe compared to the Empyrean looked as small as some minor star which being close to the moon's superior light seems insignificant. Cf. Tennyson, *Queen Mary*, V. 1:

> "a candle in the sun
> Is all but smoke—a star beside the moon
> Is all but lost."

pendent world, see 180, note.

APPENDIX

A

THE COSMOLOGY OF *PARADISE LOST*

PARTS of *Paradise Lost* are not easily understood without some knowledge of Milton's conception of the Universe. I shall attempt therefore to set forth some of the main aspects of his cosmology: to explain in fact, what he means by constantly recurrent terms such as 'Empyrean', 'Chaos', 'Spheres', and the like.

It is in Book V that he carries us back farthest in respect of time. The events described by Raphael (from line 563, onwards) precede not only the Creation of the World, but also the expulsion of the rebels from Heaven. And at this era, when the seeds of discord are being sown, we hear of two divisions of Space —Heaven and Chaos (V. 577, 578): Heaven lying above Chaos.

In Book VI the contest foreshadowed in Book V has begun. Now a third region is mentioned—Hell (VI. 53–5): a gloomy region carved out of the nethermost depths of Chaos. Its remoteness from Heaven may be inferred from I. 73, 74. Milton's working hypothesis, then—his general conception of space and its partitionment prior to the Creation—may be expressed roughly thus: above,[1] Heaven; beneath, Hell; between, a great gulf, Chaos.

Let us see what he has to say concerning each.

Heaven, or the Empyrean,[2] is the abode of the Deity and His angelic subjects. It is a vast region, but not infinite. In X. 380 Milton speaks of its "empyreal bounds"; in II. 1049 of its "battlements";[3] in VI. 860 of its "crystal wall". These fence Heaven in from Chaos. When Satan voyages through space, in quest of the new-created World, he kens far off the crystal line of light that radiates from the empyreal bulwarks, marking

---

[1] I.e. from the point of view of this World, the position of which we shall see.

[2] The terms are synonymous. *Empyrean* = Lat. *empyræus*, from Gk. ἔμπυρος. The notion was that the Empyrean was formed of the element of fire (πῦρ).

[3] Cf. Lucretius' *flammantia mœnia mundi* (I. 74) and Gray's "flaming bounds of Space" (*Progress of Poesy*).

where runs the severance betwixt Heaven and Chaos (II. 1034 *et seq.*). In the wall of Heaven are the "everlasting doors" opening on to Chaos (V. 253–6, VII. 205–9). The shape of Heaven Milton does not determine (II. 1048); perhaps it is a square (X. 381). Its internal configuration and appearance he describes in language which reminds us of some lines (574–6) in Book V. May not the Earth, says Raphael, be "but the shadow of Heaven, and things therein Each to other like, more than on Earth is thought"? Milton expands this idea, and developing to the utmost the symbolical, objective presentment of the New Jerusalem in the *Revelation*, depicts a Heaven scarce distinguishable from an ideal Earth.[1] In fact, his Heaven and his Garden of Eden have much in common; so that Satan exclaims, "O Earth, how like to Heaven!" (IX. 99). Thus the Heavenly landscape (if I may describe it in Miltonic language) has its vales, wood-covered heights and plains (VI. 70, 640–6); it is watered by living streams (V. 652); and fair with trees and flowers[2]—immortal amaranth and celestial roses (III. 353–64), and vines (V. 635). Daylight and twilight are known there (V. 627–9, 645, VI. 2–15). And soft winds fan the angels as they sleep (V. 654, 655).

These angelic beings, divided, according to tradition (see p. 153), into nine Orders, each with particular duties, perform their ministries and solemn rites (VII. 149) in the courts of God (V. 650) and at the high temple of Heaven (VII. 148). Their worship is offered under forms which recall, now the ritual of the Temple-services of Israel, now the inspired visions of St John. They celebrate the Deity who dwells invisible, throned inaccessible (III. 377) on the holy mount (VI. 5), howbeit omnipresent, as omnipotent, throughout Heaven and all space: round whose throne there rests a radiance of excessive brightness, at which even Seraphim, highest of Hierarchies, veil their eyes (III. 375–82).

It has been objected that Milton's picture is too material. But he himself takes special pains to remind us that the external imagery under which he represents his concepts is symbolical, not literal—adopted merely as a means of conveying *some* impression of that which is intrinsically indescribable. The truth, I believe, is that he has applied to Heaven the descriptions of 'Paradise' in the apocalyptic literature of the first centuries

---

[1] The Earth deteriorates after the fall of man (X. 651 *et seq.*).

[2] This is a descriptive detail most conspicuous in early Christian apocalyptic works; see next page.

of Christianity. The *Revelation of Peter* (dating perhaps from early in the second century A.D.) affords an illustration of these descriptions. St Peter is represented as asking our Lord where are the souls of the righteous dead—"of what sort is the world wherein they are and possess glory? And the Lord shewed him [me] a very great space outside this world shining excessively with light, and the air that was there illuminated with the rays of the sun, and the earth itself blooming with unfading flowers, and full of spices and fair-flowering plants, incorruptible and bearing a blessed fruit: and so strong was the perfume that it was borne even to us[1] from thence. And the dwellers in that place were clad in the raiment of angels of light, and their raiment was like their land: and angels encircled them."[2]

The second region, for which Chaos seems the simplest title, is also variously called "the wasteful Deep" (II. 961, VI. 862), "the utter Deep" (VI. 716), and "the Abyss" (I. 21, VII. 211, 234). Here rules the god of Chaos and his consort Night (II. 959–63). According to the long description in Book II. 890 *et seq.*, this region is an illimitable ocean, composed of the embryon atoms whereof all substances may be formed—whereof Hell and the World are afterwards formed. It is a vast agglomeration of matter in its primal state, "neither sea, nor shore, nor air, nor fire". Here prevails eternal anarchy of storm and wind and wave and stunning sounds. In VII. 210–14 the Messiah and His host stand at the open gate of Heaven and look forth on to Chaos; and what they behold is an Abyss "Outrageous as a sea, dark, wasteful, wild".

[1] I.e. St Peter and the other disciples who are with our Lord on the Mount of Olives. See *The Gospel according to Peter, and the Revelation of Peter* (Cambridge University Press ed., 1892), pp. 48, 49.

[2] Mr James (whose version I have just quoted) gives a similar passage from a rather later work, the *History of Barlaam and Josaphat*, wherein the Paradise of the just is revealed in a vision as "a plain of vast extent, flourishing with fair and very sweet-smelling flowers, where he saw plants of all manner of kinds, loaded with strange and wondrous fruits, most pleasant to the eye and desirable to touch. And the leaves of the trees made clear music to a soft breeze and sent forth a delicate fragrance, whereof none could tire...And through this wondrous and vast plain [he passed] to a city which gleamed with an unspeakable brightness and had its walls of translucent gold, and its battlements of stones the like of which none has ever seen. And a light from above...filled all the streets thereof: and certain winged hosts, each to itself a light, abode there singing in melodies never heard by mortal ears."

The creation of Hell, we may perhaps assume, just precedes the fall of the angels.[1] It has been prepared for their punishment when, after the proclamation in v. 600-15, they have revealed their rebellious spirit. To form Hell a part of the abyss has been taken. In II. 1002 Chaos complains that his realm has been encroached upon by Hell—"stretching far and wide beneath". Round it runs a wall of fire (I. 61); overhead spreads a fiery vault or cope (I. 298, 345). At the descent of the angels Hell lies open to receive them (VI. 53-5); then the roof closes (VI. 875), and they are prisoners. Henceforth the only outlet from Hell into Chaos is through certain gates, the charge whereof is assigned to Sin (II. 643 et seq.). At her side, as protector, stands Death, ready with his dart to meet all comers (II. 853-5). To please Satan (her sire), Sin opens the gates. Afterwards she cannot shut them; and all who will may pass to and fro between Hell and Chaos. Later on (when the bridge from Hell has been made) this change becomes terribly significant. For the inside of Hell, we hear of a pool of fire (I. 52, 221); dry land that burns like fire (I. 227-9); and drear regions of excessive cold and heat, intersected by rivers (II. 575 et seq.). Here again the picture is traditional, owing, no doubt, much to Dante, who in turn owed much to the apocalyptic descriptions before mentioned.

Immediately after the expulsion of Satan the World is created (VII. 131 et seq.). By "the World" is meant the whole Universe of Earth, seas, stellar bodies and the framework wherein they are set—in short, all that the eye of man beholds. The Son of God goes forth into the abyss (VII. 218 et seq.), and with golden compass marks out the limits of this World; so that Chaos is again despoiled of part of his realm (as he laments in II. 1001-6). The new World is a globe or hollow sphere, suspended in the abyss, and at its topmost point fastened by a golden chain (see II. 1051, note) to Heaven. In II. 1004-6 Chaos tells Satan of this Universe:

> "Another world,
> Hung o'er my realm, linked in a golden chain
> To that side Heaven from whence your legions fell."

The length of this chain, i.e. the distance of the World from the

---

[1] Cf. the English *Faust-book* (1592) where Faustus asks when Hell was made and Mephistophiles replies—"Faustus, thou shalt know, that before the fall of my lord Lucifer was no hell, but even then was hell ordained" (Thoms' *English Prose Romances*, III. 185).

Empyrean, is not stated, I believe; but the distance was not—comparatively—very great (II. 1051-3, VII. 618).

Also, between the globe (again, on its upper side, i.e. that nearest to the Empyrean) and the gate of Heaven there stretches a golden stair, used by good angels for descent and ascent when they are despatched to Earth on any duty such as that which Raphael discharges in Books V-VIII. This stair (suggested by Jacob's dream?) is not always let down (III. 501-18). And hard by the point where the golden stair touches the surface of the globe there is—in later times, after the fall of man—another stair (or rather bridge), which leads, not upward to the Empyrean, but downward to Hell: i.e. it extends over the portion of Chaos that intervenes between Hell and the World (II. 1024-33, X. 282 *et seq.*). This bridge,[1] the work of Sin and Death, is used by evil angels when they would come from Hell (its gates being open) to Earth—"to tempt or punish mortals" (II. 1032).

Hence a good angel and an evil, visiting mankind simultaneously, the one descending the golden stair, the other ascending the bridge, will meet at this point of the surface of the globe. And to enter the globe, i.e. to get through its outer surface to the inside, each must pass through the same aperture in the surface, and descend by the same passage into the interior: as Milton explains in Book III. There he describes how Satan journeys through Chaos, till he reaches and walks[2] on the outer surface of the World (III. 418-30). But how to pass to the interior? The surface is impenetrable, and there seems to be no inlet. Then suddenly the reflection of the golden stair which chances to be let down directs his steps to the point where the stair and the bridge come into contact with the globe, and here he finds what he seeks—an aperture in the surface by which he can look down into the interior. Further, there is at this aperture a broad passage plunging right down into the World—

---

[1] In the English *Faust-book* 1592 (Thoms' *English Prose Romances*, III. 194), Mephistophiles says: "We have also with us in hell a ladder, reaching of exceeding highth, as though the top of the same would touch the heaven, to which the damned ascend to seek the blessing of God, but through their infidelity, when they are at very highest degree, they fall down again into their former miseries." With the last part of this extract cf. *P. L.* III. 484 *et seq.* It seems to me highly probable that Milton studied the *Faust-book* (which was immensely popular), as well as Marlowe's dramatic adaptation of it; see II. 596, note.

[2] I.e. like a fly moving up a lamp-globe (Masson).

being, really, a continuation of the golden stair. Thus Satan, standing on the bottom step of the stair, and looking straight up, sees overhead the gate of Heaven; and looking straight down, sees the interior of the globe, leagues beneath (III. 526 *et seq.*).

Similarly on the seventh day of the Creation the angels, gazing from Heaven's gate down the stair and down the broad passage which continues the stair, see, as Satan did, into the new-made World (VII. 617-19):

> "not far, founded in view
> On the clear hyaline, the glassy sea."[1]

In short, at the point in the surface of the globe nearest to the Empyrean, there is a choice of ways: the stair leading to Heaven; the bridge to Hell; and the broad passage to the interior of the World:

> "in little space
> The confines met of empyrean Heaven,
> And of this World; and, on the left hand, Hell
> With long reach interposed; three several ways,
> In sight, to each of these three places led."[2]

And descending the broad passage what would an angel find in the interior of the globe? What is this globe as Milton, following the astronomy of his[3] time, has described it?

The globe as then conceived may best be likened (in Plato's comparison)[4] to one of those puzzles or boxes in which are contained a number of boxes of gradually lessening size: remove the first, and you shall find another inside, rather smaller: remove the second, and you shall come on a third, still smaller: and so on, till you reach the centre—the kernel, as it were, round which the different boxes were but successive shells. Now, of the globe of the World the Earth (they said) is the kernel (is it not often called 'the centre'?)[5]; and—a stationary body itself—it is encased by numerous shells or Spheres: the number of the Spheres being a subject of dispute and varying in the different

---

[1] I.e. the Crystalline Sphere.

[2] X. 320-4.

[3] I do not mean to imply that the Ptolemaic system was still generally believed in at the time when *P. L.* was published, but that it satisfied Elizabethan writers of whom Milton was the last.

[4] See the Myth of Er in the *Republic* 616, 617; and the note on *Arcades* 64 (Pitt Press ed. p. 59), where the passage is translated.

[5] Cf. perhaps I. 686; and certainly the *Winter's Tale* II. I. 102, *Troilus* I. 3. 85.

astronomical systems. Milton, accepting[1] for the purposes of his epic the Ptolemaic system as expanded by the astronomer Alphonsus X of Castille, recognizes ten Spheres. A Sphere, it should be noted, is merely a circular region of space—not necessarily of solid matter. Indeed, of the ten Spheres only one, the Primum Mobile, appears in Milton's description to consist of some material substance. Seven of them are the Spheres of the planets, i.e. the orbits in which the planets severally move.

The order of the Spheres, which fit one within the other,[2] is, if we start from the Earth as the stationary centre[3] of the Universe, as follows: first, the Spheres of the planets successively—the Moon, Mercury, Venus, the Sun, Mars, Jupiter and Saturn; then, outside the last of these (i.e. Saturn), the Firmament or Cælum Stellatum, in which are set the 'fixed stars'; then, outside the Firmament, the Crystalline Sphere; and last, the Primum Mobile enclosing all the others. Compare the famous lines (481–3) in Book III describing the passage of the souls of the departed from Earth to Heaven:

"They pass the planets seven, and pass the fixed,
    And that Crystalline Sphere whose balance weighs
    The trepidation talked, and that First Moved."

It remains to note three or four points in these lines. Milton treats the Sun and Moon as planets (v. 177, x. 651–8). Compare Shakespeare, *Troilus*, I. 3. 89, "the glorious planet Sol", and *Antony*, v. 2. 241, "the fleeting Moon no planet is of mine". The 'fixed stars' are referred to four times in the poem—but only once (v. 176) with the word 'star' added: in the other

---

[1] He was evidently familiar with the Copernican system (cf. IV. 592–7, VIII. 15–178): and the question has been asked why he did not follow it in the poem. The answer surely is obvious. The Copernican theory was new, without a scrap of literary association and with no poetic terminology: whereas the Ptolemaic view and its delightful fictions as to the Spheres, their harmonies, and the like, had become a tradition of literature, expressed in terms that recalled Marlowe and Shakespeare and Jonson and the *sacri vates* of English verse. To have surrendered this poetic heritage merely out of deference to science had been impossible pedantry—a perverse concession to the cold philosophy that "empties the haunted air and unweaves the rainbow" (*Lamia*).

[2] Cf. Marlowe's *Faustus* VI. 38, 39:
    "As are the elements, such are the spheres,
        Mutually folded in each other's orb."

[3] Cf. VIII. 33 "the sedentary Earth"; and see IX. 107–9.

138 APPENDIX

places (III. 481, V. 621, X. 661) they are called simply "the fixed". Though they are unmoved their Sphere revolves round the Earth, moving from East to West, completing a revolution in twenty-four hours, and carrying with it the seven inner Spheres.[1] The rapid motion of this Sphere is glanced at in v. 176 ("their orb[2] that flies"). The Crystalline Sphere and the Primum Mobile were not included in the original Ptolemaic system. They were added later, to explain certain phenomena which the earlier astronomers had not observed, and for which their theories offered no explanation. Thus the supposed swaying or "trepidation" of the Crystalline Sphere was held to be the cause of the precession of the equinoxes. This Sphere is described as a vast expanse of waters (see note on VII. 261). It encircles the eight inner Spheres. The original notion may perhaps be traced to the waters "above the firmament" in *Genesis* i. 7. Compare the picture in VII. 270-1 of the World

> "Built on circumfluous waters calm, in wide
>   Crystalline ocean."

The main purpose that this "ocean" serves is to protect the Earth from the evil "influences" of Chaos; those "fierce extremes" of temperature which might penetrate through the outside shell (the Primum Mobile) and "distemper" the whole fabric of the Universe, did not this wall of waters interpose (VII. 271-3).

Last comes the Primum Mobile,[3] "the first[4] convex" of the World, i.e. the outside case of our box or puzzle. It is made, as we saw, of hard matter; but for its crust of substance Chaos would break in on the World, and Darkness make inroads (III. 419-21). The first moved itself, it communicates motion to the nine inner Spheres. In Elizabethan literature allusions to it are not infrequent: we will conclude by giving three. Compare Spenser, *Hymne of Heavenly Beautie*:

> "these heavens still by degrees arize,
>   Until they come to their first Movers bound,
>   That in his mightie compasse doth comprize,
>   And carry all the rest with him around;"

[1] These have separate motions of their own.

[2] 'Orb' and 'Sphere' are interchangeable terms—when it suits Milton.

[3] Dante's *primo giro* (*Purgatorio*, I. 15).

[4] III. 419. To Satan coming from Chaos it is the first; in our calculation, as we started from the Earth, it is the last.

and Marlowe, *Faustus*:[1]

"He views the clouds, and planets, and the stars,
The tropic zones, and quarters of the sky,
From the bright circle of the horned moon
Even to the height of Primum Mobile;"

and Bacon, *Of Seditions and Troubles*: "for the motions of the greatest persons in a government ought to be as the motions of the planets under Primum Mobile".

B

ON THE CHARACTER OF MILTON'S SATAN

I have reserved for this *Appendix* notice of some points in Milton's delineation of the character of Satan. First, as to the rank which Milton assigns to him before his revolt, and the cause of that revolt. Milton speaks of Satan as an archangel[2]— "if not the first archangel" (v. 660): that is, he is inclined to give Satan preeminence over all angelic beings. But this preeminence is not emphasised so much as we might have expected.

The immediate cause of the rebellion in Heaven is the proclamation that all should worship the Messiah as their Head (v. 600–15). Satan resents the command, conceiving himself "impaired" (v. 665) thereby; and he makes its pretended injustice a means of drawing away a third part of the angels from their allegiance. They are equal, he says, to the Messiah: self-begotten, not created: not liable to pay worship; and so, playing on their pride, he wins them to his side (v. 772–802, 853–66). Meantime, in his own heart an even stronger motive is at work; to wit, ambition to be himself equal to the Deity—nay, superior. He not only disclaims submission to the Son: he strives "against the throne and monarchy" (I. 42) of the Almighty Himself; and it is as the foe rather of the Father than of the Son that the great archangel is set before us in *Paradise Lost*.

Touching both matters there was much tradition, whereof it may be interesting to cite two or three illustrations from

---

[1] Scene VI. *chorus*, ll. 5–18, in the third Quarto, 1616; the passage is not in the two earlier editions of 1604 and 1609 (Ward, p. 178).

[2] Contrast the first extract from the *Faust-book*, later on.

popular works[1] with which Milton is likely to have been
familiar. To take, for example, the English *Faust-book*: Faustus
asks: "But how came lord and master Lucifer[2] to have so great
a fall from Heaven? Mephistophiles answered, My lord
Lucifer was a fair angel, created of God as immortal, and being
placed in the Seraphims,[3] which are above the Cherubims, he
would have presumed upon the Throne of God...upon this
presumption the Lord cast him down headlong, and where
(i.e. whereas) before he was an angel of light, now dwells in
darkness."[4] Later on Faustus returns to the subject, enquiring
"in what estimation his lord Lucifer was, when he was in favour
with God": also touching his form and shape: to which
Mephistophiles replies, "My lord Lucifer...was at the first an
angel of God, yea he was so of God ordained for shape, pomp,
authority, worthiness, and dwelling, that he far exceeded all the
other creatures of God, and so illuminated that he far surpassed
the brightness of the sun, and all the stars...but when he began
to be high minded, proud and so presumptuous, that he would
usurp the seat of God's Majesty, then was he banished."[5]

The *Faust-book*, it will be seen, agrees with Milton on both
points; while, as regards one of them—Satan's rank —it is more
explicit than *Paradise Lost*. Equally explicit is Heywood's
Hierarchie of the Blessed Angels (1635). There (p. 336) we read
that of the angels Lucifer was first-created and chief:

> "As he might challenge a prioritie
>   In his Creation, so aboue the rest
>   A supereminence, as first and best."

Heywood mentions Michael, Raphael, and Gabriel, and adds
(p. 337) that great as they were,

> "Yet aboue these was Lucifer instated,
>   Honor'd, exalted, and much celebrated."

---

[1] I choose three works each of which may, I think, be regarded as
a *résumé* of many of the current traditions of demonology. Two of the
books—the *Faust-book*, 1592, and Scot's *Discourse*, 1584—were
extremely popular, and personally I believe that Milton had studied
both. Scot devotes several chapters to "Lucifer and his fall". The
third work—Heywood's *Hierarchie*, 1635—is very serviceable to an
editor of *Paradise Lost*.

[2] A common name of Satan.

[3] The highest of the Hierarchies, see v. 587. We may note the forms
'Seraphims', 'Cherubims'; see G. under 'Cherubim'.

[4] Thoms' *English Prose Romances*, 2nd ed., III. 184.

[5] Thoms, III. 187.

Reginald Scot goes even further, remarking[1] that according
to the teaching of some divines Satan even after his fall exceeded
in power any of the angelic host. It seems to me therefore something strange that Milton did not unequivocally invest Satan
with superiority over all the angels.

As to Satan's motive Heywood[2] differs from Milton, making
jealousy of mankind the cause; while Scot writes:[3] "Our
schoolemen differ much in the cause of *Lucifer's* fall [some
alleging one thing, some another, while] others saie, that his
condemnation grew hereupon, for that he challenged the place
of the Messias." This accords more with *Paradise Lost* v. 661–5.

For Milton Satan is the type of pride. The type was already
fixed. As an epithet of Lucifer 'proud' had passed into a proverb.
Thus Gower said:[4]

> " For Lucifer with him that felle
> Bar pride with him into helle.
> There was pride of to grete cost
> Whan he for pride hath heven lost; "

and Marlowe:[5]

"Faust. How comes it, then, that he is prince of devils?
Meph. O, by aspiring pride and insolence;
For which God threw him from the face of heaven;"

and Greene:[6]

> "proud Lucifer fell from the heavens,
>
> . . . .
> Lucifer and his proud-hearted friends
> Were thrown into the centre of the earth."

Milton therefore did not wholly conceive or create the character
of the arch-rebel. Tradition, literary no less than theological,
prescribed the dominant idea in that nature: enough if Milton
developed the idea in harmony with the design of his poem.
This he did. He depicts Satan as an embodiment of the spirit
of pride and ambition:[7] not the ambition which is an honourable
desire of praise—that last infirmity of noble minds—but the
fevered lust for power which springs from overmastering self-
esteem. In Satan this spirit of egotism is the poison that per-
meates his whole being, vanquishing and vitiating all that is
good in him.

[1] Nicholson's ed. p. 425.
[2] p. 339.   [3] p. 423.
[4] *Confessio Amantis*, book I.   [5] *Faustus* III. 67–9.
[6] *Friar Bacon* IX. 59, 65, 66.
[7] Cf. Satan's own words in IV. 40.

For at the outset of the action of *Paradise Lost* Satan has much that is noble and attractive in his nature. To have made him wholly evil had repelled, and lessened the interest of the poem, which turns, in no slight degree, on the struggle between the good and evil elements in him. Indeed, this very pride is not without its good aspect. Herein lies the motive power that nerves him at every crisis to face insuperable difficulties; to cherish immortal hope—though hope of revenge; and to adventure "high attempts".

On the other hand, it is this same spirit that drives him onward to his final fall. If at any moment he is minded to repent and submit—through pity for the friends whom he has ruined, or mankind whom he schemes to ruin, or himself—through sense of his ingratitude (IV. 42–5) towards the Almighty—whatever the motive—relentless, resistless egotism sweeps aside compunction, and denies him retreat. To sue for grace were to humble himself in the eyes of his followers and in his own: which must not be (IV. 79–83).

Steadily does Milton keep this idea before us. There is no possibility of missing or mistaking his intention. The very word 'pride' recurs[1] like some persistent refrain, ringing clearest at the great crises, the fateful moments when the action of the epic enters on a fresh stage: as when in the fourth Book (ll. 27 *et seq.*) Satan looks down upon Eden from his resting-place on mount Niphates, and a brief while is inclined to give up his attempt and seek re-admission into Heaven; or as when in the ninth Book (ll. 455–72) he sees Eve in the Garden and is touched by her beauty and innocence, and disarmed of his ill thoughts. Always, however, the end is the same: "the hot hell" of pride in his heart breaks anew into flame; and he goes forward to his work.[2] Had not pride led him to undertake it?

Satan's resolve to compass the fall of man is prompted by several feelings—each a phase of self-esteem. There is jealousy. Man has usurped his place—dispossessed him and his followers. At sight of Adam and Eve he exclaims (IV. 359–60):

"Into our room of bliss thus high advanced
Creatures of other mould, earth-born perhaps!"

The same feeling finds expression in almost the same words later on (IX. 148, 149). That others should receive favour from the Almighty—and, as he thinks, at his expense—wounds his pride.

[1] Cf. I. 36, 58, 527, 572, 603—with many other examples.
[2] Cf. Mr Stopford Brooke's admirable *Study* of Milton, p. 148.

Again, there is desire to assert his supremacy by undertaking an office from which the mightiest of his followers recoil in fear. Nowhere does Satan stand forth so eminent and sublime "with monarchal pride" as in the scene in the second Book where he proffers himself for the great enterprise. The counsel of Beelzebub has been applauded by all (ll. 386–9): but who will carry it out? None dare: and then Satan, proclaiming his readiness, once more confirms his sovereignty. Here too pride has ruled.

But the strongest motive remains: desire
"To wreak on innocent frail man his loss
Of that first battle, and his flight to Hell."[1]
"To spite the great Creator" (II. 385) he will bring ruin on the earth and its inhabitants: which, if not victory, were revenge. The notion flatters his self-conceit. It is born of the old pride. And Milton dwells on it with fitting insistence.[2]

Is Satan the 'hero' of *Paradise Lost*? We might think so did we not read beyond the first books. But to trace his history in the poem to its inglorious close is to dispel the impression. Milton can scarcely intend that we should regard as 'hero'—as worthy of sustained admiration—one who passes from the splendour of archangelic being to the state of a loathsome reptile.[3] The hideous metamorphosis in X. 504–32 is the necessary contrast to those scenes at the beginning of the epic in which the great rebel does appear in heroic grandeur: and we must look on both pictures. If *Paradise Lost* narrates the fall of man, it narrates too—and no less clearly—the fall of man's tempter. The self-degradation of Satan is complete: outward and inward: of the form and of the spirit: a change—ever for the worse—of shape and mind and emotion.

There is the outward sign. Before his expulsion he is preeminently a lustrous being, clothed with ethereal radiance and glory—so much does his name "Lucifer" argue.[4] And afterwards he retains something of this "original brightness" (I. 592): howbeit much has passed from him (I. 97, 591–4). But gradually what was left decreases in proportion as the evil in him prevails: so that Uriel perceives the foul passions that dim his face (IV. 124–30); while Gabriel marks his "faded splendour

[1] IV. 11, 12.   [2] Cf. VI. 905, 906.
[3] Cf. his words in IX. 163–71.
[4] Cf. VII. 131–3, and the second extract from the *Faust-book*, and Marlowe, "beautiful As was bright Lucifer before his fall" (*Faustus* v. 155).

144   APPENDIX

wan" (IV. 870), and the Cherub Zephon taunts him therewith
(IV. 835–40). Equal is his loss of physical force. On the fields
of Heaven he does not fear to meet Michael in combat (VI. 246
et seq.): in the Garden of Eden he doubts himself a match for
Adam:

" Foe not informidable! exempt from wound,
I not; so much hath Hell debased, and pain[1]
Enfeebled me, to what I was in Heaven."

In fact, he is glad that he has to deal with the woman—not the
man (IX. 480–8).

Nor this because of lost strength alone. He shuns the "higher
intellectual" of Adam (IX. 483), who would be better able than
Eve to see through his arguments and so resist temptation. He
is conscious of his own decline in intellect. The strong intelli-
gence which inspires his speeches in the first two books has
degenerated, by perverse use, into mere sophistical slyness, a
base cunning—even as wine may lose its savour and turn to
vinegar. He is no more the mighty-minded archangel: he is
naught but the serpent—"subtlest beast of all the field".
Lastly, every impulse in him towards good has died out. The
element of nobility that redeemed his character at the outset
from absolute baseness has been killed. In evil he moves and
has his being, so that himself confesses "all good to me becomes
bane"; and in destroying lies his sole delight (IX. 118 *et seq.*).

Hardly therefore shall we believe that Milton meant us to see
in the fallen and everfalling archangel the hero of *Paradise Lost*.
That position surely belongs to Adam.

C

PARADISE LOST, I. 358–75; II. 274–8, 397–402.

These[2] passages (with several in *Paradise Regained*) are illustrated
by the following in Hooker's *Ecclesiastical Polity*, I. iv. 3: "The
fall of the angels was pride.[3] Since their fall, their practices
have been the clean contrary unto those before mentioned. For
being dispersed, some in the air, some on the earth, some in the
water, some[4] among the minerals, dens, and caves, that are

[1] See I. 55, VI. 327, notes.
[2] I have to thank Mr R. D. Hicks for many of the references used
in this sketch.
[3] See p. 145.   [4] Cf. Plato's δαίμονες ὑποχθόνιοι.

under the earth; they have by all means laboured to effect a universal rebellion against the laws, and as far as in them lieth utter destruction of the works of God. These wicked spirits the heathens honoured instead of gods, both generally under the name of *dii inferi*, 'gods infernal'; and particularly, some in oracles,[1] some in idols,[2] some as household gods, some as nymphs: in a word, no foul and wicked spirit which was not one way or other honoured of men as God, till such time as light appeared in the world and dissolved the works of the Devil.'' The interest of this passage is that Hooker identifies the fallen angels (1) with the heathen—more especially classical—deities, (2) with the dæmons supposed to inhabit the four[3] 'elements'. This twofold identification accords with the apparently universal belief of mediæval writers. The precise steps whereby it was reached cannot perhaps be determined; but the process may have been on this wise.

The belief in the existence of dæmons is as old as Hesiod's time; cf. the *Works and Days*, 121-6. It is found *passim* in Greek philosophy. The character attributed to these dæmons varies in the different authorities. In a rough generalization we may say that they were regarded as semi-divine powers intermediate between gods and men. Their dwelling-place also varies: Æschylus (*Persae*, 630) describes them as χθόνιοι; Plato[4] (*Cratylus*, 398 A) as ὑποχθόνιοι. The theory which assigns the air as their special abode, and which is brought forward very prominently in *Paradise Regained*, dates from Neo-Pythagorean writers.[5] Now the tendency of Greek popular superstition and of later philosophy was to merge these dæmons in the gods: a tendency traceable as far back as Democritus.[6] He (says Zeller[7]) "may be regarded as the first who, mediating between philosophers and the popular religion, entered upon the course so often

[1] Cf. the second passage quoted later on from Zeller.

[2] Alluding perhaps to *Ps.* xcvi. 5—see later.

[3] Hooker omits the dæmons of fire (=Philo's τὰ πυρίγονα?).

[4] He is quoting Hesiod, l. c. (where, however, our texts have ἐπιχθόνιοι).

[5] I.e. from the first century B.C. onwards. "They imagine the dæmons to be souls dwelling in the space between the earth and the moon, and occupying, alike in virtue of their nature and their abode, a place intermediate between gods and men"—Zeller (*Philosophie der Griechen*, III. 2, p. 138); he cites various Neo-Pythagoreans, summarising their views thus.

[6] *Circa* 420 B.C.

[7] *Pre-Socratics*, English trans., II. p. 289.

pursued in after times, viz. that of degrading the gods of polytheism into dæmons". This course is carried further by the Neo-Pythagoreans—for whom, "as for the other philosophers of that time, dæmons take the place of the popular gods in all cases where what is attributed to the gods was found irreconcileable with a purer conception of the divinity, and yet was not altogether to be denied. Divination[1] proceeded from them, expiations were made to them: Timæus Locrus even affirms that the gods committed to them the government of the world" (Zeller)[2]. And this identification of gods and dæmons is completed in Philo Judæus[3] and Rabbinical writers. Not to multiply proofs, we may take a single illustration which will readily occur to most readers, viz. 1 Cor. x. 20, where St Paul (influenced, I presume, by Rabbinical teaching and Greek philosophy) expressly, and appropriately since he is writing to Greeks, calls the divinities of the Gentiles δαιμόνια.[4] The notion may be traced in many patristic works.

The next step is the identification of the dæmons with the fallen angels. This is made by Philo, who treats the dæmons as intermediaries or messengers (ἄγγελοι) between God and the world, and says that they are the beings whom Moses calls angels—οὓς ἄλλοι φιλόσοφοι δαίμονας, ἀγγέλους Μωϋσῆς εἴωθεν ὀνομάζειν, ψυχαὶ δ' εἰσὶν κατὰ τὸν ἀέρα πετόμεναι.[5] This identification is also a Rabbinical doctrine. It suffices for our purpose again to recall St Paul's words in Ephes. ii. 2, where Satan, chief of the fallen angels, is termed "the prince of the power of the air", i.e. lord of the dæmons of the air.

The dæmons, then, having been identified on the one hand with the heathen gods, and on the other with the fallen angels, the identification of the fallen angels with the heathen gods naturally followed. Hence it is common to find all three treated as the same in patristic and mediæval works. This is Hooker's view; it is also Milton's. The identity of the fallen angels and the heathen gods is stated so explicitly in P. L. i. 358–75 that it were superfluous to dwell on the point. The identity of the

---

[1] Cf. Hooker, ante; Nat. Ode, 175 (note in Pitt Press ed.); P. R. I. 430, 431, where the Saviour says to Satan (prince of the dæmons) "all oracles by thee are given".

[2] Philosophie der Griechen, III. 2, p. 139.

[3] B.C. 30—A.D. 40 (circa).

[4] The same word is used in the Septuagint in Psalm xcvi. 5 where the A. V. has "idols". Cf. Hooker, ante, and P. L. i. 375.

[5] De gigant. 285 A (263, 7).

fallen angels and the dæmons[1] is less emphasised in *P. L.* (but see II. 274–8, 397–402, notes). In *P. R.* it is conspicuous. As a signal illustration *P. R.* II. 121–6 may be instanced.

D

PARADISE LOST, I. 515–17

What are we to understand by the expressions "the middle air" (*P. L.* I. 516) and "the middle region of air" (*P. R.* II. 117), the meaning of which would appear to be the same? Most editors are silent on the subject; some interpret "middle" = "between heaven and earth". This view, though possible, does not appear to me wholly satisfactory, and I venture to offer another—that Milton alludes in both places to a theory, evidently current at that time, of the division of the air into three regions, and that "middle region" is really a quasi-scientific term ("*media regio*") which would be perfectly intelligible to all scholars of the 17th century. As to the history of this threefold division: the first hints of it that fell in my way were the passage in the *Adamus Exul* of Grotius and that[2] in Jonson's *Masque of Hymen (ad fin.)* mentioned in my note on *P. L.* I. 516. The combined evidence of these led to the conclusion that the threefold partition must have been a conception then recognized: not indeed a classical conception, but experience had often shown that in such matters Milton's views are post-classical, what one may vaguely call 'mediæval'. This I conjectured to be a case in point; and such it proved. The kindness of Mr R. D. Hicks enables me to throw some light on a doctrine which, in my opinion, fits the two Miltonic passages with extreme appositeness, and lends them an entirely new[3] interest. Of the references with which Mr Hicks has supplied me space will admit but two or three.

First, then, the following extracts from the works of Bartholomæus Keckermann,[4] the German *savant*, are important as coming from what may be considered a compendium of contemporary science—if indeed one should not rather say

[1] I.e. the dæmons of all four 'elements', not of air alone.
[2] See next page.
[3] New, that is (and I hope true) to most modern readers, since the explanation finds no mention in any edition of Milton; but to many of his contemporaries it would have been superfluous.
[4] *D. Bartholomæi Kechermanni Dantiscani operum omnium quæ exstant Tomus Primus. Genevæ. Apud Petrum Aubertum.* MDCXIV.

omniscience. Keckermann is speaking of the divisions of the air; and he remarks that there are two main theories as to its partition—the older and less correct which postulates two regions, the modern and more accurate which recognizes three. He says: "*Aristoteles atque adeò veteres Physici locum aeris dividunt in* πρότερον *&* δεύτερον, *id est, primum & secundum, sive superiorem & inferiorem...Recentiores autem accuratius paulò totum illud spacium* (sic) *aereum partiti sunt in tres partes sive regiones...Perfectior sive accuratior distinctio aeris est in tres regiones, nempe in Supremam, Mediam & Infimam.*" The genesis of this doctrine he traces thus: "*Distinctio ista...ab interpretibus Aristotelis primum tradita fuit, nempe ab Averroe,[1] a Themistio[2] & Simplicio,[3] & deinde latius explicata ab Alberto[4] M. & aliis Scholasticis, idque potissimum eo fine, ut doctrina meteorum clarior atque illustrior fieret*" (as for sundry other reasons).[5] He discusses at some length the characteristics of each region; and though we are most concerned with what he has to say of the middle region (*media*)—his remarks being founded on what Albertus had written—we may just note that he represents the upper region (*suprema*) as the driest and hottest, and the lower region (*infima*) as hot, through radiation from the surface of the earth heated by the sun's rays, but also moist. Now as to the "*media regio*" he writes (1) that it is peculiarly cold—(*a*) because vapours collect there from land and sea, (*b*) because of its reaction (ἀντιπερίστασις) against the heat of the upper and lower regions; (2) that, beginning where the sun's rays lose their power—its lowest point earthwards—it reaches to the tops of the loftiest mountains—its highest point heavenwards. The diameter of this belt of air is computed by some at seven English miles.

Keckermann has referred above to his authorities; let us glance at Albertus Magnus. In his *Commentary* on the *Meteora* Albertus has a chapter[6] headed, *Quare non sunt nubes in superiori regione aeris, sed in media tantum.* Here, after discussing the upper and lower regions, he adds, "*est autem in medio duarum regionum, scilicet superioris æstuosæ, & inferioris calidæ & humidæ, tertia aeris zona sive regio...quæ est valde frigida et excellentis frigiditatis*". And then he goes on to explain how vapour gathers there—*infra altissimos montes*—and condenses

---

[1] A.D. 1120–98.
[2] A.D. 330–90.
[3] *Circa* A.D. 536.
[4] A.D. 1193–1280.
[5] Cf. *op. cit.* col. 1446.
[6] *Liber* I, *Tractatus* I, *Caput* VIII.

and forms clouds, so that this middle region is the gathering-place of rain.[1] Later[2] he writes to the same effect—"*tria sunt aeris interstitia, infimum & medium & supremum...medium frigidum excellenter & humidum*". Now let us summarise the results of these descriptions of the "*media regio*", and see how they apply to the Miltonic "middle region".

(1) The "*media regio*" is the place of clouds; cf. *P. R.* I. 39–41, where Satan

> "in mid air
> To council summons all his mighty peers,
> Within thick clouds and dark tenfold involved."

(2) It is thick with heavy vapours; cf. *P. R.* II. 117, where Satan ascends "Up to the middle region of thick air".

(3) It is peculiarly cold; and 'cold' is the precise epithet used in *P.L.* I. 516. Cf. *The Death of a Fair Infant*, 16, "Through *middle* empire of the *freezing* air".

(4) It extends to the top of high mountains; and mount Olympus is the dwelling-place of the deities who "rule the middle air", *P.L.* I. 515, 516. Cf. the *Vacation Exercise*, 41, 42.

(5) It is capped by another, perhaps broader, belt of air; and in *P. L.* I. 517 Milton expressly sneers at the "highest heaven" of the classical deities as not being so very high after all—which, according to the whole system of this theory, is true enough.

It appears to me therefore that the explanation suggested fits the passages at every turn. I imagine that to many of Milton's readers, as to many of the spectators of Jonson's *Masque*, the notion of the three regions was perfectly familiar. And I have given the view at some detail because I believe that it restores a lost point of Miltonic interpretation.

---

[1] Cf. the passage in Jonson; it is a description of some scenery used in the *Masque of Hymen*, which represented "the three regions of air": the middle region "all of dark and condensed clouds, as being the proper place where rain, hail, and other watery meteors are made"; or as Averroes puts it—*in quo fiunt pluvia et nix et grando* (*Meteorologicorum Lib.* I, *Cap.* IV).

[2] *Liber* II, *Tract.* I, *Cap.* III.

E

PARADISE LOST, I. 582–7

582–7. The enumeration of proper names is a favourite device with M.—as with many other poets, notably with Virgil. Cf. *Nat. Ode*, one of his earliest poems (1629), XI. 381–411, *P. R.* III. 270 *et seq*. The charm of such passages lies in the musical sound of the names, in their historical or literary associations, and in the impression of vague remoteness and mystery that they convey. Bentley, however, with something more than his usual infelicity as a critic of M., omitted ll. 579–87 (from "what resounds" to "Fontarabbia") as being "Romantic Trash—a heap of barbarous Words". Even Keightley opined that the names are chosen "somewhat at random"; whereas, in truth, each has been carefully selected by M. for its associations. These we shall be able to trace at greater length here than would have been desirable in the *Notes*—and with some fresh illustrative matter.

582. *all who since*. He is thinking—mainly—of great Italian poems of chivalry with their accounts of contests between Christians ('baptized') and Saracens ('infidel'—see 763, note): e.g. Pulci's *Morgante Maggiore*, 1481—see allusion to it, *Areopagitica, P. W.* II. 64; Boiardo's *Orlando Innamorato*, 1495, recast by Berni, 1541—see allusion *P. R.* III. 338–43; Ariosto's *Orlando Furioso*, 1516, of which there was a famous English Version by Sir John Harington 1591—see extract from Ariosto in *Of Reformation, P. W.* II. 383; and Tasso's *Gerusalemme Liberata*. In a letter from Florence (1638), and elsewhere, M. manifests his delight in Italian literature.

583. *Aspramont*, situate 6 miles north of Nice. In Hexham's *Mercator* (1636) I find it marked in the map of Provence, and again in that of Italy. The castle belonging to the great family of the Counts of Aspramont may still be seen. Probably the literary allusion is to the *Orlando Furioso*, XII. 43, where Aspramont is mentioned as the scene of a feat of arms performed by Orlando; and M. may have known a certain Italian poem, entitled *L'Aspramonte* and published at Venice in 1532—itself, possibly, based on the French 'Chanson de Geste' *Aspremont*, which deals with Charlemagne's conquest of Apulia. In any case, it is pretty clear that 'Aspramont' was a name familiar to readers of mediæval romances of chivalry: and does not Scott tell us of jousts at the castle of Aspramont for the hand of the 'Lady of

POETIC USE OF PROPER NAMES 151

Aspramonte' (*Count Robert of Paris*)? Also, as M. in his journey to Italy, rejecting the route by Marseilles to Genoa which Sir Henry Wotton recommended (see *Comus*, p. 72), passed through Nice (so he says in the *Defensio Secunda*), he may conceivably have visited the famous castle, and viewed the scene of the exploits of Orlando and other knights. The notion that Aspremont in the Netherlands is meant need only be mentioned to be dismissed.

Montalban, or *Montauban*, another famous name. It was the castle, in Languedoc, of the Knight Renaud, the Rinaldo of Pulci's *Morgante Maggiore* and Boiardo's *Orlando Innamorato*. In the English romance "The Foure Sonnes of Aymon" (published by Caxton, about 1489), Montalban is constantly mentioned as the scene of conflicts between Charlemagne's troops and Renaud who is besieged there (see Early English Text Society's ed. pp. 395–422). Rodd in his *Spanish Ballads* (1812) gives one "The Ancient Ballad of Count Claros of Montalban" (and another "The Ancient Ballad of the Battle of Roncesvalles").

584. *Damasco*, probably the literary allusion is to the *Orlando Furioso*. In Harington's version the 'Argument' to book XVII says, "Martano at Damasco tilts"; stanzas 12–20 of that book describe the city, with the meeting of the champions there, and stanzas 58–73 their tournaments and jousts. No doubt, too, M. was thinking of Damascus as the scene of battles in times of the Crusades; cf. Greene, *Friar Bacon*, IV. 27, "The virtuous fame discoursèd of his deeds...Done at the Holy Land 'fore Damas' walls", and VIII. 113, "that famous Prince...Who at Damasco beat the Saracens". Note that M. uses the form 'Damasco' here, but 'Damascus' at 468: the one suggests the mediæval, the other the Scriptural, city.

Marocco, so original eds., cf. XI. 404; closer than *Morocco* to Arab. *Marrákush*. Wars between Spaniards and Moors are meant.

Trebisond, Gk Trapezus, in Cappadocia, was the seat of the empire of the family of the Grand-Komnenos from A.D. 1204 to 1461, when the city was captured by Mohammed. Writers of the Middle Age and later historians (Gibbon has only a brief allusion, VII. 327) celebrate the extraordinary splendour of the court and magnificence of the city. "Never", says the historian of Trebizond, Professor Fallmerayer, "was there a land more fitted to provide material for romances of chivalry (*Ritter-geschichten*)": Trebizond "became in popular romance and in

PL 8

the imagination of the Italians and Provençals one of the most famous empires of the east, and the rallying point of the youth and flower of Asia" (*Geschichte des Kaiserthums von Trapezunt*). Now the great exemplar of this romance associated with Trebizond (whose splendours would naturally be reflected on Western Europe through an Italian medium) was a certain heroic novel, *Il Caloandro*, or *Il Caloandro Fedele*, written by Giovanni Ambrosio Marini of Genoa, published at Bologna in 1641 (but I am not sure that this was the 1st ed.), and often reprinted. This work, which had some historical basis, was one of the most famous romances of the 17th cent. Twice translated into French (by Monsieur de Scudèry, brother of the novelist, and by the Comte de Caylus), it may have been Englished—as was another novel by Marini, *The Desperadoes*; and it seems to me quite likely that M. was thinking of it here, or at any rate that many of his readers would think of it. Those who knew the novel would recall the numerous jousts and tournaments which take place at the court of Trebizond, e.g. the great combat in book XXI ('tis a vast story) between the three champions of the princess Tigrinde and the three representatives of the Persian and Tartar armies—with many similar scenes. It is worth while to add that the author (Cardinal Bessarion) of the curious *Laus Trapezuntis* (printed in Tafel's *Eustathii Opuscula*, 1832) dwells on its tournaments and games as a special feature of the court; and to remember how Scott makes the Templar say to Rebecca, " I won him (his horse, Zamor) in single fight from the Soldan of Trebizond " (*Ivanhoe*, chap. xliv).

585. The historical reference is to the Moorish invaders of Spain, the literary to book II of the *Orlando Innamorato*, where we read how Agramant, 'King of Africa', assembled his troops at Biserta (ancient Utica) for invasion of Christendom, landed in Spain, and came up with army of Charlemagne, when "a bloody battle ensued".

586, 587. The event to which M. refers was this: Charlemagne, who had entered Spain to attack the Saracens, was retreating into France, A.D. 778; his army had to pass through the defile of Roncesvalles (or Roncesvaux) in N.W. Spain; Charlemagne himself, with main body, had got through the pass, when the rear-guard, through Ganelon's treachery, was attacked in the pass by the Gascons (or Basques), and cut to pieces, among those who perished being the famous Roland, whose death became the subject of numberless 'Chansons de Gestes', such as the great *Song of Roland* (see Eginhardus, *Vita*

Caroli Magni cap. 9). Now we note two things in these lines: (i) Fontarabbia is 40 miles from Roncesvalles: why does M. place the disaster at the former? Some will have it that he chose Fontarabbia because the name has a very pretty sound, and that "by Fontarabbia" was quite accurate enough—in poetry: which seems to me a feeble solution. Some again (after Newton) say that M. followed the historian Mariana and 'other Spanish writers'—names not specified. Mariana, however, does not mention Fontarabbia at all, but gives the ordinary version, that the battle was at Roncesvalles. My own belief is that there is some literary allusion not yet traced. Scott happily combines the two names, *Marmion*, VI. 33:

> "O, for a blast of that dread horn,
>   On Fontarabian echoes borne,
>   That to king Charles did come,
>   When Rowland brave, and Olivier,
>   And every paladin and peer,
>   On Roncesvalles died."

(ii) M. represents Charlemagne as having fallen in the fight, whereas he lived till 814. Here again Milton's authority is not known; though Mariana does speak of Charlemagne dying through chagrin at his defeat soon after.

Montaigne introduces the name *Fontarabie* in a short historical anecdote in his *Essay* (I. xv) entitled "of the punishment of Cowardise" in Florio's translation (1603).

F

THE ORDERS OF THE HEAVENLY BEINGS

According to a mediæval belief the Heavenly beings were divided into three Hierarchies, and each Hierarchy was sub-divided into three Orders or Choirs. These Orders comprised the Seraphim, Cherubim and Thrones (θρόνοι), forming the first Hierarchy; Dominations (κυριότητες), Virtues (δυνάμεις), and Powers (ἐξουσίαι), forming the second; Principalities (ἀρχαί), Archangels and Angels, forming the third. This system was deduced, in the main, from St Paul's words in *Ephes.* i. 21 and *Colos.* i. 16. First formulated in the treatise περὶ τῆς οὐρανίας ἱεραρχίας, which was long attributed, though falsely, to Diony-sius, the Areopagite, the notion had great influence in the Middle Ages; cf. Dante, *Paradiso*, XXVIII. 98–126. Allusions to it are frequent in Elizabethan writers. Works from which many illustrations of the system might be quoted are:—*Batman vppon Bartholome* (1582), Reginald Scot's *Discovery of Witchcraft* (1584), Thomas Watson's *Eglogue* (1590), the *Faust-book* (1592), Spenser's *Hymne of Heavenly Beautie* (1596), Bacon, *Advancement of Learning*, i. 28, and Heywood's *Hierarchie of the Blessed Angels* (1635), which deals with the subject at great length.

Milton accepted[1] the tradition and made it the basis of the whole angelical system of *Paradise Lost*.

Each of the Orders possessed some special quality. The Seraphim were the "burning" lustrous beings; cf. Spenser, *Heavenly Beautie*:

"those eternall burning Seraphins,
    Which from their faces dart out fierie light."

This conception, due probably to the false derivation of *Seraphim* from a root signifying 'to burn', determines Milton's choice of epithets for this Order of the Hierarchies. See *Seraphim* in the *Glossary*.

The Cherubim had a wondrous power of vision: hence their main duty in *Paradise Lost* is to keep watch. See IV. 778, note. And through this power of vision they enjoyed in a peculiar degree the *Visio Beatifica* or faculty of "contemplating" the Deity. In the words of the treatise περὶ τῆς ἱεραρχίας they were distinguished διὰ τὸ θεοπτικὸν αὐτῶν καὶ θεωρητικόν. And this notion is the key to that line (54) in *Il Penseroso*, the point of which has been so much misunderstood—"The Cherub Contemplation".

The archangels were, as their name implied, the "chief messengers" of the Almighty and the intermediaries between him and Man. Cf. Reginald Scot, "As for archangels, they are sent onlie about great and secret matters"; and Heywood, "The Archangels are Embassadors, great matters to declare". Hence Milton makes Raphael in book V and Michael in books XI, XII—each one of the seven archangels referred to in III. 648–53, the bearers of messages and charges from the Almighty to Adam.

---

[1] Thus in *Church Government* he says, "the angels themselves... are distinguished into their celestial princedoms and satrapies", *P. W.* II. 442. He several times uses the special terms "Orders" and "Hierarchies"—cf. *P. L.* I. 737, V. 587, 591, VII. 192; while the titles "Seraphim", "Thrones", "Dominations", "Virtues" etc. occur constantly.

One other point in which Milton follows mediæval tradition with regard to the Heavenly beings may be noticed. Descriptions like those in book III, ll. 625–8 and 636–42, are purely traditional. We must compare them with the presentment of angels in works of early Christian art. Poets and painters alike drew upon religious tradition and expressed it by certain conventional details. And this presentment of angelic beings contained a considerable element of symbolism. In *Batman vppon Bartholome* II. iii, iv, there is a long discourse on the attributes which painters assign to angels and on their symbolical significance. The following brief extracts from it illustrate Milton's pictures of Uriel (III. 625–8) and the "stripling Cherub" (III. 636–42): "When Angells are paynted with long lockes and crispe haire, thereby is understoode their cleane affections and ordinate thoughts. For the hayre of the head betokeneth thoughts and affections that doe spring out of the roote of thought and minde . . . And they be painted beardles: for to take consideration and heede, that they passe never the state of youth, neyther waxe feeble in vertues, neither faile for age. . . Truely they be paynted feathered and winged. . . [as a sign that] they be lifted up in effect and knowledge, and rauished to the innermost contemplation of the loue of God."

GLOSSARY

Milton's diction is essentially Elizabethan: the diction of the Authorised Version (1611) of the Bible and of Shakespeare. *Paradise Lost*, therefore, though published in 1667, is best illustrated from the works of the generation contemporary with Shakespeare. Hence many of the illustrations in the *Glossary* and *Notes* are taken from the writers who may collectively and conveniently be described as Elizabethan.

A marked feature of Milton's diction, as of his style, is his classical bias. He employs many words in their classical sense, just as he employs many classical idioms and figures of speech. This classicism of diction is still more conspicuous in his prose, in which he introduces numbers of long, sonorous words derived from the Latin. Sometimes he invents such words. These books of *Paradise Lost* contain numerous examples of his classical diction, e.g. *abject, admire, exercise, frequent, mood, prevent, reluctance* (see each in this *Glossary*); *suffice, afflict, offend, virtue, horrid, expatiate, arbitress, sentence, sublime, voluminous, labouring, deform, redounding, pennons, hold* (see *Notes* to I. 148, 186, 187, 320, 563, 774, 785; II. 51, 528, 652, 665, 706, 889, 933, 1043).

Another interesting feature is his partiality for Italianised forms. This is more conspicuous in his verse, perhaps because he felt so strongly, and wished his readers to be reminded of, the spell and fascination of the great Italian epics. By his own statement, he had studied Italian much before he went to Italy. His letters and prose-works reveal his love of it (I do not remember any interesting reference in his works to French literature); and several short poems testify to his very considerable mastery of the language. Instances of his leaning towards Italian are—*ammiral, harald, Soldan, sovran*; *sdein* (IV. 50), *serenate* (IV. 769); *azurn* (*Comus*, 893).

Abbreviations:

A.S. = Anglo-Saxon, i.e. English down to about the Conquest.

Middle E. = Middle English, i.e. English from about the Conquest to about 1500.

Elizabethan E. = the English of Shakespeare and his contemporaries (down to about 1650).

O.F. = Old French, i.e. till about 1600. F. = modern French.

Germ. = modern German. Gk. = Greek.

Ital. = modern Italian. Lat. = Latin.

The dates, of course, are only approximate: such divisions must be more or less arbitrary and open to criticism.

abject, I. 312, 'cast down', the literal sense of Lat. *abjectus*, the past participle of *abjicere*, 'to cast away or down'. In Tindale's *New Testament* (1534), 2 *Cor.* vii. 6 is rendered "He that comfortith the abjecte" = "those that are cast down" in the Authorised Version. Commonly *abject* is a figurative word = 'degraded'.

abyss, I. 21, 658; Lat. *abyssus*, from Gk. ἄβυσσος, 'bottomless'—ἀ-, 'not' + βυσσός, 'bottom, depth'. Shakespeare always uses the older form *abysm*, from F. *abisme*; cf. *The Tempest*, I. 2, 50, "In the dark backward and abysm of time".

admire, I. 690, II. 677, 'wonder', the literal sense of Lat. *admirari*. Cf. *admiration* = 'wonder' III, 271, and in *Hamlet*, III. 2, 339, "your behaviour hath struck her into amazement and admiration"; and *admirable* = 'to be wondered at', *Midsummer-Night's Dream*, v. 27, "strange and admirable".

advise, II. 376, 'consider'; often used reflexively in this sense, like F. *s'aviser*, 'to consider'. Cf. 1 *Chronicles* xxi. 12, "advise thyself what word I shall bring" (Revised Version 'consider').

alchymy, II. 517, 'metal'; properly *alchemy*, from Arabic *alkīmīa: al* = 'the' (Arabic article), + *kīmīa*, a corruption of χημία, used in late Gk. for the chemical transmutation of metals. Probably χημία was the Gk. form of the native name of Egypt (= 'the land of *Khem*'), and meant 'the Egyptian art'. Later, through confusion with χέειν, 'to pour' (cf. χυμός, 'sap, juice'), there arose a form χυμεία: whence in E. the old spellings 'alchymy', 'alchumie', and 'chymist' (short for 'alchymist'). From meaning the art of amalgamating metals 'alchemy' came to be used of the amalgam or metallic composition produced by the process. A certain amalgam, like gold, was called 'alchemy gold' or 'alchemy'; cf. Fletcher. *Purple Island*, VII. 39, "Such were his arms, false gold, true alchymie". This mixed metal, in which brass was the chief constituent, was much employed for trumpets—as M. evidently knew.

Alp, II. 620; formerly used, like *Alpes* in late Latin poets, of *any* high (especially snow-capped) mountain. Cf. *S. A.* 628, "Nor breath of vernal air from snowy Alp"; and Haluyt's *Voyages,* I. 112, "Certaine *Alpes or Mountaines* directly South-ward". A Celtic word; cf. Gaelic *alp,* 'a high mountain'.

amerce, I. 609; cf. *Romeo and Juliet,* III. 1, 195, "But I'll *amerce* you with so strong a *fine*", i.e. punish. F. *amercier,* 'to fine', which was derived from the O.F. phrase *estre à merci* = 'to be in the *mercy* of any one as to the amount of a fine (Lat. *merx*) which he could impose'. Here (I. 609) *amerced* = 'deprived of' (i.e. as a punishment for their rebellion). Note that F. *merci,* whence E. *mercy,* is connected with *merx* (= 'a fine' in late Latin), and not with *misericordia.*

ammiral, I. 294. The chief vessel of a fleet was called the 'admiral' because it carried the admiral or chief officer. Cf. Hakluyt, I. 401, "the sayd William met with sixe ships...and tooke of them the Admirall". In the form *ammiral* M. imitates Ital. *ammiraglia,* which Florio (1598) renders by "an admirall or chief ship". Properly *admiral* means 'ruler, commander', being derived from Arabic *Amir,* 'ruler' (cf. *Ameer* of Afghanistan and *Emir*); and formerly the full phrase "admiral *of the sea*" was used, the italicised words being dropped in course of time. The *d* in *admiral* (older form *amyrel*) arose through confusion with Lat. *admirabilis* and *admirable.*

assay, I. 619, '*try,* attempt'; M. always uses this form, from O.F. *assai,* a variant form of O.F. *essai,* whence the commoner form in E. *essay.* Lat. *exagium,* Gk. ἐξάγιον, 'a weighing, *trial* of weight'.

astonish, I. 266; formed from the older verb *astony* = O.F. *estonner,* modern F. *étonner,* from Lat. *extonare,* 'to thunder'. The original notion of *astony* (see IX. 890), *astonish,* and *astound* (I. 281) was 'to stupefy, strike senseless, as with a thunder-bolt'. Cf. the *Argument* to bk. I, line 12, and Milton's *History of Britain,* "*astonished* and *struck* with superstition as with a planet".

baleful, I. 56, II. 576, 'full of sorrow, unhappy'; commonly 'full of harm'—cf. *Comus,* 255, "baleful drugs". A.S. *bealu* = 'evil, sorrow'.

beest, I. 84. The verb *be,* from A.S. *béon* (the infinitive), was conjugated in pres. tense indicative as late as Milton's time, especially in: (i) 2nd pers. sing. with *if*; M. indeed does not use "if thou beest" elsewhere, but the idiom is frequent in Shake-speare—cf. *The Tempest,* III. 2. 137, "if thou beest a man", and

v. 134, "if thou be'st Prospero". (ii) 1st pers. plur.; cf. *Genesis* xlii. 32, "We be twelve brethren". (iii) 3rd pers. plur.; cf. *Matthew* xv. 14, "they be blind leaders". Very common was 'there be'; cf. vi. 143, *Comus*, 519, "such there be".

bullion, I. 704; F. *bouillon*, Lat. *bullio*, 'a mass of metal', from *bullire*, 'to boil'. *Bullion* is only *connected* with Lat. *bulla*, 'a seal' in so far as *bulla* itself is from *bullire*.

buxom, II. 842, 'yielding'; from A.S. *búgan*, 'to bend'; cf. Germ. *beugsam*, 'easily bent, pliant'. Originally *buxom* meant 'obedient'; cf. the *Glosse* to Spenser's *Shepheards Calender, September*, "*Buxome and bent*, meeke and obedient". Then came the sense 'yielding, pliant'; cf. Fairfax, *Tasso*, xv. 12, "with strong oars...brush the buxom wave".

Cherubim; the correct form = Heb. *Kherūbhīm*, the plural of *Kherūbh*. The oldest forms in English, as still in French, were *Cherubin*, sing., and *Cherubins*, plural. Cf. Coverdale, "Thou God of Israel, which dwellest upon Cherubin", *Isai.* xxxvii. 16; and Wyclif, "Two Goldun Cherubyns", *Exod.* xxv. 18. Later, as in the Bible of 1611, *Cherub*, sing., and *Cherubims*, plural, were used, as being closer to Hebrew. M. wrote *Cherube* for singular (a still nearer approach in sound than 'Cherub' to the *ū* of the Heb. *Kherūbh*), and the true plural *Cherubim* (adopted in the Revised Version of the Bible). *Kherūbh* is said to come from the Babylonian word for the figure of the winged bull which stood at the door of a house to keep off evil spirits. The Jews propably owed it to the Phœnicians.

combustion, I. 46; properly 'conflagration', from Lat. *comburere*, 'to burn up'; hence metaphorically 'utter confusion', or 'destruction', as here. Cf. vi. 225, and *Macbeth*, II. 3. 63, "dire combustion and confused events". In M. always a very strong word; cf. *Of Reformation*, "to threaten uproar and combustion", *P. W.* II. 417.

conjured, II. 693, 'banded (literally 'sworn') together in a conspiracy'; Lat. *conjuratus*. Cf. Surrey's translation (1557) of *Æneid*, II, "They bind themselves with the conjured bands", and Spenser, *Faerie Queene*, v. 10. 26.

couch, II. 536, 'to fix the spear in the rest' (Fr. *coucher*). The 'rest' was "a strong part of the armour at the breast, against which they placed the butt of the spear to give more force to the charge" (Keightley). Cf. Shakespeare, 1 *Henry VI.* III. 2. 134, "A braver soldier never couched lance". So Tennyson, *Pelleas and Ettarre*, "She spake; and at her will they couch'd their spears".

cresset, I. 728; a vessel of iron to hold some burning substance (e.g. grease, oil, tarred rope) and serve as a lantern or beacon; usually mounted on the top of a pole, or hung from a roof—cf. Scott, *Marmion*, "A cresset in an iron chain". F. *cresset* or *crasset*, 'a cup for holding grease'; *not* akin to O.F. *creuset*.

cry, II. 654, 'a pack'; cf. *Coriolanus*, III. 3. 120, "You common cry of curs!" The sense comes from the hounds' *cry* or notes.

dint, II. 813, 'blow', its original sense; also used of the *dent* (another form of *dint*) or impression left by a blow; cf. Shakespeare, *Antony and Cleopatra*, II. 6. 39, "targes undinted", i.e. shields not marked by blows.

disastrous, I. 597, 'boding misfortune'. *Disaster* (Lat. *dis* + *astrum*, 'a star') is one of the words belonging to astrology: thus Minsheu (1617) explains it as "some misfortune due to the *influence* (see p. 165) of the *stars*". Cf. 'ill-*starred*'.

element, II. 490, 'sky', a common Elizabethan use; cf. *Henry V*. IV. I. 105, 107, "the king is but a man, as I am: the element shows to him as it doth to me". So in *Lear*, III. I. 4 ("the fretful element").

empyreal, I. 117, II. 430, 'fiery, formed of fire', Lat. *empyræus*, Gk. ἐμπύραιος, 'in the fire (πῦρ), fiery hot, burning'. Note that M. always accents the adj. *empýreal*, but the noun *empyréan* (II. 771).

engine, I. 750; in its original sense 'contrivance', i.e. something made with *ingenuity* (Lat. *ingenium*). Later, 'implement, instrument', especially of war; so in II. 923, where it probably means 'cannon', as in VI. 484, 518. Cf. *Othello*, III. 3. 355, "you mortal engines" (i.e. cannon).

enthrall, II. 551; **thrall,** I. 149; from Icelandic *þræll*, 'a serf', Danish *træl*; no doubt, *thrall* came into England through the Danes. Strictly it meant 'a runner', i.e. on messages, the original root being that seen in Gk. τρέχειν, 'to run'. The notion that *thrall* comes from *thrill*, because the ears of serfs were *thrilled* or *drilled*, i.e. pierced, is wrong.

exercise, II. 89; in the sense of Lat. *exercere*, 'to harass, torment'; cf. Virgil, *Æneid*, v. 725, *Iliacis exercite fatis*. So in *Ecclesiastes* i. 13, "this sore travail hath God given to the sons of men to be exercised therewith" = 'to *afflict* them', as the margin reads. See *P. R.* I. 156.

fare, II. 940, 'journey, travel'; the literal sense of A.S. *faran*; cf. Germ. *fahren*, 'to travel'. So often in Spenser; cf. *Faerie Queene*, II. I. 2, "forth he fares", and II. 2. 12, "fare on foot". This notion of 'travelling' is kept in 'railway-*fare*', 'thorough-*fare*'.

founder, I. 204, II. 940; properly 'to sink to the bottom' (Lat. *fundus*); cf. F. *s'effondrer*, 'to sink down'. Cognate words *foundation, profound* and F. *fond*, 'bottom'.

frame, II. 924, 'fabric'; a favourite word with M. and with writers like Dryden and Thomson who were influenced by his diction (see II. 438, 898, notes). Cf. V. 154, "this universal frame" = the universe. Cf. too Shakespeare: "this goodly frame, the earth", *Hamlet*, II. 2. 310. Similar is the Lucretian phrase *moles et machina mundi* (V. 96).

fraught, II. 715, 'laden with'; the p. p. not of *freight* but of *fraught*, 'to load', a verb now obsolete; cf. *Cymbeline*, I. I. 126, "If...thou fraught the court", i.e. burden it. The participle was also (but rarely) *fraughted*; cf. *The Passionate Pilgrim*, 270, "Fraughted with gall". Akin probably to *freight*.

frequent; in the sense of Lat. *frequens*, 'crowded'. Cf. Ben Jonson, *Sejanus*, "'Tis Cæsar's will to have a frequent senate". M. twice uses "in full frequence" = in full assembly (Lat. *frequentia*); cf. *P. R.* I. 128, II. 130. Cf. Tennyson, *The Princess*, "Not in this frequence can I lend full tongue".

fretted, I. 717; from the verb *fret* = 'to work or design with *frets*'. A *fret* was a small band; the word comes from O.F. *frete*, 'an iron band' = Ital. *ferrata*, 'an iron grating' (cf. Lat. *ferrum*, 'iron'). "*Fret*-work" was specially used of a kind of gilding for the roofs of halls; it was a pattern formed by small gilt bands or *frets* intersecting each other at right angles. Cf. Bacon, *Advancement of Learning*, II, "Beautiful works and orders, like the *frets* in the *roof* of a house". So Milton uses the word here, and Shakespeare in *Hamlet*, II. 2. 313, "this majestical *roof fretted* with *golden* fire". Quite distinct is the other verb, *fret*, 'to adorn', from A.S. *frætwan*.

frore, II. 595, 'frosty'; from A.S. *froren*, 'frozen', the p. p. of *fréosan*, 'to freeze'. Spenser has the adj. *frory*, 'frozen', *Faerie Queene*, III. 8. 35, and *frorne* in *Shepheards Calender*, *February*.

goblin, II. 688. Derived through the French from late Lat. *gobelinus*, a diminutive of Lat. *cobalus*, 'a mountain-sprite, demon' = Gk. κόβαλος, 'a rogue', or 'a goblin supposed to befriend rogues'.

grunsel, I. 460 = *ground-sill*. Minsheu (1617) has "a Ground-sell of a doore; *vide* Threshold"; *sill* is akin to Germ. *schwelle*, 'threshold'.

gryphon, II. 943; Lat. *gryphus*, from Gk. γρύψ; also in late Latin *griffus*, whence the other form *griffin*. A third form in

Elizabethan E. was *gripe*; cfo Shakespeare, *Lucrece*, 543, "the gripe's sharp claws".

harald, I. 752, II. 518, 'herald'; always spelt *harald*—cf. Ital. *araldo*—in the original editions of *Paradise Lost*. It illustrates Milton's liking for Italian forms; see p. 159.

highth, I. 24, II. 95; always written thus by M. The form is common in Hakluyt's *Voyages*, and is said to survive in parts of America. *High-th* is curious in that it retains the *th* of the A.S. word *héhþu*, represented now by *t*—cf. *heigh-t*. For the ordinary change of *th* (in A.S., *þ*) to *t*, cf. A.S. *gesih-þ*, later *gesih-t* or *sih-t*, now *sigh-t*.

hubbub, II. 951, 'confused din'; put for *hoop-hoop*, a reduplication of *hoop*, 'a cry of surprise'—cf. O.F. *houper*, 'to shout'. Also written *whoobub*, as in *The Winter's Tale*, IV. 4. 629, "come in with a whoobub", i.e. a clamour. Cf. '*whoop*ing (or '*hoop*ing')-cough'.

influence, II. 1034, Late Lat. *influentia*, literally 'a flowing in upon'. It was an astrological term applied to the power over the earth, men's characters, fortunes etc., which was supposed to descend from the celestial bodies. Cf. "planetary influence", *Lear*, I. 2. 136, "skyey influences", *Measure for Measure*, III. 1. 9. M. generally uses *influence* with reference to this astrological notion; cf. IV. 669, VII. 374, 375 (from *Job* xxxviii. 31, "the sweet influences of Pleiades").

intend, II. 457, 'attend to, consider'; cf. Ben Jonson, *Bartholomew Fair*, V. 3, "I pray you intend your game, sir." Cf. Lat. *intendere animum*.

its, I. 254. In Elizabethan English the regular *neuter* possessive pronoun was *his*; cf. *Genesis* i. 12, "herb yielding seed after *his* kind", and iii. 15, "*it* shall bruise thy head, and thou shalt bruise *his* heel". About 1600 *its* came into use, but slowly. Bacon has *its* rarely; the Bible of 1611 never; the nine instances in the 1st Folio (1623) of Shakespeare are probably corrupt, since in every extant work published during his lifetime the old idiom *his* is invariable—cf. *Julius Caesar* I. 2. 123, 124, "that same eye...did lose *his* lustre". Milton, as an Elizabethan in his diction, avoids *its*: either (1) by personifying the noun, thus in his prose abstract words like 'virtue', 'truth', are always followed by *her*; or (2) by retaining the old *neuter* use of *his*; cf. *Comus* 246–8:

> "Sure *something* holy lodges in that breast,
> And with these raptures moves the vocal air
> To testify *his* hidden residence."

The only places in Milton's verse where *its* occurs are I. 254, IV. 813; and *Nativity Ode*, 106. I know but two instances of *its* in his prose—*Areopagitica* and *Church Government, P. W.* II. 94, 471.

justle, II. 1018 =*jostle*; connected with *joust* (often spelt *just*), from Lat. *juxta*, 'close to'. For the form (then common) cf. *The Tempest,* V. 158, "*justled* from your senses".

landskip, II. 491; here and in the three other places where it occurs—IV. 153, V. 142, *L'Allegro,* 70—spelt *lantskip* in the original editions. It was a term borrowed from Dutch artists (cf. Dutch *landschap*), and its forms in E. have been various— e.g. *landschaft, landschape, landshape, landscip*. For *landskip* (apparently the oldest form in E.) cf. Cotgrave (1611), "Païsage: Landskip, countrey worke"; and *The Spectator,* 94, "a beautiful and spacious landskip". The suffix *skip* (or *-scape*) is closely connected with the noun *shape,* hence *land-skip* (or *-scape*) simply means '*shape* of the land'. In most words *-skip* is softened to *-ship* as in *friend-ship*; cf. Germ. *freund-schaft.*

lewd, I. 490, 'lustful'. Middle E. *lewed*=A.S. *lǽwed*. Its successive meanings were: (1) 'enfeebled', *lǽwed* (=*geléwed*) being the past participle of *lǽwan,* 'to weaken'; then (2) 'ignorant'; then (3) 'bad, worthless'; then (4) 'lustful', i.e. bad in a particular way. From (2) arose also the sense 'lay, belonging to the laity', because the laity compared with the clergy were ignorant.

list, 'wish, please'; commonly a present (II. 798), but also used as a preterite by M. (II. 656, IV. 803). Shakespeare, who uses the present tense often, once has *listed*; cf. *Richard III,* III. 5. 84, "his savage heart...*listed* to make his prey". Akin to *lust,* which often meant 'pleasure', as does Germ. *lust*; cf. *Psalm* xcii. 10, "Mine eye shall also see his lust of mine enemies" (Prayer-Book).

mood, I. 550, or **mode,** 'key', 'measure', a musical term; cf. *S. A.* 662, "a *tune* harsh and of dissonant *mood*". Lat. *modus*; distinct from *mood,* 'disposition' (Germ. *muth*).

oblivious, I. 266, 'causing to forget, producing forgetfulness'; cf. *Macbeth,* V. 3. 43, "some sweet oblivious antidote". So Horace uses *obliviosus* of wine (*Odes,* II. 7. 21); and M. speaks of *obliviosæ...Lethes aquæ* in *De Idea Platonica,* 20. The usual sense now is 'forgetful'.

orient, I. 546, II. 399, 'bright, lustrous'. In Elizabethan poetry 'orient' is a constant epithet of gems, especially pearls. Perhaps, used thus, it first meant 'eastern', gems coming from the Orient or East; then as these were bright it got the notion 'lustrous', which suits, I believe, every passage where M. uses it, though in one or two places (e.g. in IV. 644) 'rising'=Lat. *oriens* is possible. Commonly he applies it to jewels or liquids; cf. "orient pearl" V. 2, "orient liquor" *Comus* 65.

panim, I. 765; another form of *pagan*, from late Lat. *paganus*, 'heathen'. Strictly O.E. *paynyme* meant 'heathendom', '*country*' of the heathen', and a 'heathen man' was *payen* or *payn*; then *paynyme* got the sense, 'heathen man', that really belonged to *payen*.

paramount, II. 508, 'lord, chief'; originally a legal term for the lord of an estate under whom land was rented. O.F. *paramont*, 'at the top, above'=Lat. *per+ad Montem*.

pavilion, II. 960, 'palace'. M. refers to *Ps.* xviii. 11, "He made darkness his secret place; his pavilion round about him were dark waters"—where, however, the sense is less 'palace' than 'tent', as sometimes in M. Cf. V. 653, and *pavilioned*= 'in tents, encamped', XI. 215. Through F. *pavillon* from Lat. *papilio*, 'a butterfly', used by late Latin writers to mean 'a tent' because a tent is spread out like the wings of a butterfly.

pioner, I. 676; O.F. *peonier*, 'footsoldier', Ital. *pedone* (from Lat. *pes*, 'foot'). For -*er*=-*eer* as a suffix in Elizabethan E. cf. "charioter" VI. 390; "mutiner" *Coriolanus* II. 254; "enginer" and "pioner" *Hamlet*, III. 4. 206 and I. 5. 163 ("a worthy pioner").

plumb-down, II. 933, 'straight down, in a vertical line'; cf. Sylvester, "direct now falls *Plumb* on their heads". *Plumb* meant (1) a mass of lead (Lat. *plumbum*), attached to a cord and used in determining whether a wall is perpendicular; (2) the vertical or perpendicular position so determined: hence the phrases 'in plumb'=vertical, 'out of plumb'=not vertical. Used adverbially, as here, 'plumb' is short for '*in* plumb'; cf. Fr. *à plomb*. In modern E. *b* has softened into *p*=*plump*, 'straight downward'.

portcullis, II. 874, a kind of grating, made of timber or iron, sliding up and down in vertical grooves, and forming part of a gateway. Here the portcullis came down over and protected the lock of the gate: Sin had to raise it before she could get at the keyhole. Lat. *porta colatica*, 'a sliding door': *colatica* from *colare*, 'to flow'—whence F. *couler*, 'to flow', *coulisse*, 'a slide, groove'.

prevent, II. 467, 739, 'anticipate, forestall'; cf. *Psalm* cxix. 148, "Mine eyes prevent the night watches", and I *Thessalonians* iv. 15, "we which are alive...shall not prevent them which are asleep ", i.e. 'rise before'. Literally 'to come before', Lat. *præ*, 'before'+*venire*, 'to come'.

prick, II. 536, 'to ride hard', literally 'to spur a horse on'; cf. Tennyson, *Gareth and Lynette*, "And Gareth crying prick'd against the cry". See Spenser, *Faerie Queen*, V. 10. 31. In *Piers the Plowman* 'prykiere'=a rider.

puny, II. 367; perhaps in the literal sense 'born later, younger', mankind having been created after the angels; cf. the *Areopagitica*, "like a puny with his guardian", i.e. a young man not yet of age (*P. W.* II. 79). But 'weak, inferior' (its usual sense now) would also suit. The term "*Puisne* Judge" shows the etymology (F. *puis né*).

purlieu, II. 833, 'outskirt', strictly of a forest, as in IV. 404. Sometimes land which had been taken from its owner and made part of a forest was restored to him or his successor. The *process* whereby this was done was called *perambulatio*='a walking over the land to settle its boundaries'; then the land itself came in legal Latin to be called *perambulatio*, rendered in French by *pourallee* (*pour*+*aller*). The form *purlieu*, from *pourallee*, was influenced by a wrong derivation from F. *pur lieu*=*purus locus*, 'a space clear of trees'.

purple, I. 451; like Lat. *purpureus*, Gk. πορφύρεος, not limited in poetry to the colour strictly called 'purple', but used of rich hues like red, rosy, crimson. In Shakespeare *purple* is applied, as here, to blood; cf. *Richard II*. III. 3. 94, "The *purple* testament of *bleeding* war", and 3 *Henry VI*. II. 5. 99, "his purple blood".

recorder, I. 551, a kind of flute or flageolet; cf. the title of a musical work published in 1686, "The Delightful Companion, or Choice New Lessons for the *Recorder or Flute*." So called from the old verb *record*='to sing'; cf. Fairfax, *Tasso* II. 97, "to hear the lark record her hymns". By "*soft*" M. implies not effeminate strains but the sweet, subdued notes of the instrument; cf. Fletcher's *Piscatorie Eclogues* VII. 3, "the *sad* recorder *sweetly* plains".

reluctance, II. 337, 'struggling against'—the lit. sense of Lat. *reluctari*. So X. 1045, "Reluctance against God and his just yoke", and VI. 58, where reluctant is used of flames struggling against, i.e. so as to force their way through, smoke. Now *reluctance* has softened into the sense 'unwillingness, loathness'.

rhyme; spelt (in the First Ed.) *rhime* in I. 16 but *rime* in the *Preface;* so possibly M. used *rhime* (i.e. *rhyme*)=poetry opposed to prose, and *rime* = rhymed metre opposed to blank verse. The spelling *rhyme* is due to confusion with *rhythm*, Gk. ῥυθμός; the word should be written *rime* (from A.S. *rím*, 'a number').

satiate, I. 179. A noticeable point in Elizabethan English is the tendency to make the past participles of verbs of Latin origin conform with the Latin forms. This is the case especially with verbs of which the Latin originals belong to the 1st and 3rd conjugations. Thus Shakespeare and Milton have many participles like 'create' (*creatus*), 'consecrate' (*consecratus*), 'incorporate', 'dedicate', where the termination -*ate*, in modern English -*ated*, = Lat. -*atus*, the passive participial termination of the 1st conjugation. Cf. **elevate** (II. 558).

So with the Latin 3rd conjugation; Latinised participles such as 'deject' (*dejectus*), 'distract', 'attent' (*attentus*), 'suspect', **suspense** (II. 418), 'addict' (*addictus*), 'pollute' (*pollutus*), with many others, are to be found in Shakespeare or Milton. Further, participles not from the Latin are abbreviated by analogy; e.g. Milton (I. 193) has '**uplift**' = 'uplift*ed*', though *lift* is of Scandinavian origin.

scape, I. 239, II. 442; originally short for *escape*, it became an independent form and should be printed *scape*, not *'scape*; cf. *estate* and *state*. *Escape* = O.F. *escaper* (modern *échapper*), literally 'to slip out of one's cape' (Lat. *ex* + *cappa*), and so 'to steal off, escape'.

scathe, I. 613, 'injure'; rare as verb, but cf. *Romeo and Juliet*, I. 5. 86, "This trick may chance to scathe you". For the noun cf. *King John*, II. 75, "To do offence and scath in Christendom".

Seraphim; then supposed to come from a Hebrew root 'to burn'; cf. Blount (1672), "Seraphim, i.e. *fulgentes aut comburentes*; so called, for their burning with divine love and charity." Hence "*fiery* Seraphim", II. 512; "*bright* Seraphim" III. 381, and in *At a Solemn Musick*, 10, "*bright* Seraphim, in *burning* row". Really *Seraphim* is from a root 'to exalt', and means 'the exalted ones'. In the history of its plural **Seraph** (I. 324) resembles *Cherub*: *Seraphins* in some old writers; *Seraphims* in *Isaiah* vi. 2, 6; *Seraphim* in M.

Soldan, I. 764, 'Sultan'; cf. Minsheu (1617), "the great Soldane, or *Sultan* among the Turks or Persians". From Arabic *Sultán*, 'victorious', Latinised as *Soldanus*, whence Ital. *soldano*.

sovran, I. 246, II. 244; spelt thus always in *P. L.*; cf. Ital. *sovrano*. The common form *sovereign* = O.F. *soverain*, later *souverain*. Lat. *superanus*, 'chief', formed from *super*, 'above'.

sublimed, I. 235. In chemistry to 'sublime' or 'sublimate' is "to raise a solid substance into vapour by heat". M. means that the material substance catching fire is raised to a state of pure flame.

success, II. 9. 123; its usual sense in Elizabethan E. is 'result, fortune'—how a person fares in a matter, or a thing turns out, whether well or ill. Cf. Shakespeare, *Troilus and Cressida*, II. 2. 117, "Nor fear of bad success in a bad cause", i.e. ill-fortune. So *P. R.* IV. I.

Syrtis, II. 939, Gk. Σύρτις, the name of certain quicksands and sandbanks off the Coast of N. Africa; the word came to mean any quicksand or sandbank—as here.

take, II. 554; a common Elizabethan sense was 'to enchant, captivate', especially by supernatural influence; cf. *Hamlet*, I. I. 163, "then...No fairy takes" (viz. at Christmas). Hence the general meaning 'charm', as here; cf. Bacon, *Of Masques*, "things...such as do naturally take the sense". So in Tennyson's *Dying Swan*, III.

umpire, II. 907; the arbitrator who decides a dispute; hence, a judge, Put for *numpire* = Middle E. *noumpere* = O.F. *non per* = Lat. *non par*, 'not equal, odd': there being two disputants, the umpire was a third man, presumed to be *impartial* (Lat. *impar* 'unequal').

uncouth, II. 407, 827; A.S. *uncuð*, 'unknown'—from *un*, 'not', + *cuð*, the p.p. of *cunnan*, 'to know'. In M. it almost always means 'strange, unfamiliar', with the implied notion 'unpleasant'; cf. V. 98, VI. 362.

unenvied, II. 23. Elizabethan writers constantly treat the termination *-ed*, which belongs to the passive participle, as equal to the adjectival ending *-able*; especially with words which have the negative prefix *un-*, and the sense 'that may not be'. Cf. *untamed*, 'that may not be tamed = untam*able*' (II. 337), *unnumbered*, 'that may not be numbered = innumer*able*', II. 903. So "unvalued" = 'invaluable', "unavoided" = 'inevitable', *Richard III.* I. 4. 27, IV. 4. 217. The use of the participial and adjectival endings was less regular then than now.

utter, I. 72; the comparative of A.S. *út*, 'out', and an older form of *outer*. Lawyers still speak of "the *utter* bar" in contrast with "the *inner* bar". In *Ezekiel* x. 5 the Bible used to read "*utter* court".

vans, II. 927, 'wings'; Ital. *vanni*, from Lat. *vannus*, 'a winnowing-*fan*'. Cf. *P. R.* IV. 583, "plumy vans" (said of angels' wings), and Tennyson's *Love and Death*, "Love wept and spread his sheeny vans for flight". For *van=fan* cf. *vat=fat* as in 'wine-*fat*'.

waft, II. 1042; often used (as here) by Elizabethan writers with the sense 'to journey, or carry, over water'. Cf. 2 *Henry VI.* IV. I. 114, "I charge thee waft me safely cross the Channel"; and *P. R.* I. 104.

warp, I. 341; a nautical term (Scandinavian) applied to a process in seamanship too complicated to be explained here. M. uses it to describe 'undulatory forward motion'.

welkin, II. 538, 'sky'; properly a plural word = 'clouds'; cf. cognate Germ. *wolke*, 'a cloud'. The termination *-in* (for *-en*) is the plural ending which we get in *brethren, children, oxen*).

wont, I. 764, were wont; preterite tense, 3rd person plural. The verb *won*, 'to be accustomed to', now used only in p.p. *wonted* or *wont*, from A.S. *wunian*, was then conjugated; cf. *Nativity Ode*, 10.

INDEX OF WORDS

This list applies to the **Notes** *only; words of which longer explanations are given will be found in the* **Glossary.** *The references are to the pages.*

Printed in Great Britain
by Amazon